Tsewa's Gift

Wampurái Peas plants manioc cuttings in a recently burned swidden.

SMITHSONIAN SERIES IN ETHNOGRAPHIC INQUIRY

Tsewa's Gift

Magic and Meaning in an Amazonian Society

Michael F. Brown

Smithsonian Institution Press
Washington and London
1985

Library of Congress Cataloging-in-Publication Data
Brown, Michael (Michael F.)
  Tsewa's gift.

  (Smithsonian series in ethnographic inquiry)
  Bibliography: p.
  Includes index.
  1. Aguaruna Indians—Religion and mythology.
2. Aguaruna Indians—Magic. 3. Aguaruna Indians—Ethnobotany.
4. Indians of South America—Peru—Religion and mythology.
5. Indians of South America—Peru—Magic. 6. Indians of South
America—Peru—Ethnobotany.
I. Title. II. Series.
F3430.1.A35B763   1986   299'.8   85–40401
ISBN 0–87474–294–3 (alk. paper)

 The paper used in this publication meets the minimum requirements
of the American National Standard for Permanence of Paper for
Printed Library Materials Z39.48–1984.

Designer, Christopher Jones
Editor, Mary L. McNeil

Contents

Acknowledgments

M y research among the Aguaruna Jívaro of the Alto Río Mayo, Peru, was supported by grants from the Henry L. and Grace Doherty Charitable Foundation, the Wenner-Gren Foundation for Anthropological Research, the Centro Amazónico de Antropología y Aplicación Práctica, and Williams College. A postdoctoral fellowship at the Smithsonian Institution, under the direction of Dr. William H. Crocker, provided me with congenial surroundings in which I could finish writing this book. I thank all of these institutions for their generous assistance.

Various Peruvian friends were kind enough to welcome me into their homes during my absences from the Alto Mayo. I especially want to acknowledge the hospitality of Alejandro Camino and Patel de Camino in Lima, John Chang Luzula and Obertila Pinedo de Chang in Lamas, and Luis Uriarte and Annette Rosenvinge de Uriarte in Iquitos.

Genus and species determinations for plants collected in the Alto Mayo were made by William Anderson and Bronley Gates of the University of Michigan Herbarium and Timothy Plowman of the Field Museum of Natural History. Most of the identifications in the text, however, were based on lists of Aguaruna plant names and their Linnaean equivalents generously provided by Brent Berlin of the University of California, Berkeley. These identifications are the result of Dr. Berlin's ethnobiological research in several Aguaruna communities on the Alto Río Marañón and its tributaries. Any inaccuracies that result from the application of his data to the flora of the Alto Río Mayo are mine alone.

Colleagues who were kind enough to comment on the manuscript at various stages of its gestation include Alton Becker, Richard I. Ford, Gillian Feeley-Harnik, Kenneth Kensinger, David Langston, Michael Taussig, Martha Works, and Aram Yengoyan. I am particularly indebted to Ivan Karp and William L. Merrill of the Smithsonian Institution for giving so freely of their critical insights during the final stages of writing.

Robert Lewis, a staff illustrator with the Smithsonian's Department of Anthropology, prepared the figures that accompany the text.

Margaret L. Van Bolt, my *compañera* in the Alto Mayo, cheerfully shared the challenges of fieldwork for more than a year. Much of what I was able to learn about garden magic was the result of her rapport with the women of Huascayacu, Alto Naranjillo, and Shimpiyacu. She also contributed several of the photographs that appear in the book.

Samuel Bazán Paz, Adolfo Juép Nampín, Teodoro Timías Dosinta, Kayáp Jiukám Tsapík, Eladio Jiukám Wasúm, Vicente Weepiu Ampám, and Shajián Wajai Besént each did his best to help the visiting *kurínku* learn what it means to be *awajún*. My admiration for all the Aguaruna people of the Alto Río Mayo is, I trust, readily apparent in the pages that follow.

Publisher's Acknowledgments

Portions of chapter 3 appeared in "The Role of Words in Aguaruna Hunting Magic," *American Ethnologist* 11:545–58, 1984. Portions of chapter 4 appeared in "Aguaruna Jívaro Gardening Magic in the Alto Río Mayo, Peru," *Ethnology* 19:169–90, 1980. Both are excerpted with permission.

List of Illustrations

List of Plates

List of Tables

Orthographic Note

The Aguaruna orthography used in this book was developed by the Summer Institute of Linguistics and is now employed by the Aguaruna themselves. The pronunciation of vowels and consonants follows Spanish usage, with the following exceptions:

a —Preceding u, it approximates the Spanish o; preceding i, it approximates the Spanish e.
b —Varies between b and mb.
d —Varies between d and nd.
e —Represents the high central vowel [ɨ].
g —In the final position of a syllable it is the same as the English ng.
sh —Pronounced as in English.
w —Pronounced as the Spanish hu, with one exception: before i it is pronounced with the v of vaca.
h —Denotes a glottal stop. (See Larson 1966:91–93 for details)

All accents fall on the first syllable unless otherwise noted. Nasalizations have been deleted. There are some slight phonetic differences between Aguaruna as spoken in the Alto Mayo and the Alto Marañón, but these are so minor that I have generally followed the spelling used by Mildred Larson (1966).

Introduction

The heavy rains of Peru's northern *montaña* usually keep the Aguaruna Indians indoors, where they attend to domestic chores and drink manioc beer warmed over the fire. Neighbors gather to share conversation and perhaps even to dance, provided there is enough manioc beer and a festive mood prevails.

On one rainy day, I talked with Shajián Wajai about the means by which human beings think. "Do people think with their heads or their hearts?" I asked him. The verb *anentáimat*, "to think," is similar to the noun *anentái*, "heart," and some people had told me that this is because we think with our hearts. Yet it is not unusual for Aguaruna parents to exhort a child to let advice "enter your head," perhaps in recognition of the prevailing non-Indian belief about the seat of intellect. So my question to Shajián was a plea for clarification. He drank from a bowl of beer that his wife held out to him, then said deliberately, "The people who say that we think with our heads are wrong because we think with our hearts. The heart is connected to the veins, which carry the thoughts in the blood through the entire body. The brain is only connected to the spinal column, isn't it? So if we thought with our brains, we would only be able to move the thought as far as our anus!"

Behind Shajián's piquant humor lies a great concern with the nature, quality, and uses of human thought. Many of the Aguaruna childrearing practices of the past were intended to make the heart strong, the thoughts "straight" or correct. One important aspect of developed thought is the ability to accomplish the practical activities by which the Aguaruna define themselves as human beings. In the course of completing these tasks, people employ many procedures that are not easily accommodated within the category "technology": they perform songs to attract game and help their gardens grow; they alter their diet so that the foods they eat will not interfere with the project at hand; they attempt to manipulate the emotions of loved ones through the power of special animal, vegetable, and mineral substances. Because the efficacy of these procedures is not explained by reference to cause and effect relationships that are acceptable in Western scientific terms, we usually classify them as "magical."

Despite the fact that magic has stirred the interest of anthropologists since the birth of our discipline, the number of full-length ethnographic studies of magic is surprisingly small. Theoretical essays on magical thought draw heavily on two ethnographies—E. E. Evans-Pritchard's *Witchcraft, Oracles, and Magic Among the Azande* (1937) and Bronislaw Malinowski's *Coral Gardens and Their Magic* (1935)—for their inspiration. As admirable as these classic works are, they represent only a minute portion of the ethnographic record. There is still a pressing need for fine-grained accounts of magic as it is understood and practiced in specific societies.

This book examines the magical practices of the Aguaruna, a native people of the Upper Amazon. In the course of this examination, I will attempt to show how magic makes sense to the Aguaruna, given their representations of reality. As we shall see, the Aguaruna do not think of magic as an activity totally different from religion, mythology, or even instrumental action. Indeed, one of the objects of this study is to establish that from the native point of view magic does not differ qualitatively from practical activity, nor is its logic independent of prevailing notions of material causality.

At this point, the attentive reader may be asking, "If magic is not clearly distinguished from other pursuits, why use the term at all?" This question admits of no easy answer. "Magic" has long been viewed as a problematic label. The publication of essays that attempt to distinguish magic from religion, science, or technology is almost a cottage industry in the field of anthropology. More recently, critics have charged that "magic" is a catchall for "those operations which the agents consider efficacious but which the scientific observer thinks deluded" (Peel 1969:73). Jeanne Favret-Saada (1980:195) argues that this negative definition of magic is simply a sly means of defining magical practitioners as exotic "others" so that the anthropologist is absolved of the need to probe deeper into truly different ways of seeing the world.

Nevertheless, "magic" does serve as a convenient, if flawed, term for a congeries of phenomena that are difficult for Western observers to understand. After exploring various alternatives, including a complete purging of the term from this book, I have decided to pay reluctant homage to our intellectual history by using "magic" to label the beliefs and practices I document here. A working definition that has the rare virtue of brevity is provided by J. Van

Baal (1971:55–56): magic consists of "ritual acts that are directed toward concrete or practical ends." A more poetic formulation, and one I find closer to the Aguaruna way of looking at the matter, is found in Michael Taussig's *The Devil and Commodity Fetishism in South America* (1980:15). "Magic," Taussig writes, "takes language, symbols, and intelligibility to their outermost limits, to explore life and thereby to change its destination."

In common anthropological usage, "magic" encompasses such phenomena as sorcery, shamanistic healing, the manipulation of human sentiments, and ritual procedures that accompany practical work, all of which are found in Aguaruna society. Since a detailed analysis of the Aguaruna's entire magical repertoire would result in a text of unwieldy proportions, I have chosen to focus on magical intervention in subsistence activities and marital relations—kinds of magic that the Aguaruna practice almost exclusively in private.

Provision for private magic—that is, ritual undertaken in isolation—is rarely made in theories of ritual performance. Many anthropologists choose to focus on the effects that the ritual healers produce in their patients through the mind-body connection or placebo effect. Alternatively, they develop theories that draw attention to the social aspects of rituals—their rhetorical content and the unconscious messages they may communicate. There is no question that ritual can be an important form of social action. Nevertheless, it is illuminating to look at ritual procedures that have shed at least some of their social skin, their tissue of political and economic and interpersonal contingency. In private magic, we have the opportunity to observe collective representations being put to work by individuals for practical ends (cf. O'Keefe 1982:14).

Interpretations of Magic

Though much maligned by his intellectual descendants, Sir James Frazer is usually credited with being the first to adopt a systematic approach to the study of magic. In *The Golden Bough*, Frazer brings together a bewildering array of magical practices recorded all over the world and organizes them according to a limited number of themes. Frazer's work introduces two inductive laws of magic, the Law of Similarity and the Law of Contagion, which in multiple reincarnations are still with us today in most analyses of magical acts. By thus reducing the apparent diversity of magic to a series of variations on the themes of similarity and contagion, Frazer's intent is to demonstrate that magical thought is based on an ordered system of natural laws not unlike those of science, the difference being that the order of magic is "merely an extension, by false analogy, of the order in which ideas present themselves to our minds." Science, in contrast, rests on "patient and exact observation of the phenomena themselves" (Frazer 1958 [1890]:825).

Two landmark studies of the 1930s recharted the course of ethnological approaches to magic. Evans-Pritchard's *Witchcraft, Oracles, and Magic Among the Azande* (1937) argues that, first, the practitioners of magic do not necessarily confuse magical rites with practical action; second, that a system of magical beliefs may be internally coherent and logical; and third, that the people who subscribe to such beliefs are able to maintain a skeptical attitude toward their own traditions, although this skepticism is sufficiently limited that the fallacies of the system are never brought to light. Malinowski's *Coral Gardens and Their Magic* (1935) asserts that the Trobriand Islanders, like the Azande, do not confuse magical action with practical, instrumental action. For Malinowski, however, magic is not an intellectual process, a means for understanding the causes of good luck or misfortune, as it is for Evans-Pritchard; rather, it is an emotional response to uncontrollable forces—disease, plant growth, the weather, and so on. The irony of *Coral Gardens* is that while Malinowski is committed to a psychological explanation of magic, he takes us on an engaging journey through Trobriand intellectual life as revealed in the complex tropes used in gardening spells. Over the years, Malinowski's documentation of the intellectual aspects of magic has proved as influential as his theories of magic's putative psychological origins.

Throughout much of the 1940s, 1950s, and 1960s, witchcraft and sorcery attracted more attention than humbler magical pursuits, and in many of these studies (e.g., Kluckhohn 1944, Marwick 1965) the principal issues are the psychological causes and social effects of magic rather than its internal logic. The question of why the members of a given society do not or cannot see the inconsistencies in their system of beliefs, first raised forcefully by Evans-Pritchard, thus remained dormant until resurrected by Robin Horton and others in the late 1960s. Horton (1967) systematically reviews the similarities and differences between the intellectual systems that support magical and scientific modes of thought. While noting that the two have much in common, Horton argues that "traditional thought" of the sort that supports magic lacks a concern with formal logic—thinking about thinking—and is thus prevented from seeing beyond itself, thereby arriving at the kind of uncompromising skepticism that is supposed to characterize Western science. Claude Lévi-Strauss, whose concerns are similar to but more far-reaching than Horton's, takes the view that magic is "science yet to be born" (Lévi-Strauss 1966:11). Using words that echo Frazer's, Lévi-Strauss points out that both magic and science are based on meticulous observation of the natural world, but while magic calls upon "perception and imagination," science is a step removed from those faculties (1966:15).

The modes of thought that underlie magic (or any other form of ritual) are not universally regarded as germane to the understanding of its meaning. Edmund Leach (1968:523) states that "the actor's own view is inadequate" for the interpretation of ritual; he bluntly asserts that "the rite is prior to the explanatory belief" (ibid.:524). Leach quite rightly points out that a ritual such as the Roman Catholic Mass is relatively invariant in its form, while the beliefs that motivate worshipers may vary greatly. Thus Leach, like other advocates of what has come to be known as the "symbolist" interpretation of ritual, attempts to "establish the explanatory priority of ritual action over the rationalizing beliefs which accompany it" (Skorupski 1976:43).[1]

The insights of the symbolist approach are acquired at considerable cost. One is bound to feel vaguely dissatisfied with an "explanation" that has little or nothing to say about the motives that cause members of a given society to act the way they do. John Skorupski (1976:48) notes that the thoughts of the participant are of more than passing human interest; they are, in fact, essential to an understanding of ritual in any comprehensive sense.

To the extent that symbolist theories of magic address themselves at all to the question of motive and belief, they advance the argument that magical practitioners think of themselves as engaging in "expressive" acts rather than "instrumental" ones. Through magic they are trying to *say* something rather than *do* something. They do not intend their magic to work in the same sense that they intend more prosaic practical acts to work. John Beattie (1970:245) makes this point when he says that the magician knows that "when he was making magic he was performing a rite, not applying laws of nature, however dimly apprehended." S. J. Tambiah echoes this view in his celebrated reinterpretation of Malinowski's account of Trobriand spells:

> It is a truer tribute to the savage mind to say that, rather than being confused by verbal fallacies or acting in defiance of known physical laws, it ingeniously conjoins the expressive and metaphorical properties of language with the operational and empirical processes of technical activity. . . . Let me emphasize that there is only a simulation involved here (Tambiah 1968:202).

The expressive/instrumental distinction upon which this argument rests begins to look less plausible when examined closely. How, for example, do we know when an act is instrumental and when it is expressive? Leach, who shares with Beattie and Tambiah the conviction that one must distinguish between these two types of phenomena, defines them in the following way. Instrumental acts (or "technical acts," as Leach prefers to call them) "serve to alter the physical state of the world out there—digging a hole in the ground, boiling an egg," and so on (Leach 1976:9). Expressive acts, he continues, "simply say something about the state of the world as it is, or else purport to change it by metaphysical means" (ibid.:9). As an example of the difference between instrumental and expressive acts, Leach contrasts the Sinhalese peasant who uses a hammer to drive a stake into the ground with one who stands still and utters a spell when faced with a charging elephant; the latter expressive action is "palpably quite different *in kind*" from the former instrumental action (ibid.:30, emphasis in original). This case illustrates the muddle into which Leach has gotten himself, for surely the man who stands still as the elephant charges is doing something quite "instrumental" from our point of view and, no doubt, from his. Nor can Leach's formulation be reconciled with accounts that, following Marx, demonstrate the expressive quality of practical labor itself (e.g., Sahlins 1976, Chevalier 1982, Feeley-Harnik 1984). Purposeful acts always "say something about the state of the world" even as they endeavor to change it.

It is in the analysis of the use of objects for magical ends that symbolist theories face their greatest challenge. Leach mentions direct physical contact as an important defining characteristic of instrumental acts, yet even a brief review of the literature turns up cases in which direct contact is essential for "expressive" magical procedures to have an effect. Obvious examples include the practice of bringing a love charm into contact with the object of one's affection or the procedures by which plant substances are rubbed on a hunter's weapon. Tambiah (1968:194) argues that this use of objects merely mimics technology by "clothing a metaphorical procedure in the operational or manipulative mode of practical action." Although I wouldn't deny that metaphor or analogy figure in this process—surely they do—it is clear that one cannot assume a priori that the performer sees this metaphorical act as inherently different from an operational act.

If, as Clifford Geertz (1973:34) suggests, the function of social science is to "seek complexity and order it," it is imperative that we document the connections between magical acts and the ideas that give them life. This is not necessarily to subscribe to a simple-minded literalism that makes thought completely determinative of action. Ideology may well mystify reality in some instances. But human action always takes place in a world charged with meaning, and any account that fails to investigate systematically the complex connections between acts and motives is, in a very important sense, impoverished.

The convention in anthropology has been to contrast "magical," "mystical," or "symbolic" thought with the kind of common-sense, "rational" thought that people apply in practical matters. Yet, as I shall show in this book, magic is by no means a closed system of symbolic relations, cut off from lived experience. It has, as Marcel Mauss and Henri Hubert (1972 [1902]:141) said long ago, "dealt with material things, carried out real experiments, and even made its own discoveries." A satisfying theory of symbolization must come to grips with the undeniable links between magic and its material effects, between symbolic thought and practical reason.

Attempts to redefine the links between symbolic processing and practical activity tend to work on two levels: the cognitive or psychological and the sociological. Dan Sperber (1975, 1980, 1982) is prominent among those who have focused attention on the cognitive domain. Sperber denies that symbolic thinking is ontogenetically prior to (and therefore more primitive than) rational thinking; rather, it works in tandem with rational thought to process information and solve problems. In the absence of factual data, the mind searches long-term memory for "symbolic evocations" or loosely associated thoughts that are then interpreted by the "rational device." Although many aspects of Sperber's ambitious program cry out for clarification, it does represent a powerful argument that symbolism is an integral part of all cognition, not just a process relegated to "religious" or "magical" behavior. Symbolic thought, Sperber asserts, is a "particularly creative form of problem solving" (1980:43).

Sperber's insights complement the poststructuralist concern with the relationship between thought-of and lived-in orders. In a provocative analysis of economy, ideology, and culture change among the Campa of Amazonian Peru, Jacques Chevalier (1982) expresses his misgivings about the predilection of social scientists to assume a "differentiation between elements of action and those of meaning, or between the realm of material activity and the psychological process of human signification" (1982:4). Chevalier instead proposes to look at culture as a process of "practical signification," in which signs acquire material concreteness and actions accrue symbolic meaning.

In the chapters that follow, I assess the symbolic content of Aguaruna magic without losing sight of its connections to technology and "production" in the broadest sense. Specifically, I wish to show how the Aguaruna accommodate "instrumental" and "expressive" acts within one general framework of causality. Put in slightly different, and perhaps more pretentious, terms, my goal is to interpret magical thought and action in terms of Aguaruna ontology, or theories of the nature of existence.

The approach followed here is frankly literalist in that it seeks to illuminate magical acts and utterances in terms of Aguaruna notions of their intended purpose. This is not to say, however, that every statement about magic need be taken at face value. Like all human beings, the Aguaruna are able to say things "in quotes"—to perform acts or make statements that require a symbolic rather than a literal interpretation. But the greatest care must be taken before asserting that a given declaration is issued in inverted commas, lest we construe a statement encapsulating some truly different way of looking at the world as a "merely poetic" utterance.

In chapters 1 and 2, I offer a brief overview of Aguaruna social life and world view, paying particular attention to ideas of how human beings come to control events in their world. Chapters 3 through 5 detail the use of magical techniques in three important arenas of daily life—hunting, horticulture, and domestic relations. In each case, a description of the activity's technical and social context is followed by an analysis of the magical procedures pertinent to that domain. I particularly want to call attention to the web of cognitive associations linking specific magical acts to practical activity. In chapter 6 I pull together the diverse threads of ethnographic fact to argue that the Aguaruna see no fundamental disjunction between magic and technology. Their magic is a process in which the symbolic and practical orders inform one another. Aguaruna magic and technology share a common concern with—indeed they are constituted by—ordering behavior that has an instrumental intent.

The Aguaruna and Amazonian Ethnography

Although this work primarily addresses certain questions of anthropological theory, it is also intended as a contribution to the ethnography of those Amazonian peoples whom the Spanish called "the Great Nation of the Jívaro." The Aguaruna, who number around

FIGURE 1. **Approximate Distribution of Jivaroan Linguistic Groups**

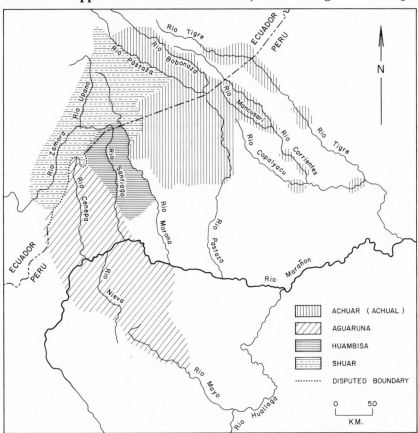

twenty-five thousand (Uriarte 1976), are a prominent member of this language family. Other Jivaroan societies include the Shuar, the Huambisa, and the Achuar (also known as the Achuarä or Achual).[2] Contemporary Jivaroan peoples primarily inhabit upland tropical forest regions in eastern Ecuador and north-central Peru.[3] (See Figure 1.) Aguaruna populations are found in the southern and western reaches of this area, along the Alto Río Marañón and its tributaries and, in lesser numbers, along tributaries of the Río Huallaga. My own field research was conducted in several communities located in the valley of the Alto Río Mayo, a Huallaga tributary in northern Peru.

All Jivaroans are known in the popular and ethnographic literature for their bellicosity and, more specifically, for the now-abandoned practice of shrinking the severed heads of slain enemies for ritual purposes. The Shuar of Ecuador, the most extensively studied Jivaroan group, are the subject of general ethnographic accounts by Rafael Karsten (1935), Matthew W. Stirling (1938), and Michael J. Harner (1972). Harner's monograph provides a good overview of Shuar culture as it was in the late 1950s and early 1960s, and most of his observations can be extended to the Aguaruna as well.[4]

The Aguaruna of Peru are the subject of one general ethnographic study (Brown 1984c) as well as many scholarly contributions of a more specialized nature. Henning Siverts (1972) has written a passionate account of the destructive effects of rapid culture change on Aguaruna communities in the Alto Río Marañón, and Martha Works (1984a, 1984b) documents the transition to market-oriented agriculture among the Alto Mayo Aguaruna. Mildred Larson (1966, 1978; Pike and Larson 1964) conducted linguistic research among the Aguaruna for many years. Aguaruna ethnobiology is analyzed in meticulously crafted studies by Brent Berlin (1976), Brent Berlin and Elois Ann Berlin (1975, 1977), and James S. Boster (1980, 1983), which were inspired by the pioneering work of J. M. Guallart (1962, 1964, 1968a, 1968b, 1975). Several volumes of Aguaruna myths were collected by T. Akuts Nugkai et al. (1977, 1979) and A. Chumap Lucía and Manuel García-Rendueles (1979). The present study of Aguaruna magic is in many respects complementary to the existing literature. By focusing attention on a domain in which encyclopedic knowledge of the natural world meets more abstract notions of being and becoming, I hope to shed light on Aguaruna ethnobotanical and ethnozoological concepts. The role of myths as explanatory texts and rich sources of imagery is explored in some detail. I also try to bring the prevailing image of Jivaroan fierceness into better perspective by describing an area of Jivaroan life characterized as much by the creation of harmony as by the expression of hostility.

Although Jivaroan languages have no close relatives among other Amazonian tongues, Jivaroan culture shares much in common with upland groups of western South America. The Aguaruna, like many of their neighbors, live in semipermanent villages usually comprising fewer than 150 people. Their political system is acephalous and egalitarian in nature. Aguaruna subsistence patterns are not dramatically different from those of such well-known groups as the Canelos Quichua (Whitten 1976), the Amahuaca (Carneiro 1970), the Sharanahua (Siskind 1973), or the Cashinahua (Kensinger 1975). In common with other lowland Amazonian societies, the Aguaruna possess a rich mythology that informs all facets of daily life. In contrast to many of the societies of Brazil and eastern Peru, however, the Aguaruna lack a tradition of large-scale, centrally organized rituals. Such rituals as existed in the past were primarily associated with the vision quest and the preparation of trophy heads obtained during intertribal warfare. Since the abandonment of large-scale hostilities, ritual life has been confined to shamanistic healing sessions, small domestic healing rituals performed by nonspecialists, and the magical rites described here.

Studying Aguaruna Magic

In December 1976, I arrived in Huascayacu, an Aguaruna village located on a small tributary of the Alto Río Mayo. My choice of Huascayacu was purely serendipitous. Two weeks earlier, while traveling in the sierra near the town of Chachapoyas, I had met a farmer giving a party to celebrate the sale of his land in the highlands and the removal of his family to a jungle plot in the Alto Mayo. Under the influence of the copious amounts of cane liquor that he and his relatives were drinking, he told me that his new farm was near two villages of *chunchos* (a pejorative term meaning jungle Indians), probably Aguaruna, and he offered to take me to them. Under the influence of equally copious amounts of the same cane liquor, I accepted his invitation instantly. My original fieldwork proposal had been to conduct a study of exchanges of medical information across ethnic boundaries. Because my planned field site had, for various reasons, proved unsuitable, I was actively searching for an alternate location where I could begin work. The Alto Mayo seemed to be just such a place.

My new friend, who undoubtedly soon forgot the entire episode, was startled to find me at his door in the Alto Mayo a fortnight later. He kindly located someone who could guide me to Huascayacu, a village located about three hours on foot from the mestizo settlement of Atumplaya. My guide and I came upon a party of Aguarunas clearing the trail, and they invited us to drink manioc beer. With the assistance of Teodoro Timías, the village's bilingual teacher, I explained that I wanted to live in the community "to learn about Aguaruna language and culture." This request was baffling to my hosts but not completely without precedent: they had heard about the activities of American missionary-linguists sent by the Summer Institute of Linguistics to other Aguaruna villages, and they assumed that my work would be similar. I suspect that it was a combination of traditional hospitality and simple curiosity that convinced them to grant me permission to stay. This was their opportunity to study a *kurínku* (gringo) at close range, and they were not about to let it slip away. Months later I realized that luck also played a part in my cordial reception. Huascayacu was far enough away from the areas of intensive colonization by non-Indians that the villagers had thus far been spared the tense confrontations with outsiders that were then afflicting other villages in the Alto Mayo. Consequently, they were much less suspicious of me than were their kinsmen elsewhere.

The community loaned me a small, unoccupied house in the center of the village, and I arranged to take meals with several families in the community. During my first months in Huascayacu, I occupied myself after the manner of most ethnographers new to their field site: following the events of daily life, measuring gardens, collecting genealogies, and learning to conjugate verbs under the sardonic tutelage of naked seven year olds. Most villagers had only a limited command of Spanish, so I had little choice but to learn Aguaruna. After about eight months, I was able to ask coherent questions and, with steadily greater frequency, understand the answers. About this time I also had to abandon my original research design, as it was clear that Aguaruna-colonist exchanges of medical knowledge were still limited and mostly confined to the use of commercially made pharmaceuticals by the Aguaruna.[5]

To broaden my perspective on the current situation of the Alto Mayo Aguaruna, I moved to the community of Alto Naranjillo in November 1977. There I became actively interested in the question of magic while pursuing information on the use of hallucinogenic plants. I was intrigued by the fact that certain visions were said to be more than just a way of seeing things; the Aguaruna thought of them as a means of *doing* things, of affecting the world through specific experiences. While reviewing months-old tapes of songs with knowledgeable informants, I discovered that some songs were attributed a similar power to affect the world. Knowledge is power in ethnographic inquiry: as I learned more about magical procedures, songs, and charms, I was able to ask better questions and eventually penetrate some, though undoubtedly not all, of the secrecy that surrounds this aspect of traditional lore. In this enterprise I was greatly assisted by Margaret Van Bolt, who came to the Alto Mayo in June 1977. Her conversations with Aguaruna women provided information about garden magic that would have been impossible to gather had I been working alone, because of the social constraints on private conversations between men and women.

Although I tried on various occasions to use interview protocols and formal elicitation methods, they inspired in the Aguaruna the

Tsewa's Gift

most profound ennui. People responded much more enthusiastically to questions asked in the course of informal visits in the early morning or late afternoon, times of day devoted to socializing. I obtained certain kinds of secret information in private conversations with knowledgeable people. The Aguaruna usually perform magical rites in private, which made it difficult and in some cases impossible for me to make firsthand observations of the procedures described in the following pages. To confirm the accuracy of accounts that I could not verify myself, I cross-checked statements with as many people as possible. While much of my information was gathered in Huascayacu and Alto Naranjillo, I managed to visit eight of the nine Aguaruna communities of the Alto Mayo and interview people from each in order to arrive at the broadest possible spectrum of opinion.

One of the most difficult problems of this research was to obtain accurate glosses of magical songs, the language of which is exotic even to the Aguaruna. Most adults could explain the general meaning of a given song, but few were able to interpret every trope on a word-by-word basis. The translation method that I finally employed involved several steps: recording the song, making a transcription and preliminary translation with the aid of a bilingual assistant, returning to the original performer to inquire about specific phrases or figures of speech, and then seeking the opinions of others about the meaning of difficult passages. This procedure often generated additional comments that were incorporated into the analysis as it progressed.[6] (More detailed information about translation procedures and examples of the original Aguaruna song texts can be found in Appendix II.)

During the months that I spent in the Alto Mayo, the Aguaruna treated me in a manner that was remarkably generous, patient, and good-humored. That is not to say that our relations were entirely free of tension. Given the serious problems they face as a result of the incursion of non-Indians into the region, it would be a miracle if they had not felt at least some suspicion about my presence. Yet I always felt that they were willing to share their traditional lore with me so that I, however imperfectly, could explain it to others. The emphasis that I place on Aguaruna song and narrative in part reflects my admiration for their consummate skill as musicians and orators.

When I left the Alto Mayo in October 1978, after twenty-one months in the field, I was confident that I had established the broad outlines of the magical procedures associated with horticulture, hunting, and domestic relations. The interpretation of this information, however, proved more difficult than I had anticipated. Because magic is practiced in private, it is not amenable to the style of analysis that stresses the social impact of rites (e.g., Victor Turner's [1967:260–72] interpretation of the Ndembu *Mukanda* ritual). Approaches that focus on words and acts as expressive or performative phenomena seem to do violence to the beliefs of the practitioners, who are clearly convinced of the instrumental efficacy of their rites. In developing my own interpretation, then, I have tried to follow a course that takes into account both the symbolic aspects of magic and the instrumental intent that is its raison d'être.

In the summers of 1981 and 1984, I was able to return briefly to the Alto Mayo to catch up on recent events and to ask for clarification of points related to magical procedures. The changes that had taken place since 1978 were astonishing. The Marginal Highway of the Jungle (*Carretera Marginal de la Selva*) connecting the Alto Mayo to major cities on the Peruvian coast, which opened to traffic in late 1977, was now a bustling thoroughfare that transported colonists and businessmen to the Mayo and produce to the Pacific coast. Although my Aguaruna friends humored me by answering questions about magic and other traditional practices, it was apparent that their interests had turned to more exotic matters: bank loans, mechanized agriculture, or the advantages and disadvantages of purchasing a bulldozer for the community. It became clear to me that in my zeal to make sense of Aguaruna magic, I had inadvertantly contributed to the stereotype of Jivaroans as a "timeless people." The assumption that culture consists of patterns that endure over time is at the heart of anthropology, of course. But as Johannes Fabian (1983) has pointed out, this assumption threatens to deny to the culture under study its ability to adapt and progress. Despite their tenacious adherence to certain traditional values, the Aguaruna emphatically refuse to become anachronisms. In an afterword to this book, I describe some of the changes taking place in the Alto Mayo and the Aguaruna response to them.

My fieldwork from 1976 to 1978, and especially my brief follow-up visits, made me acutely aware of the difficulties raised by intracultural variation in belief and practice. Jivaroan societies are highly atomistic, lacking the sort of centralized political or religious institutions that can impose uniformity of belief. The people of the Alto Mayo voiced markedly different opinions about the nature of powerful beings (i.e., "spirits"), the proper ways to use magical charms, and the reasons for the efficacy of magical acts. This variability is promoted by the fact that a great deal of magical knowledge is founded on individual experiences—dreams, visions,

omens, experimentation with magical objects—that, while culturally patterned, inevitably differ from person to person. In this study,
I endeavor to draw attention to the form underlying different opinions without violating their diversity. Nevertheless, whether any
account can truly do justice to the legendary independent-minded-
ness of the Aguaruna—their proud and stubborn determination to
respond creatively to experience in terms they find acceptable—is
doubtful indeed.

CHAPTER 1

Alto Mayo

The Mayo is a river with two lives. The Alto Mayo moves sluggishly, doubling back on itself constantly in the manner of old Amazonian watercourses. Below the town of Moyobamba, this listless meander becomes the Bajo Mayo, a torrent that drops through a series of formidable rapids until it empties into the Huallaga near Tarapoto. The available maps of the region place the entire river within the Department of San Martín in north-central Peru.

It is only the first of these two incarnations, the Alto Mayo, its physical features and its native people, that shall concern us here. The limits of the Alto Mayo valley are defined on the east by a narrow chain of mountains, to my knowledge nameless, that form the final barrier to the Amazon Basin. To the west lie the Andean foothills, and beyond them the eastern cordillera. Despite its altitude (800–1,500 meters above sea level) and its relatively modest rainfall (1,500mm per year), the native vegetation of the valley is tropical rain forest. Unlike many other parts of Amazonia, however, there are no clearly marked rainy and dry seasons. Precipitation peaks between January and April, but significant amounts of rain may fall during any month. Owing to the favorable climate and soil, vast portions of forest have been removed to accommodate cash-crop agriculture in the past ten years. Undisturbed forest is now primarily confined to land belonging to Aguaruna communities and a few upland watershed areas protected by the government.

Alto Mayo Ethnohistory

Little is known about the early history of the Alto Mayo except that in late Peruvian prehistory (A.D. 1100–1470) it was inhabited by a group of Indians known as the Muyupampas, who were apparently allied with the small pre-Inca state of Chachapoyas to the north-

FIGURE 2. **Department of San Martín, Peru**

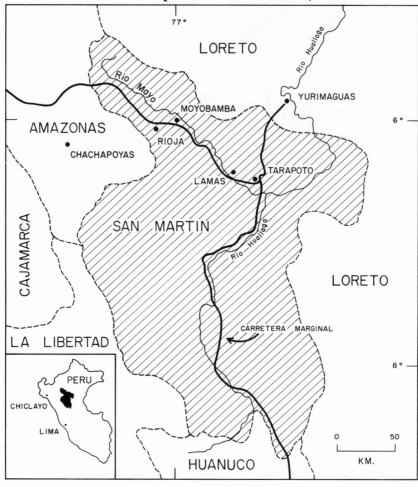

west. The Muyupampas, along with the people of Chachapoyas, were eventually conquered by the Inca Tupac Yupanqui shortly before the arrival of the Spanish (Garcilaso de la Vega 1966:480). The fate of the Muyupampas subsequent to the arrival of the *conquistadores* remains a mystery. Like the Cumbaza and Suchichi Indians of the Bajo Mayo, they may have been assimilated or eliminated soon after contact. Spanish settlers arrived in the Alto Mayo in the 1540s, but despite the political importance of Moyobamba in the early years of the colonial Province of Maynas the Spanish established settlements only in the immediate vicinity of the present-day towns of Moyobamba, Rioja, and one or two smaller villages.

Thus the upper reaches of the Mayo had little direct contact with non-Indian settlers until the twentieth century. Information is scarce as to what native population, if any, lived in the more remote forested areas of the Alto Mayo between the sixteenth century and the first half of the twentieth century. Recent ethnohistorical research conducted by Grohs (1974:84) has produced fragmentary evidence suggesting that some Cahuapanas and Chonzo Indian populations may have inhabited the forests immediately east of the Alto Mayo.

Permanent Aguaruna settlements in the Alto Mayo were established in the 1940s, although individual families may have been using the Mayo as a hunting and refuge territory since the early twentieth century.[1] The first families to settle in the area came from the Potro, Cahuapanas, and Apaga rivers, tributaries of the Alto Río Marañón. Those who were among the earliest to arrive recall that the area was uninhabited and, as a consequence, rich in fish and game. The abundance of fish and game is one of the most frequently cited motives for the migration to the Alto Mayo, although a desire to escape intratribal vendettas in the Potro-Cahuapanas area is also mentioned. As they came, Aguaruna families settled along the Mayo and its tributaries, including the rivers Huascayacu, Naranjillo, Túmbaro, Cachiyacu, Naranjos, Valles, and Huasta.

Adults who participated in the migration to the Alto Mayo say that it was some years before they come into contact with local "Christians" (kistián), that is, non-Indians. Santiago Pijúsh described what he was told about the first encounter with the man who was to become his family's patrón:

> Long ago, no one lived here. In Putjuk [the Río Potro] my relatives heard that there were many peccaries and spider monkeys here. Some people came to see if this was true. They found many fish in the rivers.
>
> They made gardens way upriver, on the Río Huascayaquillo. Little by little, they moved here from Putjuk, settling upriver.
>
> One day they found a trail made by Christians. They were afraid, but my grandfather Kujak followed the trail until he arrived at a place where the Christians had tied a machete to a tree with a vine. He took down the machete, examined it, then left it where he had found it.
>
> When the Christians returned, they noticed that the machete had been moved. They followed my grandfather's tracks until they came upon my relatives. Both groups, Aguarunas and Christians, ran away because they feared one another.
>
> Then one of the Christians, Rosalio, said, "I'm going to talk to them. They aren't our enemies. I'll see if they'll work for me." He

went to look for my relatives, but couldn't find anyone. One day he found Grandfather Kujak, and they talked. My grandfather had learned a little Spanish in Majanú [the Alto Río Marañoń]. They made friends. Rosalio invited Grandfather Kujak to his house. They talked a lot. Kujak and the others began to buy things from Rosalio. Rosalio traded them cloth for meat. Little by little they came to know the Christians.

These first contacts were established in the early 1950s, and they intensified as the mestizos sought to take advantage of the forest products and cheap labor provided by the Aguaruna. Some households relocated so that they could work for *patrones* on a daily basis. Much of the Aguaruna-mestizo trade was controlled by four or five men from Rioja and Moyobamba. Some of these *patrones* engaged in the abuses that are so common in trade relations throughout the Amazon. The Aguaruna were allowed to become indebted and then forced to work at far below the going wage labor rate to pay off their debts. Several *patrones* established unions with Aguaruna women, fathered children, and then abandoned them. Still, the Aguaruna were spared the overt violence inflicted by *patrones* elsewhere in the Peruvian Amazon, and some older people recall this period as a time of relative affluence when they could obtain boxes of beads or ammunition in exchange for only a few animal pelts.

Events broke the hold of the *patrón* system in the early 1970s. A series of laws favorable to native peoples was issued by the left-leaning military government of Peru following the coup of 1968. These laws outlined procedures by which Indians could have their villages designated as "native communities" (*comunidades nativas*) and obtain inalienable land titles to be held in common by community members. In 1970 the Summer Institute of Linguistics (SIL) sent two bilingual Aguaruna teachers to survey the Alto Mayo villages in preparation for the establishment of primary schools. The two teachers, Adolfo Juép and Israel Katíp, convinced community leaders that they no longer had to brook the abuses of the *patrones*. Meanwhile, the *patrones* denounced Juép and Katíp before the local authorities, arguing that the SIL had sent in "outside agitators" to stir up the Indians. Both teachers were detained, and Israel Katíp spent two months in the Iquitos jail until the trumped-up charges against him were dismissed in court. The happy conclusion of this case marked the end of *patrón* influence in the Alto Mayo.

Most of the communities petitioned for, and were granted, land titles in the mid-1970s. (One community, San Rafael, was not awarded its title until 1983.) Land grants in the Alto Mayo were much more generous than those awarded Aguaruna communities

FIGURE 3. Location of Aguaruna Communities, Alto Río Mayo

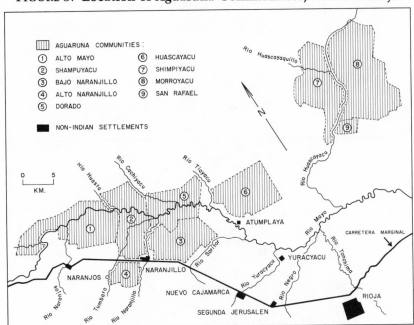

AGUARUNA COMMUNITIES:
1. ALTO MAYO
2. SHAMPUYACU
3. BAJO NARANJILLO
4. ALTO NARANJILLO
5. DORADO
6. HUASCAYACU
7. SHIMPIYACU
8. MORROYACU
9. SAN RAFAEL

NON-INDIAN SETTLEMENTS

elsewhere: the average size of the Alto Mayo communities is 6,400 hectares, as compared to approximately 3,000 hectares per community in the more densely populated Alto Río Marañón.[2]

The population of the nine Alto Mayo communities was approximately 1,100 in 1978.[3] Although the relatively favorable man/land ratio enjoyed by the Alto Mayo Aguaruna has allowed them to maintain an adequate standard of living, it has also attracted Aguaruna immigrants from the Marañón and excited the envy of non-Indian colonists hungry for land in the wake of the extraordinary influx of peasants from the highlands.

The turbulent past of the Alto Mayo Aguaruna is summarized in a long narrative by Miguel Daicháp, an elderly and highly respected resident of Shimpiyacu. This account, which I present in abridged form, is a delightful concatenation of local history, rhetorical embellishment, and acute observations of the peculiar and sometimes dangerous world of non-Indians. The precise identity of the imposing "gringos" of the narrative—whom Miguel describes as great speakers and jokesters—remains a mystery.

> Back then we lived on the Río Cahuapanas. All my family lived there. Then the *kurínku* (gringos) arrived. They came from where there are

PLATE 1. *Miguel Daicháp sits with hand in front of mouth, a gesture characteristic of formal speech. He holds a rusted Winchester rifle obtained from Peruvian traders, probably in the 1940s or 1950s.*

churches, from where cloth is manufactured. Then they went on to Moyobamba. When they got there, the Christians put them in jail. But people from Iquitos came to Moyobamba and asked the gringos, "Why have they put you in jail?" The Iquitos people said to the Moyobamba people, "Why have you done this to those who make cloth? Now where are you going to buy your cloth?" The Moyobamba people were afraid and ran away. They had to pay compensation to the gringos. The gringos were tall and substantial-looking. They wore special coats, and when they walked the coats sounded like this: "saku, saku, saku." They were great talkers and they loved to joke around.

When there was a lot of feuding in Cahuapanas, my friend [unidentified] said to me, "Come here to the Río Huascayacu [a tributary of the Alto Mayo]." We left our gardens in Cahuapanas and came here. I came here, and made my garden in Pumpu, where my son-in-law and daughter lived. That's how it was. Then we went farther upstream on the Huascayacu to cut gardens, and there we stayed permanently. But I'm from Cahuapanas originally.

One day my friend went hunting, and he discovered Sullaquiro [a mestizo hamlet]. The Christians tried to grab us but we escaped. Later we lived closer to Sullaquiro, but the "lieutenants" [soldiers? police?] began to bother us. A lot of lieutenants arrived to fight. They grabbed us one after another to cut our hair. They took my friend prisoner. They wouldn't let him alone, not even to urinate or defecate. The lieutenants took him out to defecate, but they held on to him all the while. He let down his trousers, but all of a sudden he stood up and shouted, "*Carajo, carajo, sacha curaka, senchi senchi!*" [Loosely translated, this means "Damn, damn! Forest chief! Strong, strong!"] He began to run away. He fought with the lieutenant. The lieutenant shouted, "Listen, friend, listen!" He knocked the lieutenant down. He hit him with his elbow. The lieutenant groaned "Ayau!" and didn't move. My friend escaped.

They sent a paper. The head of the Moyobamba Christians wrote a paper and sent it to the government. The government said, "Why do you bother the Aguaruna? They suffer a lot and come only to buy cloth."

The lieutenant had died. Another had died, too. Their families began to talk, saying, "When people fight with the Aguaruna they end up getting killed."

Then the government said, "If you Christians kill the Aguaruna, then the Aguaruna can kill you in revenge. Why do you bother them?" Now we walk safely in Moyobamba.

The Alto Mayo Aguaruna, 1978

Although the Aguaruna lived in semidispersed neighborhoods rather than in villages until the mid-twentieth century, contemporary communities are more centralized, often consisting of a group of houses around a school and soccer field. Average village size in the Alto Mayo was about 120 people in 1978. The formation of nucleated villages reflects several factors: the need for houses to be near the village school so that children can attend classes regularly, an increasing emphasis on communal work projects, and pressures from government officials, who feel that the "natives" should adopt a settlement pattern more in keeping with the patterns of Hispanic culture.[4]

The Aguaruna themselves have mixed feelings about village life. They seem to like the opportunities for convenient socializing that settlements offer. At the same time, they are sensitive to the drawbacks of living at close quarters with neighbors. Philandering is infinitely easier in a village than it is in a dispersed settlement, which leads to suspicion and edginess on the part of men. Fears of witchcraft increase as well. People in populated settlements find it more difficult to carry out agricultural tasks as the swiddening cycle moves gardens farther and farther away from their houses. The Aguaruna are also fastidious about what Americans primly call "waste management," and some people find villages simply too dirty for their tastes. In every community I visited, there were one or two households of people who preferred to live at some distance from the village so that they could enjoy greater privacy and easier access to gardens and game. The need to defend community lands against appropriation by non-Indian colonists has also contributed to a centrifugal movement of households in recent years. After consultation with other community residents, household heads build a house near the community's boundaries so that they can keep a careful watch on neighboring colonists who might be tempted to establish themselves on Aguaruna land.

Individual households are the most cohesive social unit in Aguaruna society. Approximately 60 percent are independent nuclear families, while the rest are a mixture of independent polygynous families and extended families, the latter typically consisting of a man, his sons-in-law, and their respective wives and children.

Aguaruna communities consist of households linked by ties of consanguinity and marriage. The Aguaruna reckon kinship bilaterally—that is, they see themselves as being equally related to their mother's and father's kin. Individuals consider themselves to be members of loosely structured, egocentric kindreds rather then permanent corporate groups such as clans. A person's kindred (patáa) may include people in all the villages of the Alto Mayo, but there is a tendency to reside with genealogically close or "true" kinsmen (*dekás patáa*) rather than more distant relatives. Given the flexibility of Aguaruna kinship reckoning and patterns of residence, it is difficult to make normative statements about the composition of Alto Mayo communities. The most stable communities seem to be organized around groups of agnatic kin (people related through males), typically a middle-aged man and his brothers and sons. Nevertheless, men may also enjoy cordial and solidary relations with their mother's brothers, brothers-in-law, and male cross-cousins. Women prefer to settle as close as possible to their sisters and, if possible, their fathers, brothers, and mother's brothers. The preferences of men and women regarding residence are not entirely incompatible, owing to a pattern of marriage to bilateral cross-cousins that gives some communities an endogamous character. Various strategic factors, however, may make marriage outside the community, or even outside of the region, attractive to some men.

Through interregional marriages and frequent visits, relations are maintained with distant Aguaruna communities in the departments of Amazonas and Loreto.[5] Residents of some Alto Mayo communities are also in almost daily contact with non-Indians. As of 1978, though, there was little intermarriage and no cases of ethnic "passing," that is, a shift of self-identity from Aguaruna to "Christian."

Political authority in Aguaruna communities is formally vested in a village headman, called *apu* or *kakájam*, who represents the community in intervillage meetings and in relations with agencies of the government. The real influence of headmen depends upon such factors as the number of their close kinsmen in the community, their leadership abilities, and their personal temperament. Communities usually have several adult men who take prominent roles in decisionmaking. Relocation of households is a common reponse to disputes, and political alignments in the Alto Mayo are constantly undergoing revision as new conflicts develop and old ones are forgotten.

Bilingual teachers, trained by the SIL but now employed by the Peruvian Ministry of Education, wield considerable influence in the communities. They have been instrumental in the formation of nucleated settlements, the introduction of cash-crop agriculture, and the conversion of some people to evangelical Protestantism. All nine Alto Mayo communities now have bilingual primary schools; eventually the population will be rendered literate in both Spanish and Aguaruna.

Despite the economic changes of the past decade, the subsistence system of the Alto Mayo Aguaruna continues to be based on a mixture of agriculture, hunting, fishing, and the collection of forest products. Many aspects of traditional technology have, however, fallen into disuse. The manufacture of cotton cloth is nearly a forgotten art, and there is fear among some adults that the same fate awaits pottery technology. The spacious, oval house described by Michael J. Harner (1972:41–46) is rare, having been replaced by a more modest rectangular structure that is divided internally into two or more rooms. A shortage of raw materials and a desire to emulate "Christian" material culture has prompted a few people to construct houses with corrugated iron roofs and separate cooking shacks after the pattern followed by local mestizos.

The tradition of belligerence that usually takes center stage in ethnographic accounts of Jivaroan peoples still figures in Aguaruna life, though less in the form of overt violence than as a social attitude. Intertribal warfare lives on only as a dim memory in the minds of the oldest residents. Intratribal homicides are now rare, but animosities based on past killings continue to ripple beneath the surface of village life. On the day of my departure from the Alto Mayo in 1978, a senior man from Alto Naranjillo requested that I bring him a cannon from the United States so that he and his sons could finish off their enemies on the Río Cahuapanas without having to go to the trouble of walking there to do the killing in person. Manuel García-Rendueles, an anthropologist and Jesuit priest who spent several days visiting me in 1978, held the residents of Alto Naranjillo spellbound with tales of some violent political demonstrations he had witnessed in Chiclayo on his way to the Alto Mayo. His listeners eagerly described, in the most graphic terms, how they would have responded to the police assault had they been the demonstrators.

The Aguaruna are well aware of their reputation for ferocity among non-Indians. On several occasions between 1976 and 1978, men decorated themselves in feathers and paint (something that they do only rarely now) to scare off Andean immigrants who had started to make agricultural fields on Aguaruna land. The appearance of a dozen armed and painted Indians was the worst nightmare imaginable for these colonists, many of whom can barely conceal their fear of all things having to do with the jungle, including its original inhabitants.

Still, most Aguaruna leaders realize that they cannot win a violent encounter with heavily armed police and soldiers. When I left the Alto Mayo in 1978, attempts were being made to forge stronger links between communities so that the Aguaruna could present a united front in negotiations with local and national authorities.

Owing to disagreements with certain factions in the Alto Río Marañón, there was little enthusiasm for affiliation with the Aguaruna-Huambisa Council, a powerful pan-tribal organization already in existence. By 1981 the Alto Mayo Aguaruna had founded an independent intercommunity organization called OAAM (Organización Aguaruna del Alto Mayo), with headquarters in Bajo Naranjillo. Initially successful in fostering cooperation among the nine Alto Mayo communities, OAAM has more recently been weakened by internal strife.

Young men with experience in the non-Indian world tend to be the driving force behind intervillage political organization. Some older men, equally suspicious of non-Indians and former enemies in other Aguaruna villages, prefer to withdraw with their families farther into the forest. Many people simply tire of the interminable public meetings called whenever government officials arrive to confer with community residents. Some of these encounters have an almost surrealistic quality. On one occasion in 1977, an official of SINAMOS (the now-defunct agency responsible for "social mobilization") arrived unexpectedly in the village of Huascayacu and called a meeting. The purpose of the meeting was to have the residents elect a village representative to the newspaper *El Comercio* in Lima, which the military government had designated as the voice of the peasants. The eloquent visitor spoke (in Spanish, through a translator) about the "transcendant nature of this post in the communications sector." A representative was duly elected, the official departed hastily, and everyone promptly forgot the whole episode. As far as I know, no one in the village had ever seen a copy of *El Comercio*.

Katán Jiukám, a man in his late fifties who resided with his wife and children in an isolated ravine, is typical of men who continue to reject village life. In 1977 Katán's house was an hour's walk from other Aguaruna houses and perhaps four hours from the nearest road. He confided to me that he liked to live apart because in his remote forest site he needn't worry about the neighbors' pigs getting into his wife's garden or sorcerers approaching him unawares. His isolation kept him close to areas of good hunting and far from mestizos who might steal his goods. The intransigence of Katán and others like him is frequently criticized by younger members of the community, who see the reluctance to accept village living as old-fashioned. Katán's view is different: "Here," he told me, "I can still live well."

CHAPTER 2

Seen and Unseen

Any fantasies that one might harbor about coming to live with an Amazonian tribe existing in pristine isolation are soon shattered by a visit to an Aguaruna village. One might well see, as I did on my first day in Huascayacu, a woman serving beer from a traditional fired bowl (*piníg*) while wearing a dress of trade cloth emblazoned with the insignias of American professional basketball teams. On Sundays it is not unusual to hear a halting version of the hymn "Amazing Grace," sung with Aguaruna lyrics, coming from the schoolhouse where a bilingual teacher conducts an evangelical worship service for a handful of earnest converts. Although few men own wristwatches, many know the names of desirable Japanese and Swiss brands. They never seemed to tire of reminding me that my own inexpensive timepiece was not a member of this elite corps.

Despite their enthusiastic appropriation of foreign material culture, however, the Aguaruna inhabit an intellectual world that remains characteristically Jivaroan. The purpose of this chapter is to provide a general overview of a system of thought in which magic is a plausible, even a necessary, way to realize personal goals. In summarizing a subject that almost by definition resists summarization, we could well lose sight of our objective—to understand Aguaruna magic on its own terms. Let me therefore begin by recounting the sort of ethnographic anecdote in which anthropologists commonly traffic. The story contains some puzzling elements that will, I hope, be rendered less opaque by chapter's end.

Ankuash's Snakebite

Early one afternoon in February 1977, Ankuash Tentéts was bitten by a small palm viper as he walked down a forest trail. Ankuash hastily returned to the vicinity of his house and advised his family of his misfortune by shouting to them from the nearby bush. In a few minutes, his widowed mother-in-law, Chipa, had bathed, donned her cleanest dress, and joined him there. She arranged a small shelter for him and then set about building a fire.

Meanwhile, in Ankuash's house women were weeping, fearing that his death was imminent. The news of his accident spread through the village in minutes. Rosalia, his wife, went from house to house asking kinsmen for remedies. When she came to my house, she asked whether I had "Christian" medicine for snakebite. As it happened, I did. Yet the thought of actually administering antivenin terrified me. I had never given an injection before, nor could I be sure that the antitoxin would not set off an allergic reaction as deadly as the poison itself. I agreed to look at Ankuash anyway. Rosalia took me to her house, then pointed out the path to Ankuash's shelter. She did not accompany me there.

Ankuash was pale and nervous. Next to the shelter, Chipa prepared an infusion of alum (*alumbre*), a snakebite remedy favored by neighboring colonists. I asked to see the wound. Ankuash pointed to his left leg, just above the ankle. There was one blue point, like a tiny bruise, but no redness or swelling. The viper's fangs had not broken the skin. Immensely relieved, both for his sake and mine, I told him that he didn't need my medicine. He was going to recover.

Despite the absence of alarming symptoms, Ankuash passed the night in the shelter. Chipa, I was told, kept him awake until dawn so that he would not dream. The four fires she built around the shelter burned brightly. At first light, Ankuash colored his ankle black with charcoal. Entering his house for the first time since the accident, he said, "Snake, you have not killed me. I am alive, and now I return to my own house."

The response of Ankuash and his household to this encounter with a deadly snake illustrates the Aguaruna strategy of drawing upon both nontraditional and traditional lore as they confront a health crisis. The search for herbal or pharmaceutical remedies presents a Western observer with no major difficulties of interpretation, but what are we to make of the apparently "ritualistic" aspects of the treatment? Why doesn't Ankuash enter his house? For what purpose does he isolate himself from his family? What effect can his dreams have on his recovery? The answers to these specific questions follow from broader canons of Aguaruna ontology, important elements of which are embodied in myth.

Being and Becoming in Aguaruna Mythology

Structure and process in the Aguaruna world are based on the interaction of the easily recognized features of daily life with forces that,
while difficult to perceive, are nonetheless real for their obscurity.
The ability of people to see, understand, and communicate with the
hidden component of reality is directly proportional to their individual knowledge. Curing shamans (*iwishín*) are generally held to
have the most comprehensive knowledge of the unseen world, but
to some extent all people attempt to develop their own knowledge
throughout their lives. The Aguaruna firmly believe that each person must acquire an understanding of the properties of the hidden
world if he or she is to survive and prosper.

The fundamental realities of Aguaruna life were established in
the distant past under circumstances described in a body of myths
collectively known as *duik muun augbatbau*, "ancestor stories."[1]
At the risk of oversimplifying a complicated subject, I wish to point
out two important themes, woven throughout these mythic texts,
that are germane to a discussion of human understanding: first, the
civilizing role of knowledge; and second, the disparities between
the inner and outer identity of things.

Aguaruna mythology describes the transformation of the world
of the ancestors from one of poverty and ignorance to a state of
relative prosperity through the acquisition of knowledge. The earliest ancestors had no knowledge of cultivated plants, fish poisons,
or hunting technology. This state of intellectual darkness was so
complete that women did not even know how to give birth to their
children until they received instruction from the common mouse.
In terms of understanding the hidden world, the ancestors were
similarly deficient. One man told me with a chuckle that instead
of singing directly to the spirits to obtain visions that protect them
from enemies, the ancestors sang such phrases as "Where does my
wife urinate? Where does she defecate?" in the vain hope that this
would intimidate their foes.

With the help of culture heroes and animals in human form,
people acquired the knowledge that enabled them to assume a more
human style of life. They obtained cultivated plants and learned the
songs that encouraged their growth. They acquired the blowgun,
pottery, and knowledge of medicinal plants. They discovered that
certain plants induced visions that extended people's lives. Using
this accumulated knowledge, the Aguaruna either eradicated the
terrible monsters of antiquity or converted them to less harmful
beings. Not all the transformations of mythical times were favorable. One story explains that the dead always came back to life until

this happy state of affairs was ended by the hornet, who speared a dead person in such a way that corporeal death became permanent (Akuts Nugkai et al. 1977, II:214). Nevertheless, the general direction of change from mythical times to the present is toward increased understanding of and control over the environment. Aguaruna myths stress the civilizing power of knowledge itself, since it is knowledge that allows human beings to triumph over poverty and evil.

In his discussion of the world view of the Canelos Quichua, with whom the Jivaroan Aguaruna have many cultural affinities, Norman Whitten notes that the Quichua see personal knowledge as resulting from a combination of encyclopedic practical information and something that he calls vision, that is, "flashes of insight in which one realizes the relationship of dream content to previous knowledge, experiences, or sets of encoding devices" (Whitten 1978b:845). The learning process thus consists of a continuous integration of practical knowledge and vision. I think that this situation holds for the Aguaruna as well, although they do not make a consistent linguistic distinction between practical knowledge and visionary insight as the Quichua apparently do. The people in the Alto Mayo who are most commonly described as "wise" (yacha) are those known to possess considerable practical knowledge and to have consolidated this knowledge through the use of hallucinogenic plants. It is not enough simply to know facts; one must learn to think well by bringing together the body, the emotions, and the intellect in the epiphanous context of the visionary experience. Adults sometimes remark that their children control more knowledge (e.g., the ability to read and write) because they attend school, but that they are often "stupid" (anentáimchau, literally "without thought") because they no longer undergo the rigorous training linked to the use of hallucinogenic plants. This lack of thought manifests itself in such antisocial behavior as fighting with close kinsmen, attempting suicide, maintaining an unseemly interest in sexual adventures, and otherwise affronting traditional morality.

Another important theme in Aguaruna mythology, as elsewhere in the Amazon, is physical transformation and its implications. Humans change to plants, animals, or celestial bodies. Monsters are converted from one form to another. Even though these changes occurred in ancient times, beings and things may retain some portion of their primordial identity.

Just as frequently mentioned in Aguaruna myths is the ability of animals to adopt human form or of spirits to adopt animal form. In one myth, the jaguar takes human form to marry an Aguaruna woman (Akuts Nugkai et al. 1977, II:174). In another tale, the vulture dons a "shirt" that gives him the appearance of a person so that he can deceive the Aguarunas who have stolen the magic stones that lead him to carrion (Jordana Laguna 1974:117). Ancient warriors (ajútap) appear to human beings as jaguars, foxes, possums, or even mice. These myths thus establish a world order in which the outward appearance of a being or an object may be at variance with its hidden, inner identity. This idea is embodied in the Aguaruna belief that all things have the potential to be something more than they appear to be. People with sufficient knowledge are able to penetrate this outer form to perceive the more important inner quality. As we shall see, the hidden qualities of objects and beings are important in certain aspects of Aguaruna magic.

Powerful Beings

The Aguaruna world is populated by many powerful beings whose influence is felt in all facets of human life. Several of these beings stand out as particularly important in that they are formidable sources of spiritual knowledge and key cognitive points of reference around which people organize their experience.

I never succeeded in eliciting an Aguaruna term that means "god" or "supernatural being" in a generic sense. The Aguaruna commonly classify these entities as "people," yet they are clearly distinguished from ordinary people by the degree to which they possess wonderful powers over the forces of nature. This is not to say, however, that the Aguaruna construe them as being somehow divorced from natural laws and processes.

From the point of view of women, the most important powerful being is Nugkui, who has been defined as the "earth mother" (Harner 1972:70) or the "feminine undersoil master of garden soil and pottery clay" (Whitten 1978b:843). A myth explains that long ago the ancestors had no cultivated plants, nor had they pots in which food could be cooked. They subsisted on a miserable diet of mashed balsa wood and a few other wild foods, which were "cooked" by being warmed in the armpits. One day a woman collecting snails saw the peeled skins of manioc tubers floating down a river from somewhere upstream. She followed the river until she came upon Nugkui (who is described as an ordinary-looking woman) washing tubers on the riverbank. The woman tried to convince Nugkui to return home with her and provide food for her hungry family. Declining this invitation, Nugkui instead offered the woman her young daughter. Once settled in her new home, the daughter of

Nugkui was magically able to summon vast quantities of food, and by the same means she provided the ancestors with many beautiful clay pots in which the food could be served.

This condition of dietary superabundance lasted until the mischievous children of the household cajoled Nugkui's daughter into summoning demons and fierce animals for their entertainment. One such being, the *iwanch*, proved so frightening that the children threw ashes into the eyes of the little girl to make her send the apparition away. Thus abused, Nugkui's daughter rose to the roof of the house and called for her mother. A tall bamboo plant next to the house bent down to receive her, and she hid inside its stem. The adults of the household, returning from the garden, cut open the bamboo to look for the little girl's hiding place. Inside the stem, they found an infant who, as they soon discovered, could summon only malformed and defective cultigens. Enraged by this state of affairs, the woman brutally kicked the infant. The child climbed into the woman's anus to escape further punishment, and the myth explains that since that moment human beings have been plagued by intestinal gas.

With the disappearance of Nugkui's daughter, people were reduced to their original poverty. Nugkui eventually took pity on their plight and, appearing in a woman's dream, directed them to a cache of cultigens that were then propagated. Now, however, plants required human toil to grow. Thus the ancestors went from a condition of exaggerated poverty to one of exaggerated abundance, finally arriving at a state of balanced or conditional abundance predicated on their own labor.

Nugkui continues to live in the present, inhabiting the topsoil and deep caves. She helps garden plants grow quickly; according to some informants, she also controls the availability of certain game animals, especially the collared peccary. Some people insist that Nugkui is not a single person but rather a group of beings. They reason that because Nugkui has a daughter she must also have a husband. Nevertheless, it is more common for people to refer to Nugkui as if she were a single person, and in subsequent discussion I will follow this usage for the sake of convenience.

As a being who is instrumental in the growth of cultivated plants, Nugkui is frequently mentioned in the course of ritual acts directed toward garden productivity. In magical songs, Nugkui is a key symbol of fertility and success in such feminine endeavors as horticulture, pottery manufacture, and the care of domestic animals.

The being whose powers complement those of Nugkui is Etsa, the sun. In the mythical past, while Etsa still retained his human form, he established much of the material and social order that exists today through a series of proclamations or spells. The Aguaruna often say that a given practice exists "because Etsa said that it would be this way." Although Etsa is perceived as being instrumental in the shaping of Aguaruna moral order, many of the deeds attributed to him in mythology are negative in character. It was Etsa who gave snakes the poison that they now use to kill people. He also decreed that men will forever be suspicious of their wives, and that housebuilding will be an arduous and time-consuming task.

In due course, Etsa rose into the heavens to become the sun. His direct influence in earthly matters seems to have ended with this transformation, and the Aguaruna do not think of the sun as an active spiritual force of any consequence. I recorded no songs or prayers directed to the sun, though magical song texts sometimes use Etsa as a symbol of masculinity and success in male subsistence tasks and handicrafts.

In the mythology of the Ecuadorian Shuar, Etsa is sometimes replaced by a culture hero named Shakáim, the latter being a transformation of the former (Pellizzaro 1978b:3–5). Magical songs recorded in the Alto Mayo make frequent allusions to Shakáim, yet the Aguaruna did not consistently connect Shakáim with Etsa. They did, however, usually describe Shakáim as a masculine being who is a partner of Nugkui and who complements her feminine powers.

A third important being is Tsugki, whose home is at the bottom of the whirlpools and rapids of great rivers such as the Marañón, and who may occasionally appear above the water in the form of a rainbow. The Aguaruna's first contact with this being is described in a myth, which explains that an attractive woman (variously described as Tsugki or Tsugki's daughter) once lured a man to her home in the depths of the river. After the man was harassed by the anaconda that resided there, the couple decided to live on land in the man's house. There, too, contentment eluded them, for the man's mother beat the woman after seeing her appear in the form of a boa or anaconda. The offended woman returned to her riverbottom home, later coming to wreak vengeance by means of a terrible flood and an army of dolphins and anacondas. Only her husband was spared annihilation.

Aguaruna consultants vacillated as to whether Tsugki is the woman's father or the woman herself. Published sources are similarly contradictory: J. L. Jordana Laguna (1974:44) describes Tsugki as female, whereas Michael Harner (1972:154) states that Tsugki is male. Norman Whitten (1978b:846) argues that for the Quichua, Tsugki has both male and female manifestations. Pita Kelekna (1982) reaches a similar conclusion in her analysis of Achuar data. This sexual ambiguity accounts for the contradictions in Aguaruna comments about Tsugki, and suggests that Tsugki has a mediating role with respect to Etsa and Nugkui.

Like Nugkui, Tsugki is a living being who continues to influence human activities in diverse ways. Most sources on the Shuar identify Tsugki as the mythical first shaman and the ultimate source of shamanistic powers, a view that is commonly though not universally shared by the Alto Mayo Aguaruna.[2] The healing songs of shamans frequently allude to Tsugki or one of its animal manifestations. As we shall see later, Tsugki is also attributed special powers in amorous matters. Whitten (1978b:846–47) characterizes the power of Tsugki as unstructured and elemental, hence its association with such dangerous domains as witchcraft and sexuality. Through appropriate cultural channels, however, this diffuse power can be directed to legitimate ends.

A class of powerful beings who frequently intervene in human affairs are ancient warriors or *ajútap*, a word derived from *ajút*, meaning "old, ancient." *Ajútap* appear most frequently in the visions of people who have endured the rigors of fasting and sexual abstinence while making repeated use of psychotropic plants, especially ayahuasca (*Banisteriopsis* sp.) and several species of the solanaceous genus *Brugmansia*, a close relative of Jimson weed. An *ajútap* adopts one of various guises when it appears to a human being. It may come as a jaguar, a fox, an eagle, or one of several other birds, mammals, or reptiles, and in certain cases it may manifest itself as a cometlike ball of fire. The arrival of an *ajútap* is terrifying because the apparition is accompanied by fierce winds and deafening roars. If the vision-seeker can muster enough courage to touch the *ajútap*, it will disappear with a final peal of thunder, only to appear again later in human form. The *ajútap* then gives the person an important revelation. In the case of a man, the revelation usually is that he is destined to be a great warrior, invulnerable to his enemies. *Ajútap* appear to women more rarely than they do to men, but when they do it is usually to tell the woman that she will assist her family in warfare, perhaps by acting as a spy, or that she will excel in some more conventional female task such as gardening (cf. Harner 1972: 135–43).

Although opinions vary, most people in the Alto Mayo believe that the *ajútap* live in a great house in that part of the sky which produces storms and fierce winds. As I shall explain shortly, human beings are able to produce new *ajútap* souls at death, so that the numbers of *ajútap* are constantly increasing.

Of growing importance in contemporary Aguaruna thought, but almost irrelevant to a discussion of traditional magic, is Apajuí (literally, "our father"), a word conventionally translated into Spanish as *Dios* or God. It is difficult to say whether a high god figured in Aguaruna religious thought in precontact times. The available evidence suggests that if the concept existed at all it was limited to that of a deistic creative force.[3] Missionary teaching has advanced the idea of a more immediate and intrusive God. Aguaruna converts to Christianity now direct American-style prayers to Apajuí, and they often use such phrases as "We'll see each other again if Apajuí wills it."

Although Aguaruna Christians reject some aspects of traditional religion, I spoke with none who doubted the existence of Nugkui, Tsugki, Etsa, or the *ajútap*. Apajuí rules over other supernatural beings, but his power is necessarily more diffuse and therefore less useful to human beings in their everyday tasks. Apajuí resides in the highest heavens, where he receives the souls of the dead and serves judgment on them according to their sins.

Powerful beings provide a framework upon which the Aguaruna organize cosmographic knowledge. The most important part of the Aguaruna world is the surface of the earth, where human beings live. The spaces below the surface—the soil domain of Nugkui, the underwater domain of Tsugki, the interior of mountains inhabited by demons—are dark, mysterious, and often dangerous to humans. The heavens, both the lower sky dominated by ancient warrior souls and the upper sky where Apajuí and the souls of the dead live eternally, represent the site of future life, the existence after death. As the interface between the dark powers of the spaces below and the transcendent freedom of the spaces above, the surface of the earth has the most complex reality of all. Here the forces from above and below converge to aid or confound human activities.

Souls

At the heart of Aguaruna world view are beliefs about the nature and properties of souls. Human beings, animals, plants, and some inanimate objects have souls. The souls of human beings are usually denoted by the word *wakán*; the souls of plants, animals, and things are most commonly indicated by the word *aents*, literally "person." A *wakán* is the aspect of a human being that continues

---

to exist after death. The *aents* or "person" of a plant, animal, or thing is an anthropomorphic entity that is normally hidden inside the exterior form of the being or thing, but which may reveal itself to the knowledgeable human observer. I gloss both *wakán* and *aents* as "soul" because as far as I could determine they refer to an identical concept—namely, an enduring, hidden essence that when made visible has the form and characteristics of a human being. The current external state of a being or thing is determined by, or at least intimately related to, the current state of its soul.

Majority opinion has it that all human beings possess two souls: an eye soul (*iwaji*), which ascends to heaven after death, and a shadow or demonic soul (*iwanch*) that remains on earth in various guises after a person has died. Both of these souls have specific manifestations that are visible while a person lives. The eye soul is the reflection of a person that one sees when looking into someone else's eyes. The Aguaruna remark that when a person is healthy his pupils and irises shine brightly, but that with ill-health they lose their brilliance. At death the pupils and irises lose all lustre, a sign that the eye soul has left the body. The visible aspect of the shadow or demonic soul is the shadow that one casts on the ground.[4] When a person dies, the shadow soul becomes an anthropomorphic monster or takes one of three animal forms: deer, owl, or the blue *Morpho* butterfly. All of these forms of the shadow soul are called *iwanch* and considered menacing, but the anthropomorphic monster form is the most dangerous to human beings. People recount many tales of *iwanch* who have attacked human beings, sometimes fatally. Reactions to the *iwanch* are a curious mixture of derision and fear—derision because *iwanch* are hideously ugly and live in a way that inverts the rules of human conduct, fear because *iwanch* delight in beating drunken men and kidnaping women and children. *Iwanch* sightings are a frequent occurrence, especially just after someone has died and the soul of the deceased is thought to be in the vicinity.

Christian teachings and cross-cultural contacts in general have tended to influence soul beliefs to the point that there now exist significant differences of opinion about the number and qualities of human souls. A small but growing minority of Aguaruna state that humans have only one soul, which either goes to heaven or remains on earth to be punished for its sins. The concept of *iwanch*, the shadow soul and the forms that it takes after death, now is used to denote the Christian Satan. Thus traditional ideas about *iwanch* coexist with the idea that *iwanch* are temptors of men and inexorable opponents of God.

The exact function of souls within the human body is the subject of similarly divergent speculation. Most people express the opinion that souls animate the body. Less universally, it is believed that souls confer sensibility. As one man said, "The reason that we feel a thorn when we step on it is because we have a soul." People sometimes remark that a person who is about to die cannot taste his food. This is because his soul is preparing to leave, or has already left, his body. People do generally agree that the condition of the soul affects the condition of the body, thus making it possible to act on the former to obtain some desired result in the latter. Sorcerers, for instance, can wreak havoc on their victims by organizing an attack on their victims' souls.

In investigating Aguaruna soul concepts, I encountered a frustrating vagueness and inconsistency in comments on the precise way that souls affect bodily states. For example, there exists a category of childhood illness called "fright" (ishámkamu) that some Aguaruna explain in terms of soul-loss.[5] They say that when a small child is attacked by a dog, falls off a bed, or suffers some other frightening experience, his or her soul may be thrown out of the body, creating a pathological condition that manifests itself in fever, loss of appetite, convulsions, and eventually death. Everyone accepts the validity of the illness category "fright," but some people deny that the condition has anything to do with souls. Instead, they argue that a frightening experience makes the heart beat irregularly; this rapid and irregular heartbeat is responsible for the observed symptoms. Similar intracultural variation exists with respect to beliefs about which of the two human souls (i.e., the eye soul or the shadow soul) has the greater influence on the state of the body.[6]

Animals as well as people possess souls, although there are various opinions about the souls' form and function. One common view is that animal souls have the same form as the animals themselves. Thus when animals die, their souls ascend into the sky to be hunted in the afterlife by the souls of dead human beings. The souls of animals sometimes attack newborn children, and in describing these attacks people note that the animal soul has the same qualities as the animal's body. Bird souls peck the infant's body with their beaks, boa souls squeeze the infant's soul in their powerful coils, and so on. Yet in some cases, these same species are attributed anthropomorphic souls, which appear to people in human form.

The Aguaruna show less concern with the souls of plants than they do with those of animals. Occasionally, someone will assert that all plants have souls and that these souls cause plants to bear flowers and set fruit. More commonly, though, people confine their remarks to discussions of the souls of plants that are culturally important. These include the tuberous cultigens manioc, cocoyam, achira, and arrowroot; the medicinal plants ginger and *pijipíg* (*Cyperus* spp., a sedge); the intoxicants tobacco and *Brugmansia*; and three trees (*mente, bakaig,* and *wampúsh*) that are linked to the activities of sorcerers. All of these plants harbor "people" or souls.

A limited number of inanimate objects also possess souls. Foremost among these is stone in its various forms. Large boulders or escarpments in the mountains have "souls," "mothers," or "demons" (the expressions are used interchangeably) that sometimes appear to people as they travel in remote parts of the forest. Several kinds of pebbles are used in ritual procedures connected with horticultural, hunting, warfare, fishing, and courtship, and some people sustain that these pebbles have souls. The degree to which the natural elements are seen as animate was never clearly established during my fieldwork. The sun, moon, rain, and thunder were all people in mythical times, but today there is little concern with them as sentient beings. The Aguaruna do occasionally deliver a special chantlike speech to the rain so that it will not overtake them until they can find shelter, which may suggest that rain is still seen as animate. I was told about one abstract state that has a soul: the "soul of hunger" (*nujan wakaní*). The soul of hunger is found in food that is cooking or waiting to be served. Should anyone other than the cook lift the lid of the pot to see what is inside, he or she might catch a glimpse of the soul of hunger, which has the form of an unnaturally thin child. The person who sees this will be perpetually hungry, unable to be satisfied by food no matter how much he eats.

To summarize this discussion of soul beliefs, the Aguaruna hold that living things and some inanimate objects have an invisible, transcendent aspect that corresponds more or less to the Western idea of a soul. Souls are often anthropomorphic and possess human powers of communication. The well-being of the soul is closely tied to the well-being of the physical body within which it resides. As a corollary to this, manipulation of the soul may effect changes in the state of the body.

Dreams and Visions

Manipulation of and communication with souls are usually carried out in the naturally occurring dreams of sleep or in the visions induced by psychoactive plants. The most informative visions occur after consuming a hallucinogen, but ordinary dreams may also convey important clues about future events that will affect the dreamer. The Aguaruna generally interpret the content of dreams and visions by using a set of conventional dream symbols passed on from generation to generation.

The Aguaruna use several species of psychoactive plants to induce visions. Some informants include varieties of ginger (*Zingiber officinale*) and the sedge *pijipíg* (*Cyperus* spp.) among the plants that cause dreams, but this opinion is not universal, nor has the presence of psychoactive compounds in these plants been substantiated scientifically. With the exception of the variety of ayahuasca called *datém*, which is usually collected in the forest, all of these species can be observed under cultivation in the Alto Mayo.

Those people who venture an opinion about why some plants have an intoxicating effect argue that the plants are powerful because they are unusually "bitter" or, in some cases, "nauseating." This comment reflects the Aguaruna view that bitter substances are therapeutic and invigorating, while sweet substances are debilitating. The intoxicating power of psychoactive plants is innate, yet people can increase this power by using the plants frequently and by respecting various taboos associated with their cultivation (Brown 1978:131).

TABLE 1
**Psychoactive Plants Used by
the Aguaruna of the Alto Río Mayo**

Common name	Aguaruna name	Scientific name	Principal uses
Tobacco	*tsag*	*Nicotiana tabacum*	Inducing trance for shamanistic healing, magical songs, vision quest
Ayahuasca	*datém, natém*	*Banisteriopsis caapi*	Vision quest, shamanistic healing
Ayahuasca	*yaji*	*Banisteriopsis cabrerana*	Shamanistic healing
Toé	*baikuá*	*Brugmansia* sp.	Vision quest
Toé	*bikut*	*Brugmansia* sp.	Vision quest
Toé	*tsuak*	*Brugmansia suaveolens*	Bonesetting, inducing healing trances

Harner (1972) has described eloquently the use of hallucinogens in traditional Shuar culture, and his observations hold for the Aguaruna as well. Most of the men of the Alto Mayo began taking tobacco water, ayahuasca, or varieties of the nightshade *Brugmansia* in their childhood so that they could experience the visions thought necessary for survival in a dangerous world. The use of hallucinogens has declined dramatically in the past decade or so, owing to the influence of missionary-trained bilingual teachers and the cessation of organized intertribal warfare. Nevertheless, men continue to recognize the important role that the visions obtained in their youth had in promoting their moral education and physical well-being, and in helping them make the transition to the responsibilities of adult life.

Ignoring for a moment the special case of shamans, the Aguaruna acknowledge two major classes of visions: those in which an *ajútap* appears and speaks to the dreamer, and visions in which the dreamer sees an image of his or her future. The first kind of vision (usually referred to as *waimakbau*) confers knowledge of one's invincibility in warfare. The second kind of vision (called *niimagbau*) is not associated with warfare but rather with prosperity and good health. In a *niimagbau* vision, a man or woman sees the many children he or she will have, the fine domestic animals he or she will tend, abundant gardens, the robust good health of close relatives, and so on. The Aguaruna insist that the fact of having had this kind of vision ensures that the desirable state of affairs revealed in the vision will eventually come to pass. I was told by several people that at various points in their lives—when they perceived that things were not going as well as they might, perhaps because of a string of unsuccessful hunting expeditions or frequent illness among the members of their household—they tried to turn their luck by seeking *niimagbau* visions. With persistence, most managed to obtain a vision, and their situation immediately took a turn for the better.

Either of the two major types of visions may occur unexpectedly in the dreams of sleep, as well as under the influence of psychotropic plants, but more commonly the dreams of sleep serve to inform people of less dramatic events that will touch upon their lives, such as the arrival of unexpected visitors or the outcome of the next day's hunt. As we shall see, dreams are also an important means of monitoring the efficacy of magical procedures once they are in progress.

In a way that is difficult for the Aguaruna themselves to explain, visions and dreams have a formidable creative power that goes be-

yond mere communication. The Aguaruna insist that without ex-
pending the considerable effort required to obtain a *niimagbau* vision, one's own future is extremely insecure. The person who does
succeed in having the vision is doing more than seeing a preor-
dained future. The future exists as a set of possibilities that are
given shape by the effort to bring them into consciousness within
the visionary experience. The notion that dreams have a creative or
directive power is something that surfaces in various aspects of
Aguaruna behavior, especially in the practices that come under the
general rubric of magic.

Shamanism

Some Aguaruna have a knowledge of the hidden world that sur-
passes that of ordinary people. Those who are socially recognized as
having special knowledge are known as *tunchi*, a term that I shall
gloss as shaman. There are two principal types of *tunchi*: curing
shamans (*iwishín, tajímat tunchi*) and bewitching shamans or sorcerers (*wawek tunchi*).[7] The two categories are not totally discrete,
however, since curing shamans are also potential sorcerers, and
their enemies may refer to them in precisely those terms. The main
difference between curing shamans and sorcerers is that the former
are publicly recognized and openly engage in shamanistic activities,
while the latter pursue their activities in secret.

Shamanistic power for curing or the pursuit of sorcery is based
on possession of spirit darts called *tsentsak*, which are held in the
shaman's upper torso. Sorcerers propel these darts into the bodies
of their victims, thereby causing illness. Curing shamans use the
power of their own darts to find and remove the darts of sorcerers
before the victims have been irreversibly afflicted.

Aspiring shamans commonly acquire spirit darts from someone
who already has shamanistic powers. They may be given as a gift or
in exchange for money or trade goods. Both the dart-giver and the
dart-receiver must be intoxicated by some psychoactive plant (usually tobacco or ayahuasca) at the time the transfer is made. The
dart-giver produces a salivalike substance called *kaag*, which is the
medium for his spirit darts, and a portion of this is swallowed by
the dart-receiver. Subsequently, the new shaman must spend several
weeks taking hallucinogens and observing severe restrictions on his
diet and sexual activities. Fasting and abstinence increase the
power of his spirit darts and his control over them; indeed, the
power of a shaman is directly proportional to the length of time

Tsewa's Gift

that this regimen can be maintained. At the end of this period of seclusion, the shaman is ready to cure or kill according to his disposition.[8]

Spirit darts are sometimes obtained by means other than the transfer of darts from one person to another. The plant *tsuak* (*Brugmansia suaveolens*) possesses spirit darts that can be acquired by someone who is willing to take this powerful hallucinogen many times in succession. Two other plants, a variety of *pijipíg* (*Cyperus* sp.) and a second plant called *chukcha* (unidentified), are also mentioned as potential sources of darts. An even more elaborate method of obtaining shamanistic power from a certain tree was described to me as follows:

> The tree called *mente* [possibly *Chorisia* sp.] can be used to become a sorcerer. A person must find a *mente* tree and clear away the plants around its base. Then he must drink a lot of tobacco water until he is very intoxicated. He lies down at the base of the tree. Suddenly, a great storm comes, the wind howling "weh, weh, weh." The tree shakes. Some branches of the tree will fall close by, but the person must not be afraid.
>
> Then from the heights of the tree comes a *wiakuch* [the soul of the tree, a well-dressed person with European features]. His shoes sound "tak, tak, tak." He opens the door and comes out. He says, "Son, what are you doing here?" The person replies, "I come here so that I can be a sorcerer." "All right," says the soul of the tree, "come inside."
>
> Inside the tree is a city. The person sits down in a chair, next to a table. The soul of the tree gives him tobacco, then asks, "What do you want?" "I want spirit darts," the person answers. Telling him to open his mouth, the soul of the tree gives him darts one by one. He puts some in his ears, too. "All right, now you are ready," says the soul of the *mente* tree. This is how one obtains spirit darts from *mente*.

People sometimes come to possess spirit darts involuntarily. This can occur when a sorcerer places darts in the mouth of a sleeping person. Later the recipient of the darts inadvertently causes illnesses in others. The condition can be diagnosed by a curing shaman and remedied by removing the darts from the body of the unwitting witch.

The healing sessions of curing shamans are the only public rituals currently practiced in the Alto Mayo, aside from the desultory evangelical worship services occasionally organized in a few communities. Typically, a healing session is held when a shaman is asked to diagnose the illness of a kinsman who has failed to respond to herbal remedies or commercial medicines. The family of the patient is responsible for preparing the ayahuasca (which for curing sessions consists of a mixture of *yaji* and *datém*) that will enable the curer to look for evidence of sorcery. Shamans in the Alto Mayo also use tobacco water and, in the case of one shaman at least, cane alcohol to arrive at the state of intoxication needed to treat a patient.

On the day of the curing session, the patient and concerned kinsmen come to the house of the shaman to await nightfall. At dusk the shaman drinks the ayahuasca and waits for its effects to manifest themselves. The house is usually filled with casual conversation and gossip. Neighbors stop by to chat. When it is quite dark, the shaman begins to shake his fan of *sampi* leaves, which make a dry rattling sound. He whistles softly to himself as the ayahuasca begins to affect his perception. Casual conversation ceases. The shaman yawns in a peculiar, drawn-out way as beings called *pasuk* enter his body. *Pasuk* are spirit shamans who live in the forest. Each human shaman controls one or more *pasuk*, who enter his chest as he summons them.

When sufficiently intoxicated, the shaman examines the body of the patient in search of the unmistakable glow of sorcerer's darts. The absence of darts means that the patient has an ordinary illness—usually one of the infectious diseases introduced into the region by non-Indians—that can be cured by drugs. (The best-known shaman in the Alto Mayo frequently prescribes pharmaceuticals in conjunction with the removal of spirit darts. At the time of my fieldwork, he was most partial to penicillin and several vitamin preparations.) If darts are discovered, the shaman tries to remove them by sucking and fanning the affected part of the body. After the removal of the darts, the patient is told to observe specific dietary restrictions that will aid recovery.

Although the principal object of a curing session is to treat one or more patients, its significance extends beyond the realm of medicine in the strict sense. Shamans who take ayahuasca are able to see events happening at a distance, both in space and time. How they are able to do this is a matter of dispute, but most people adhere to the theory that the *pasuk* spirit shamans bring them information from faraway places. Members of the patient's family, or anyone else who happens to be present, may take advantage of the shaman's knowledge by asking questions about the future: "Is my brother sick or well?" "Will my uncle die soon?" "Will our enemies attack us here?" The family of the afflicted person exhorts the shaman to identify the source of the spirit darts he has removed. Shamans usually resist this pressure, since their sorcery accusations

PLATE 2. *An* iwishin, *or* healing shaman, *intoxicated by* ayahuasca, *looks for spirit darts in the bodies of two sick women. In his left hand he holds a rattle-fan of* sampi *leaves.*

may make them targets for assassination. Occasionally, a shaman does identify a sorcerer, an act that precipitates a complex series of social consequences, which can sometimes include the murder of the accused by the victim's family.

The moral ambivalence of shamanism—the fact that it can be used both to kill and to cure—leads to mixed emotions about the presence of curing shamans in a given community. I have often heard people remark that their community is good "because we don't have shamans," by which they mean both publicly recognized curing shamans and hidden bewitching shamans. These same people, however, will sing the praises of a curing shaman when they need his skills for the treatment of a serious illness. The ambivalence of the Aguaruna toward curing shamans is expressed in sorcery accusations directed toward them and, more rarely, in violence.

Harner (1972) found that Shuar shamans were able to accumulate substantial wealth in the form of trade goods by exacting fees from patients and apprentice shamans who called upon their expertise. In the Alto Mayo, however, I saw little evidence that curing shamans are any wealthier than their peers. This situation could change if the flow of mestizo patients to Aguaruna shamans that began during the late 1970s continues to increase. Curers had no qualms about asking non-Indians for fees that were three or four times greater than those they would consider asking of an Aguaruna kinsman.

A social role represented in some Alto Mayo communities, but not marked by a specific term, is that of diviner. I first became aware of the activities of diviners during an extended visit to the community of Shimpiyacu, where I stayed in the same household as a woman who was in the final weeks of pregnancy. One day she began to suffer from severe abdominal cramps, which were treated by a variety of herbal medicines and ritual procedures. Later that day at a village gathering, the oldest resident of the community was asked whether the woman would recover or die. The man paused a moment, then sighed loudly with a strange percussive sound. Those present told me that this sigh (called *maiyáijamu*, literally "yawn") meant that the woman would recover. The absence of the sigh would have been a sign of an unfavorable outcome. With further inquiry, I learned that people who are able to predict the outcome of an illness through *maiyáijamu* can determine foods that a sick person should avoid. Their divinatory powers can also be extended to such questions as whether visitors will be arriving, the probability of enemy attack, and so on.

Opinions about how divinatory powers work vary widely. Some Aguaruna say that people with this ability possess *pasuk*, the spirits mentioned earlier in connection with shamanistic healing. Because *pasuk* are themselves formidable shamans, they can see things at a great distance or predict the outcome of an illness episode. In a way that was not clearly explained by my informants, a *pasuk* informs the diviner of the correct answers to the questions that have been posed. Unlike the shaman, who has a more active control over his *pasuk*, the diviner is seen as a passive vehicle for the *pasuk*'s intelligence.

Some people vigorously deny the connection between *pasuk* and divinatory powers. One man argued that the elderly have the power to know things simply because "they are the last of their brothers and sisters to remain alive," the implication being that by virtue of their longevity they reveal themselves as well supplied with spiritual knowledge. A woman who is herself a diviner explained that she was granted this power in a vision during her adolescence. Gravely ill with an unknown sickness, she was given an infusion of the powerful hallucinogen *tsuak* (*Brugmansia suaveo-lens*). The soul of the plant appeared to her in the form of an old man. He sighed loudly—the *maiyáijamu*—as a sign that she would recover. Then he told her that she, too, would be able to predict things when asked by other people. Just as the soul of the plant had said, she found that after her recovery she had divinatory powers. She denied emphatically that her gift had anything to do with *pasuk*. The sighs, she insisted, simply came by themselves.

These objections notwithstanding, the evidence suggests that there is a connection between *pasuk* spirits and divination. The characteristic diviner's sigh is identical to the sound made by shamans at the beginning of curing sessions, a sound that was identified to me as a sign that the *pasuk* are entering the shaman's chest. Because the *pasuk* are so closely associated with shamanism, and by extension sorcery, the link between divinatory powers and *pasuk* is denied to avoid the suspicion that people with this ability are secret sorcerers.

The roles of shaman and diviner illustrate cases in which accumulated visionary experience is turned to practical ends. Through their efforts to perceive that which resists perception, people ultimately make new connections among diverse experiences, thus becoming active shapers of reality.

Ankuash's Snakebite Reconsidered

Several of the most prominent themes discussed in this chapter reveal themselves in Ankuash's response to his skirmish with the snake. His troubles originate in mythological times, when Etsa equipped snakes with dart poison, which they then began to use to hunt humans with deadly efficiency. To end their reign of terror, Etsa set a trap for them. He created an attractive woman from the *etse* tree and placed her in a location where the snakes were sure to pass on their hunting trips. As each snake came upon this woman—who, as Aguaruna storytellers love to emphasize, was lying spreadeagle on the ground, smelling of sweet perfume—he succumbed to her charms and engaged in sexual intercourse. The few snakes that resisted the *etse* woman's attractions found the strength of their poison undiminished. The rest were rendered harmless (Chumap Lucía and García-Rendueles 1979:104–15).

Just as the snakes lost their killing force through sexual contact, people bitten by poisonous snakes will expire rapidly if they do not scrupulously avoid contamination by sexual fluids, smells, and sights, or even by contact with the ordinary domestic refuse that, in the Aguaruna scheme of things, follows logically from the sexual union of man and woman. If two men are walking in the bush and one is bitten by a snake, the victim should resist looking at or touching his companion. This contact could be disastrous if the other man has recently engaged in sexual relations. The victim cannot enter his house because, as I was told, "in the house there's the smell of manioc beer and food, and of people who have had sex." To prevail in what is perceived as a battle with the snake's destructive force, one shuns all polluting, and hence debilitating, associations.

This is why Ankuash remains isolated in his lonely shelter. The presumption is that Chipa, a widow, is free of sexual contamination and can safely attend him after a change of clothes and a precautionary bath. If she had been unavailable, another elderly person or perhaps an adolescent would have been called. (In retrospect, I think that I was allowed to examine him because I was at the time living as a bachelor in the village.)

Snakes embody uncanny forms of attraction. A snakebite victim is likely to be visited by other snakes, the Aguaruna say, and so must be protected from further assault by surrounding his shelter with campfires that burn though the night. Worse still, a snake may appear in the victim's dreams to bite him yet again. A snake's dream attack is likely to be fatal. This is why Chipa keeps Ankuash awake through the night even though he doesn't appear to be ill.

When Ankuash enters his house and makes his final declaration, "Snake, you have not killed me," it seals the snake's own fate. It has lost the encounter with its human opponent and will soon die. There are, of course, more familiar elements of this treatment episode that I have neglected here: herbal and mineral preparations given to the patient orally or as enemas, the search for injectable antivenin, and so on. These are considered neither more nor less important than the exotic precautions described above. All are significant parts of Ankuash's struggle to overcome his reptilian adversary. A concern with contacts and associations, souls and dreams, is not perceived as in any sense incompatible with medical technology. In Ankuash's world, thought, matter, and energy interpenetrate; they are not mutually exclusive phenomena.

CHAPTER 3

The Uses of Affinity

In September 1977, I accompanied Eladio Jiukám, the headman of Huascayacu, and several other men on a trip to the village of Shimpiyacu for a social visit. The overland journey to this isolated community took us through miles of mountainous, uninhabited forest that showed abundant signs of game. In the late afternoon of the first day, Eladio heard a rustling off to our right. Everyone fell silent. As we watched, two peccaries moved toward us, obviously unaware of our presence. I looked in Eladio's direction and saw that he and the other men were sighting down their machetes as if they were pointing firearms. No one had a shotgun! The muscles in Eladio's neck knotted with tension as the peccaries rooted with their snouts in the soil only yards away. In a few moments they caught our scent and quickly trotted off.

Oscar Ampám, the one man who was armed, had earlier slipped on ahead of us to scout for game. The men looked up the trail expectantly, hoping that Oscar would double back to see why we had not followed him. Everyone's spirits rose when we heard a shotgun blast minutes later. "My nephew Oscar is still young," Eladio told me with a smile, "but he is a good hunter."

It is almost a cliché to say that the native hunters of the Upper Amazon, the Aguaruna included, are masters of their craft. They are thoroughly familiar with the habits of the fauna of their region. Using a blowgun and poisoned darts, they kill small and medium-sized game with quiet efficiency. Their marksmanship with firearms is excellent. Nevertheless, good marksmanship and a knowledge of animal behavior are not enough to ensure hunting success. People note that a good hunter sometimes goes for days without seeing an animal, while, as in the incident described above, another man may stumble across game when he is not even looking for it.

Part of a hunter's inventory of skills are procedures that attract game and make it easier to kill. These procedures correspond to our category of "magic" because they are not informed by theories of cause and effect that are acceptable in Western terms.

After a brief survey of the technical milieu of hunting, I shall describe the various facets of hunting magic as it is practiced in the Alto Río Mayo. These procedures consist of patterned acts and utterances, and I set myself the task of identifying the cognitive associations that link them to the immediate goal of hunting success. This includes the isolation of certain key symbols used as building-blocks in the construction of an order in which men and animals are drawn inexorably together.

Aguaruna Hunting Technology

Studies of neotropical subsistence systems emphasize the importance of animal protein in the diet of the native populations of the Amazon Basin. The shifting vegeculture practiced throughout much of Amazonia is remarkably productive insofar as carbohydrates are concerned, but it contributes only a modest amount of protein to the diet. This deficiency is made up by the exploitation of faunal resources—fish, land mammals, and birds. Because the density of game animals and, in some regions, fish is fairly low in the neotropics, scholars (e.g., Meggers 1973, Gross 1975, Ross 1978) have argued that protein resources, not carbohydrate resources, are the limiting variables in the distribution of human populations in the Amazon.[1]

Aguaruna dietary patterns conform closely to this model: protein comes largely from faunal resources, carbohydrates from horticultural products. A study conducted by Brent and Elois Ann Berlin (1977:Table 3) demonstrates that while two crops, manioc and plantains, provide nearly 80 percent of the per capita intake of carbohydrates, 70 percent of the protein in the Aguaruna diet comes from fish, birds, and mammals. The relative importance of hunting and fishing varies widely among Aguaruna populations, but in the communities of the Alto Mayo hunting provides more protein than fishing because the accessible rivers are mostly too shallow to support large fish populations.

As Eric Ross (1976) has noted in his study of Achuar subsistence strategies, Jivaroan populations usually emphasize the pursuit of small and medium-sized game rather than larger animals such as deer, tapir, and capybara. Jivaroans themselves explain this pattern in terms of food taboos that prohibit consumption of these species.

Tsewa's Gift

TABLE 2
Commonly Hunted Birds and Mammals
of the Alto Río Mayo, 1976–78

Common name	Scientific name
Mammals	
White-lipped peccary	*Tayassu pecari*
Paca	*Cuniculus paca*
Armadillo	*Dasypus* sp.
Agouti	*Dasyprocta aguti*
Collared peccary	*Tayassu tajacu*
Capuchin monkey	*Cebus macrocephalus?*
Howler monkey	*Alouatta seniculus*
Coati	*Nasua rufa*
Deer	*Mazama* sp.
Spider monkey	*Ateles* sp.
Tapir	*Tapirus* sp.
Birds	
Spix's guan	*Penelope jaguacu*
White-winged guan	*Zenaida asiatica*
Andean guan	*Penelope montagnii*
White-tipped dove	*Leptotila vereauxi*
Cuvier's toucan	*Ramphastos cuvieri*
Razor-billed curassow	*Mitu mitu*
White-headed piping-guan	*Pipile cumanensis*

Principal Source of Species Determinations:
Berlin and Berlin 1977:35, 37.

Ross argues that the taboos are a cultural response to an ecological fact, namely, that large mammals are more likely to frequent riverine habitats that were traditionally inaccessible to most Jivaroan populations. In any case, smaller mammals are preferred by the Aguaruna, and they figure more prominently in the diet. Table 2 is a list of the most commonly eaten mammals and birds of the Alto Mayo. The order of the species principally reflects the current availability of each, but it is also more or less in line with Aguaruna food preferences. Two highly regarded species, however—the spider monkey and the curassow—have been exterminated in the immediate vicinity of Alto Mayo villages. Table 2 does not include the many species of small birds killed with blowguns by boys and eaten as quick-roasted hors-d'oeuvres.

Men hunt using a mixture of introduced and indigenous technology. The shotgun (usually a 16-gauge, single-shot model of U.S. or Canadian manufacture) is the most important hunting weapon. Blowguns, used with either poisoned or unpoisoned darts, are still used to bring down birds and, to a lesser extent, monkeys. With the exception of a simple trap made of a piece of iron pipe loaded with powder and shot and connected to a tripwire, I never saw any snares, deadfalls, or other traps in use.

Aguaruna men commonly hunt alone or in the company of one of their wives. They prefer to hunt in the early morning hours and return home in the early afternoon. Hunters sometimes use dogs to help them locate paca, agouti, armadillo, and peccary. Those villages that are suffering local shortages of game periodically organize group hunting expeditions of several days' duration, during which three or more hunters travel to some isolated area of the forest where game is still plentiful. A few communities are now practically depleted of game; families in these communities have been forced to intensify their fishing activities and use their domestic animals for home consumption rather than as a source of cash income.

Given the unique ecological situation of each community and the large number of variables that affect hunting anywhere, it is difficult, if not impossible, to arrive at a meaningful measure of hunting success versus time invested. What is certain is that hunters sometimes return home with little or nothing to show for their efforts.[2] The relative uncertainty of hunting contrasts markedly with the reliability of horticulture, which produces substantial quantities of food on a daily basis. Aguaruna hunters try to reduce the uncertainty of hunting by attracting game, by rendering the animals passive so that they can be more easily killed, and by avoiding practices that can cause a serious case of "bad luck" (*shimpankámu*), a condition that manifests itself as the inability to find game. Singing is an important attracting technique, and it is with song that I shall begin my description of hunting magic.

Magical Songs

The Aguaruna draw a sharp distinction between magical songs and social or secular songs. Songs with the power to act directly upon the natural and social worlds are called *anen*. The category *anen* encompasses songs used in hunting, horticulture, and courtship, and it is sometimes applied as well to those songs used by vision-seekers while under the influence of hallucinogenic plants. Unlike social songs (*nampét*), which are often invented on the spur of the

PLATE 3. *Tiwiján Jiukám sets off to hunt with his shotgun.*

moment, magical songs are learned by rote. They are ancient, powerful, and almost invariably reserved for private use.

To learn *anen*, one approaches an older person who is willing to share his or her knowledge. Songs are sometimes purchased by offering cash or trade goods to the person whose knowledge is sought. A close kinsman, on the other hand, may be willing to teach magical songs without payment. Whatever the circumstances, instructor and pupil contrive to isolate themselves in some secluded spot where they will not be interrupted while the songs are being taught.

Instruction in *anen* songs is always associated with the consumption of tobacco by the pupil. According to Aguaruna accounts, the instructor prepares green tobacco water by chewing a wad of tobacco leaf and then squeezing the saliva and tobacco juice into the hand of the pupil, who ingests it either orally or through the nasal passages. My informants emphasized the importance of both the tobacco (which produces intoxication) and the transfer of saliva (a key substance in many magical spells) in teaching *anen* to another person.[3] Tobacco smoke is sometimes used instead of tobacco juice, especially when transferring hunting songs. In the latter case, the instructor blows the smoke through a bamboo tube into the mouth and lungs of his pupil (cf. Harner 1972:60).

When the intended recipient of the song is slightly intoxicated by the tobacco, the tutor sings the *anen* repeatedly until the pupil has memorized the words and melody. The Aguaruna insist that without the ingestion of tobacco the song would have no power, nor would the song's new owner be able to commit it to memory. Long and difficult *anen* may require several transfers of tobacco until they are learned correctly.

To keep a newly acquired song, one must maintain a restricted diet and sexual abstinence for a period ranging from three or four days to a week. This fast prevents the song from "escaping" from its new and unfamiliar owner and serves to increase the efficacy of the song when it is later used for practical ends. Fasting and abstinence are so important in the process of learning *anen* that there even exist other *anen* to prevent the loss of a song should a person break the fast prematurely. The following is an example of one of these *anen*, in this case to be used by a woman who has had sexual relations with her husband:

A.1 New ginger [i.e., the new *anen*]
  I have put inside
  That which cures anger [i.e., an *anen* that calms jealousy]
  Do not leave me
  I am a woman of good fortune

[The song] recently growing
Have I erred?
I am not flirting
It is a lie
Do not leave me
I am a woman of good fortune
Do not leave me

As the first line of this song suggests, *anen* are sometimes spoken of as if they were objects with a palpable, physical presence rather like that of the *ajútap* visions described in the preceding chapter. People think of them as having a life and permanence that contrasts with the transitory nature of social songs.

The circumstances in which these songs are performed vary according to their intended purpose. Ideally, a person who wishes to use *anen* consumes a small amount of tobacco water, taken through the nasal passages, before singing. This is because the intended recipient of the song, be it plant, animal or person, will "hear" the words better if the singer is intoxicated. "Hearing" in this context means that the recipient will conform more dramatically to whatever form of behavior the singer desires. Songs performed without benefit of tobacco can still be effective, but their power is less than those performed in an intoxicated state. Magical songs can be sung either aloud or silently—that is, in one's thoughts alone. A hunter, for example, might briefly sing a hunting *anen* aloud before entering the forest, then in his thoughts as he tracks game. The same verb (*anenjut*) denotes both manners of performance, and they are both equally efficacious. Certain magical songs, those intended to attract women, are sometimes played by men on the mouth bow or flute.

Along with social songs, *anen* share the elements of repetition, parallelism (i.e., the use of parallel grammatical structures), regular rhythm, and special poetic language (Wistrand 1969). There are, however, some formal characteristics that clearly distinguish magical from secular songs. First, they lack the conventional refrains of social songs (*janu yamai yanu* for men's songs, *ja je ja je* for women's, neither having a strict, literal translation), and they tend to be more monotonous and chantlike in character, though the differences in melodic structure are of degree rather than of kind. *Anen* also employ an obscure or archaic vocabulary not encountered in ordinary speech or in the lyrics of secular songs. This is particularly true of hunting songs, which use esoteric synonyms for many common species of animals and birds.

TABLE 3
**Synonyms for Common Animal Species
Mentioned in Magical Hunting Songs**

Animal	Common Aguaruna name(s)	Magical song synonym	Origin
White-lipped peccary	yugkipák	atukís	—
Paca	kashai	majás	regional Spanish, majáz
Agouti	kayuk, wichiká	piúnak	possibly Spanish, peón
Armadillo	iruích, shushuí	shushúmpi	—
Spider monkey	washi	chupa	Quechua, chupa ("tail")
Jaguar	ikamyawaa	tumushí	—
White-headed guan	kuyu	pawa	Spanish, pava ("turkey hen")
Razor-billed curassow	bashu	pawi	Spanish, pavo ("turkey cock")

Some of these magical-song synonyms are apparently borrowed from Shuar, another Jivaroan language, while others come from Spanish and jungle Quechua. This use of esoteric language makes certain phrases incomprehensible to all but the most informed Aguaruna. The general meaning of the songs, though, was accessible to all the performers I interviewed.

Knowledge of *anen* is still widely distributed in the Alto Mayo, but interest in and familiarity with these songs seems to be in decline. People who have been influenced by Protestant missionary teachings generally disapprove of them because their use is associated with intoxication, something that Aguaruna Christians categorically reject. Young men and women enrolled in school have less time to spend learning traditional lore, including *anen*, and they profess ignorance in this field. People who do know *anen* are not always inclined to demonstrate this knowledge publicly because the songs are considered to be valuable personal possessions that need not be shared freely. Moreover, *anen* linked to courtship and domestic relations can be used to manipulate other people, so familiarity with them may be held in an unfavorable light. I discovered that it was difficult to induce people to record *anen* unless I specifically asked them to "imitate" (*dakumát*) the songs. "Imitation" implies familiarity with the words and melody of *anen* but not necessarily the ability to use them for magical ends.

Men of the Alto Mayo commonly call hunting songs "spider monkey songs" (*washi anen*), a usage that reflects the fact that the spider monkey is a highly desired, even quintessential, game animal. A myth explains that Tsewa, the headman of the spider monkeys, was the original source of hunting implements and magic. In ancient times, the ancestors lacked knowledge of proper hunting methods and were forced to hunt by clubbing sleeping monkeys in trees. Tsewa, who is described as sharing characteristics of both a spider monkey and a person, befriended an Aguaruna man, taught him hunting songs, and made him a gift of a blowgun. They exchanged social visits, and good relations were established between them. Finally, though, the man used his new-found knowledge to hunt members of Tsewa's own household. In a rage, Tsewa rammed the blowgun into the man's anus. The man himself became a spider monkey and the blowgun its long tail. But it was too late for Tsewa to take back hunting songs, for they had already been learned by human beings (Chumap Lucía and García-Rendueles 1979:277).

One of the facts established by this myth is that hunting songs and weapons originated in the animal world and are therefore part of the natural order that has been revealed to human hunters. The myth, and others like it, also sets forth the idea that in mythical times humans enjoyed more intimate relations with animals. As I shall presently show, a desire to recreate the mythical closeness between people and game animals through the use of verbal imagery is at the heart of some of the metaphors found in hunting songs.

According to the men of the Alto Mayo, the principal function of hunting songs is to attract game to the vicinity of the hunter. A secondary purpose is to make the animals "friendly" and therefore more likely to reveal their presence by emitting some sound. As one man said, "When a man knows magical songs, he uses them as he hunts. Then the spider monkeys begin to call, and he will always kill some. The curassow calls 'pish' and is more easily found."

Because the primary purpose of hunting songs is to attract, it is hardly surprising that various forms of attraction are prominent themes in the songs. In song A.2, for example, the singer likens himself to a bird called *wiisham*, which is said to have a beautiful call that both charms the listener and inspires confidence[4]:

A.2 I am your *wiisham*
    Friend *wiisham*
    Wiisham that loves

Friend *wiisham*
Your *wiisham*
Wiisham that loves
Friend *wiisham*
Wiisham of the curassow
Unerring *wiisham* [i.e., with darts that cannot miss]
Spider monkey *wiisham*
I attract the spider monkey
Spider monkey *wiisham*
Your *wiisham*
Friend *wiisham*
Wiisham that loves
I do not err with spider monkey
Your *wiisham*
Friend *wiisham*

The man who recorded A.2 stated that the *wiisham* is mentioned repeatedly "so that the singer will attract monkeys like the *wiisham* attracts men." Yet he also remarked that this song is supposed to be performed when hunting in the company of one's youngest wife, suggesting that there is an implicit sexual dimension to the attraction sought by the singer. This erotic subtext is more clearly evident in A.3, a song that a man uses while hunting with a widow he has recently taken as a wife.

A.3 I befriend the widow
I befriend the widow
With the friend I join
Unerring with spider monkey
Attractive Kagkuí [a woman's name?]
I befriend, I befriend
Attractive Kagkuí
I befriend, I befriend

The verb here translated as "to join with," *tsanít*, is glossed by the phrase "to form a friendship with" in Mildred Larson's Aguaruna-Spanish dictionary (1966). But in common speech, the verb is often used to denote sexual liaisons. The immediate sense of the song, according to the people I queried, is that the hunter seeks to avoid the possibility that the woman's presence might frighten away game. In the words of one man, the *anen* is saying to the animals: "Join with the widow Kagkuí, who attracts monkeys. She is your friend. Don't fight with her or fear her." The woman is thus used as sexual bait to attract game.

Sex and hunting are inextricably linked in Jivaroan thought, as they are in other parts of the Amazon (Kensinger 1983). Michael

Tsewa's Gift

Harner (1972:81–82) reports that the Shuar consider hunting trips to be an ideal opportunity for husband and wife to enjoy sexual intimacy, a view that is shared by the Aguaruna. Aguaruna men will sometimes talk in a sentimental way about the hunting trips they made with a young wife, the man carrying his firearm or blowgun, the woman tending to the hunting dogs. My own observations indicate that these trips are fairly rare, mostly for practical reasons—because women need to perform garden work or look after children, for example. Nevertheless, the husband-wife hunting team remains a cultural idea and a key image in hunting songs. This connection is expressed in mythic terms through the complementarity of Etsa, the sun's human form (often referred to as Shakáim in hunting *anen*), and Nugkui, the powerful feminine being who taught women how to cultivate plants (Brown and Van Bolt 1980:171). Each is a powerfully condensed "master image" (Whitten 1978b: 839) that stands for competence in male and female tasks. Together they exemplify the complementary skills that allow society to perpetuate itself. The collaboration of an Etsa-like man and a Nugkui-like woman produces a productive synergism, with results that are greater than the sum of the parts.[5]

The way that notions of male-female complementarity can be used to construct an imagery of hunting success is evident is A.4, which is a more elaborate version of A.3:

A.4 Gatherer *wiisham* [four times]
    Wiisham that loves curassow
    Wiisham that loves curassow
    Gathering, gathering *wiisham*
    Gathering, gathering *wiisham*
    Wiisham that loves game
    Wiisham that loves game
    Wiisham that loves the deer
    Wiisham that loves the tinamou
    Gatherer *wiisham* [four times]
    Wiisham that loves game
    Wiisham that loves curassow
    Wiisham that loves the guan [*kuyu, Pipile cumanensis*]
    Hawk, hawk
    Unerring *wiisham*
    Wiisham that loves game
    Gatherer *wiisham*

    Hawk, hawk
    Attract the curassow
    Attract the curassow

I will have a miscarriage for curassow
To the Nugkui woman [i.e., the singer's wife]
I will give a miscarriage for curassow [three times]
Make me find deer
To the Nugkui woman
I will give a miscarriage for curassow
I will give a miscarriage for curassow

Tsewa, Tsewa [mythical spider monkey]
Make me find spider monkey [three times]
I will have a miscarriage for spider monkey
I will have a miscarriage for spider monkey
I will have a miscarriage for monkey fat
I will have a miscarriage for monkey fat
To the Nugkui woman
I will give a miscarriage for monkey fat [three times]
Tsewa, Tsewa
Make me find spider monkey [four times]
Hawk, hawk
Attract the spider monkey [four times]
Make me find the curassow
Make me find the guan
Attract game

One of the ways that A.4 differs from the songs previously cited is that it invokes the names of two beings, the hawk (*chikiwí pinchu*, unidentified) and Tsewa (the mythical spider monkey), enjoining them to send game to the hunter. The Aguaruna speak of all birds of prey as having a unique, even miraculous, ability to locate game, and it is this quality that explains the allusion to the hawk in a hunting song. (The possibility that this particular hawk may be one that preys on monkeys was not investigated in the field. If this turns out to be the case, the intent of the allusion becomes even more obvious.) Tsewa, the ultimate source of magical hunting songs, also has special attracting powers that are sought by the hunter. People insisted that Tsewa and the hawk are mentioned "because they always find game," that is, because they are paragons of hunting skill. No one interpreted the song as a direct plea for the assistance of supernatural agencies.

The meaning of "miscarriage" in A.4 needs clarification. The Aguaruna insist that pregnant women are subject to intense food cravings that, if left unsatisfied, can induce miscarriage. When a pregnant woman feels a strong desire for specific foods, her husband does his best to satisfy that desire if it is at all possible in order to prevent a miscarriage. The idea central to miscarriage, that an unfulfilled desire can result in physical harm to the desirer, is even extended to illnesses of men. There is, for example, a category of illness called "vagina miscarriage" (*chuki usupágbau*) that may afflict a young man experiencing a strong desire for a woman who spurns his affection. This illness manifests itself by a set of symptoms similar to those of true miscarriage (e.g., intense abdominal pains) and is treated by a similar set of techniques.

The allusions to miscarriage in A.4 mean that the hunter's desire to find game is very strong, and that he might suffer harm if it is not satisfied immediately. This miscarriage is then transferred to his wife ("To the Nugkui woman / I will give a miscarriage for monkey fat"). As I noted earlier, women are consistently identified with Nugkui in magical songs, but in this case the identification is particularly significant given the Aguaruna's belief that Nugkui cannot suffer a miscarriage, owing to her legendary ability to produce any sort of food simply by calling for it. In fact, the name of Nugkui is invoked in chants used to treat miscarriage precisely for this reason. Nugkui never lacks for food, so by definition she cannot have a miscarriage caused by unfulfilled food cravings. The implication is that if a man transfers his strong desire for meat to a "Nugkui woman," she will use her Nugkui-given powers to help him find game. In a subtle way, A.4 gives further evidence that the male-female conjugal unit is important to the successful search for game, an idea that is more clearly expressed in magical practices associated with hunting dogs.

Hunting dogs were once the object of considerable ritual activity, including an entire feast specifically intended to endow a dog with strength and skill (Karsten 1935:170). Dogs are cared for principally by women and sleep on platforms next to the fireplace at the women's end of the house. When a woman accompanies her husband on a hunting trip, it is she who handles the dogs. Knowledge of songs for hunting dogs seems to be distributed among both men and women, although the only examples I recorded happened to be sung by men. The following song, A.5, was performed by a hunter who explained that it is to be sung at dawn after a man has instructed his wife to feed the dog in preparation for the day's hunt.

A.5 Nugkui woman, Nugkui woman
    Instead of lying sleepily
    You arise
    To my wild dog *putúkam* [*Ictyon venaticus*]
    The chewed manioc
    May you give
    The mouth of new tobacco
    May you give

The hand of new tobacco
May you give

The son of the wild dog *maigkú* [*Atelocynus microtus?*]
Ja ja ja jata [onomatopoeic: barking dog]
I will let loose
The branch of new *Brugmansia*
Being difficult to harm
Ja ja ja jata
I will let loose
The son of *tsajak* [a mythical race of large dogs?]
Keen, keen its sense of smell
Ja ja ja jata
I will let loose

Brother-in-law jaguar
Far away, where you should sniff
There let you sniff
I too, I too
At the farthest edge of my hunting place
There let you search
My wild dog *putúkam*
I will make rise
Brother, brother [i.e., the dog]
What do you think can happen to you?
Sadly you awake
Is it your own bad dreams?
Scraping hesitantly your claws
You are
You go, you go

I, I
Having dreamed armadillo
I awake
Having dreamed agouti
I awake
Having dreamed paca
I awake
Having dreamed peccary
I awake

A Shakáim man, a Shakáim man
I too say
I too following
Nugkui woman, Nugkui woman,
You, you
Do you confuse
The wild dog *putúkam*?
Sad you arise, arise [as if from a bad dream].

Tsewa's Gift

I, I
Having dreamed armadillo
I awake
Having dreamed agouti
I awake
Having dreamed paca
I awake
Having dreamed peccary
I awake

A.5 opens with the command that the woman, again referred to as a "Nugkui woman," feed chewed manioc to the hunting dog. She is then told to give the dog "the mouth of new tobacco" and "the hand of new tobacco." These two metaphors were subject to various interpretations by Aguaruna consultants, but most felt that here tobacco stands for magical songs in general, since the transfer of tobacco juice is so closely associated with the acquisition of such songs. The most likely interpretation is, therefore, that the singer urges his wife to use her newest and most powerful songs to bring luck to the hunting dog. This stanza shows an elegant progression of images: "chewed manioc" becomes "the mouth of new tobacco" (i.e., tobacco recently chewed to prepare tobacco juice essential for the transfer of songs), then "the hand of new tobacco" (i.e., the hand that transfers the juice to the recipient of the song). Simultaneously, something ordinary (chewed manioc) is changed metaphorically to something powerful (chewed tobacco).

At no point in A.5 is the hunting dog referred to by the ordinary word "dog" (*yawáa*). Instead, a variety of pseudonyms are used, at least two being the names of wild canines. The more prominent of the two is the *putúkam* (*Ictyon venaticus*), a species noted for its speed and keen sense of smell. Reportedly, *putúkam* are sometimes captured, tamed, and taught to perform as hunting dogs (Guallart 1962:159). The use of the names of wild dogs instead of the ordinary word "dog" summons an imagery of swiftness and cunning that the common word cannot convey.

The last two stanzas of A.5 allude to the dreams of the hunter, his wife, and the dog itself. Dreams are important omens of hunting success, and are often a critical factor in determining whether a man will set off into the forest to hunt. Favorable dreams take various forms: a dream in which one embraces an attractive woman is an omen that one will find paca; a dream of handling a string of beads foretells that a hunter will soon be cleaning peccary tripe, and so on. People sustain that through these dreams a man "kills the soul" of a game animal. To take advantage of the soul-killing, the hunter must immediately arise and set off in search of the animal.

The final stanzas of A.5 imply that both the dog and the woman have had unfavorable dreams. The singer, on the other hand, has had good dreams: "Having dreamed armadillo, I awake / Having dreamed agouti, I awake," and so on. These lines declare the hunter's infallibility, in effect saying, "The bad dreams of others are irrelevant, since my good dreams will prevail."

To summarize the properties of the hunting *anen* known to the Alto Mayo Aguaruna, it can be said that the songs consist of a densely constructed series of images built upon an esoteric lexicon and highly figurative language. People consider the songs to be both aesthetically pleasing and practically efficacious. A key image of the songs is the conjugal hunting unit—Shakáim man and Nugkui woman—which is a cultural ideal representing the fruitful collaboration of husband and wife. This order is prominent in the songs because they attempt to create a second, auxiliary order that flows from it: the hunter successfully providing meat for his family. The erotic connotations of husband-wife hunting empower the metaphors of attraction found in the songs, as do the allusions to mythological times when men and animals enjoyed greater intimacy.

Let me present one last song that shows a slightly different approach to the construction of a favorable hunting order. Instead of focusing attention on attraction alone, A.6 describes the entire process of finding and then successfully killing spider monkeys. Its logic is that of "anticipatory effect" (Tambiah 1968:200) in that it reviews the stages of a specific task before the task is actually performed:

A.6 The spider monkeys come
The spider monkeys come
From that hill they come
The spider monkeys come
With their stiff children they come
Without seeing me they come
From this hill they come
From that hill, too, they come

Sons, sons [to the singer's own sons, who accompany him]
Do you speak to spoil my luck?
Spoiling my luck speak you thus?
You speak to attract spider monkey
You speak to attract

I will shoot the spider monkey [using a blowgun]
High, high, I will shoot

High, high, I will shoot
Turning, turning, I twist kapok onto the dart
Turning, turning, I twist kapok onto the dart
This monkey I will shoot
High, high, I will lift it [with the force of the dart]
Like manioc pierced
High, high, I will lift it
I will shoot to its *wampa* fruit [i.e., intestines]
I will shoot to its *wampa* fruit

Piercingly I will shoot
Piercingly I will shoot
I go, never missing the spider monkey
I go, never missing the spider monkey

The first image in A.6 is that of a large troop of monkeys coming toward the hunter without fear, unaware of his presence. The meaning of the second stanza is more obscure but was explained to me as being a sort of rhetorical question in which the singer asks his sons whether they are using their own magical songs to somehow confound his luck. The answer, of course, is that they, too, are silently singing to attract the monkeys. By asking the question, the verse calls attention to the combined attracting power of the several hunters present. The third stanza describes the preparation of the blowgun darts, the unerring aim of the marksman, and the force of the dart as it strikes the monkey, piercing to its vital organs. The song, then, consists of an enumeration of desired events that are ultimately translated from the mental to the physical world in a highly ordered manner.

How do the Aguaruna themselves explain the action of hunting songs? By and large they don't; it is enough to know that the songs were handed down from ancient times and that their attracting powers are continually revalidated through the personal experience of individual hunters. A few men ventured the opinion that the soul of an animal hears the song, feels attracted, and draws the corporeal aspect of the animal in the direction of the singer. This interpretation was disputed by other people, but as we shall see in later discussion, the linking of magic to soul manipulation is a common, though not universally accepted, explanation of various forms of magical action known to the Alto Mayo Aguaruna.

Game Grabbers

We ask ourselves, "Why does this man kill so many animals?" It's because he has a stone. The stone makes him a good hunter. I once found a white stone in the flesh of a paca near the pelvis. It was for

PLATE 4. *Residents of Huascayacu return from a group hunting expedition into remote, virgin forest. Young men hold long blowguns, while older men carry shotguns. Both men and women are carrying baskets, slung by tumplines, in which they transport food and dry clothing.*

hunting paca. I also found one in the stomach of an armadillo. Each animal has its own stone.

When men say they have good luck because they know more about hunting, they lie. If they find game, it's only because they have a *yuka* stone. (From interviews with Aguaruna men, 1981.)

Like hunting songs, certain material objects have the power to attract animals or otherwise help a hunter in his search for game. The generic term "game grabber" (*kuntin achitai*) is occasionally used to denote the entire spectrum of hunting charms, although it is more common to call different kinds of charms by their specific names. In the Alto Mayo, game grabbers are made from objects of animal, vegetable, and mineral origin.

As one would expect, men have a more comprehensive knowledge of hunting charms than women. They tend to be secretive about this knowledge, apparently because they fear that a public admission that they own charms might invite theft. I usually found it impossible to gather information about this subject unless I framed questions in general terms ("How does one acquire a hunt-

Tsewa's Gift

ing charm?") rather than as a personal query ("How did you obtain *your* hunting charm?").

I recall with some embarrassment my first day of residence in the Aguaruna community of Huascayacu, during which I worked on making my small house habitable. I had brought some nails to use for hanging up clothing and gear, and as I had no hammer I naturally began to cast about on the ground in search of a stone with which to pound the nails into the house's support beams. A passing villager asked me what I was doing, and after listening incredulously to my reply sent a child to fetch a small sharpening stone from the house of my nearest neighbor. Later I came to learn that much of the alluvial soil of the Peruvian Amazon has no naturally occurring surface stones. Because stones are needed for sharpening steel tools, many Amazonian Indians must buy them from mestizo traders at exorbitant prices—or prices that seem exorbitant to North Americans accustomed to thinking of stone as a plentiful substance. The people of the Alto Mayo do not have to purchase stones, but the residents of some communities must undergo the inconvenience of walking a considerable distance to find a good whetstone and carry it back to their village. Stone is thus an essential and, in some instances at least, a scarce commodity for the Aguaruna. Yet the significance of stone extends beyond the purely technological and economic. Lithic materials serve as the dwellings of souls and spirits. Large boulders and escarpments, for example, house demons who frighten male travelers and kidnap their women:

> My brother-in-law Pascual, who is a shaman, told me that he once saw the chief of the rock demons (*kayái iwanchi*). The demon wore pants and a great hat, a sombrero. He called to Pascual, saying, "Come over here." He knew a lot. The demon made Pascual stop in his tracks. He was unable to move. The demon spoke in Spanish. They had a conversation in Spanish. Pascual asked him, "Where do you come from?" The demon said, "I'm from the mountain of the anaconda." Pascual was afraid. The demon was standing in the doorway of his house, and with his power he attracted people. That's how demons grab people as they walk past. Pascual said to him, "Many people are coming behind me." As he watched, the demon disappeared into his house. . . .
>
> This demon possesses a soul. He never dies or becomes ill. When he gets too old, he changes into a baby again. He lives forever.

Men seek visions of *ajútap* spirits at rocky waterfalls deep in the forested hills because some *ajútap* are believed to live in such remote places. Small stones of various kinds have the ability to move by themselves and assume human form in dreams.

In describing a very similar set of beliefs found among the Canelos Quichua, Norman Whitten (1976:42) calls stone a "transformational" material that can "bottle up and release animistic substances." He bases this assertion on a variety of data, ranging from the observation that the Quichua use ancient petroglyphs as sources of contemporary spiritual revelation to the fact that mineral substances provide the colors used to transform the outward appearance of Quichua pottery. The Aguaruna, too, think of stone as a material that can be used to change things. The most obvious example is the stone axe, which was used before the introduction of steel tools to convert forest to garden. The Aguaruna also recognize three principal categories of "magical" stones, that is, rocks or pebbles that can be used by knowledgeable people to effect changes in the world. A class of stones called *namúg* (in some contexts *namúji*) is used by shamans and possibly by some nonshamans to inflict harm on an enemy. A second category of stones called *nantag* is used by women to promote the growth of their garden plants. A third type, *yuka*, is used by men in hunting and love magic (Brown 1985).

Yuka are stones that attract either game animals or human beings of the opposite sex. A given *yuka* stone can be used for either hunting or courtship, but not for both. People find *yuka* in the entrails (or in some cases in the mouths) of mammals, birds, and fish. *Yuka* that attract game are most commonly encountered in terrestrial mammals and birds, including the white-lipped peccary, capuchin monkey, armadillo, dove, and guan. The *yuka* used in love magic tend to be found in aquatic mammals, fish, and reptiles. Descriptions of *yuka* vary widely, but most people say that they are small, shiny pebbles, their color either white, black, or red. Some *yuka* reportedly also have an unusual shape or surface texture (cf. Karsten 1935:164–65).

When a man finds a stone in the entrails of a land mammal or bird he has killed, he has strong reason to suspect that it is a *yuka* that, if properly treated, can be employed as a powerful game grabber. The correct procedure for developing the power of the stone is to seal it immediately in a container—a small gourd or a tube of bamboo are common choices—along with a quantity of red face paint (*jampu*). The finder then abstains from sexual intercourse and restricts his diet by avoiding meat, salt, palm grubs, and other preferred foods for a period of about seven days. The Aguaruna say that this fast purifies the hunter and strengthens the attracting power of the newly acquired stone. If during the period of fasting and abstinence the hunter has dreams of game animals, it is interpreted as an omen that the stone is indeed a strong *yuka* that will attract game. At the end of the fast, the hunter puts the vessel containing the stone into his palm fiber bag and sets off to hunt in the early hours of the morning. A short distance from his house, he draws red lines on his face with the paint that has been in the vessel holding the *yuka*. (The design painted on the face was usually described as consisting of a straight line on each cheekbone and a line down the bridge of the nose. No one attributed any significance to the design itself.) Setting off once again, the hunter will soon find that mammals and birds are drawn to him. The Aguaruna insist that a really strong *yuka* brings game in unprecedented numbers and renders them submissive so that they are easily killed. After the initial testing of a *yuka*, the hunter may use it on subsequent trips without any special procedures, as long as he takes care not to touch the stone immediately after sexual intercourse. A new stone that seems to have no effect or an old stone that has been ruined by improper treatment (say, by being handled by someone who has recently engaged in coitus) is simply discarded.

I found it impossible to obtain a precise explanation of how *yuka* and other charms attract game. No one claimed that *yuka* had the power to manipulate souls, an interpretation that was offered for the action of hunting songs, nor were charms explicitly associated with a specific supernatural being. From the Aguaruna point of view, the distinctive properties of *yuka* seem to be that (1) they are stone, a rare and unique substance that has transformational capabilities, (2) they have demonstrated a strong affinity to game because they appear unexpectedly in animal entrails, and (3) they have souls or spirits that can appear in the dreams of the stones' owner. The third quality is not recognized by everyone, however. Those who do believe that *yuka* have souls told me that when a man fails to care properly for a stone, he may have a dream in which a person appears and says, "I am taking my child back because you have mistreated it." The next morning, he will find that the *yuka* has vanished. This soul or "person" seems to be construed as a manifestation of, rather than a cause of, the stone's power:

> The stone comes from an animal. The animal is the stone's father.
> The animal is the person of the stone. The animal is its soul.

The logic of unexpected affinity that is central to beliefs about *yuka* stones also figures in the use of certain insects as game grabbers. The one most frequently mentioned by Alto Mayo men is the "game bird fly" (*chigki anchiji*), which is found in the feathers of game birds, where it apparently lives as a parasite (cf. Karsten

1935:165). A hunter who finds one of these insects puts it in a container of red paint such as is used to house *yuka* stones. Again, a period of dietary restriction and sexual abstinence turns the insect into a charm that attracts the bird species from which it was obtained.

The Ethnobotany of Attraction

The people of the Alto Mayo can identify well over fifty species of plants that are used as medicines, hallucinogens, or charms. About a dozen of these are regularly tended in gardens, and some are true cultigens. The Aguaruna recognize that these cultivated plants have wild ancestors but insist that the cultivated varieties are much stronger because they have been treated in ways that bring their strength to maximum expression. In other words, the relationship between people and plants is seen as synergistic: the two agencies working together have an effect greater than the sum of their individual effects (Brown 1978). While certain plants thus have an intrinsic power to attract animals, this power must first be discovered by people and then given strength and direction through cultivation.

At least six folk genera of plants are sources of hunting charms. They are listed in Table 4 in order of relative importance.

The herb *pijipíg*, a taxon that apparently includes species of two genera of sedges, is a ubiquitous plant in Aguaruna gardens, and it is also widely cultivated among other societies of the Upper Amazon under the name *piripiri*. Varieties of *pijipíg* are used as fertility enhancers and menses regulators by women (E. A. Berlin 1977:5–6), while others are used to attract members of the opposite sex, to provide antidotes for various illnesses, and reportedly even to induce visions that result in the acquisition of bewitching darts. Only one kind of *pijipíg* has the power to attract animals. A hunter mixes the root of this *pijipíg* with red face paint and applies it when beginning the day's hunt.

People usually obtain cuttings of *pijipíg* by purchase or trade and then cultivate them in house gardens. The Aguaruna claim that some people tend particularly powerful kinds of *pijipíg* in secret garden plots, but I could not determine how common this practice is. The motives for cultivating a plant secretly include a desire to protect the plant from theft or contamination and the wish to keep one's ownership of the plant from public knowledge.

The herb *tsumáik*, like *pijipíg*, has multiple uses, principally in the attraction of game, fish, and members of the opposite sex. I

TABLE 4
Hunting Charms of Botanical Origin

Aguaruna generic name	Number of folk species used as hunting charm	Scientific name(s)
pijipíg	1	Carex sp. Cyperus sp.
tsumáik	3 +	Justicia sp. Alternanthera bettzichiana
ushu	4 +	Caladium bicolor
tapíg	2	Unidentified
tsentsém	2	Unidentified
tuyúk	?	Psychotria sp.

recorded the names of three kinds of *tsumáik* used for hunting. The first is "dog" *tsumáik*, the leaves and flowers of which are made into an infusion that is given to hunting dogs to improve their tracking ability.[6] Two other kinds, "peccary" *tsumáik* and "paca" *tsumáik*, are rubbed directly on the hands and face of the hunter or mixed with red face paint. The latter two kinds of *tsumáik* attract the animals after which they are named.

A third plant, *ushu*, has no uses other than as a hunting medicine or charm. Men apply the juice of *ushu* to their eyelids and the barrel of their shotgun before hunting. When game is near, the *ushu* alerts them to the animal's presence by making their eyelids itch. (Here it is worth noting that the plant family of which *ushu* is a member, the Araceae, includes many species that contain skin irritants such as calcium oxalate.) As is the case with *tsumáik*, different kinds of *ushu* have affinities with distinct animal species.

Three other plants, *tapíg*, *tsentsém*, and *tuyúk*, are occasionally mentioned as sources of medicines that attract game, but they are less widely used than *pijipíg* or *tsumáik*.

People proved just as reluctant to speculate on the ultimate origin of the powers of these plants as they were to interpret the reasons for the potency of *anen*. A typical comment was that the plants work "because they call (*ujuínat*) the animals." I recorded narratives that do shed some indirect light on this issue, however. These accounts describe a series of procedures used to obtain a powerful hunting charm alternately identified as *pijipíg* or *tsumáik*.[7] An example follows.

A strong plant for hunting is obtained like this. One must kill the vulture *ayumpúm* (probably the King Vulture, *Sarcoramphus papa*). The vulture is left where it has fallen, and one builds a closed shelter over it so that other buzzards won't eat it. After the vulture's body has rotted, it is burned. From the ashes several plants of *pijipíg* will grow.

A man must take one of these plants and carry it with him as he hunts in the forest. If he encounters a boa, it means that this *pijipíg* attracts boas. It is thrown away.

He picks another plant from the ashes. Perhaps this time he meets no animals while hunting, but instead dreams of women that night. This means that the plant attracts women. Then he tries another *pijipíg* from the ashes. This time he finds toucans, many toucans. This *pijipíg* attracts birds. The man takes this plant, chews it up, and uses the saliva to clean the barrel of his blowgun. When he blows through the blowgun in the direction of the birds, they sit as if they were asleep. He can kill them one by one. They won't fly away. He takes this *pijipíg* and cultivates it.

Other men will ask for this plant, but one should refuse to give it away, saying "If you want some, you too can kill the vulture *ayumpúm*."

The connection between carrion birds and magical substances is clarified by a myth explaining that vultures possess special stones which lead them to dead animals (Chumap Lucía and García-Rendueles 1979:549–53). Vultures thus symbolize uncanny attraction and the secret possession of powerful agents. The procedure undertaken to produce the hunting charm uses the symbolism of carrion birds as grist for a transformational mill such as Lévi-Strauss has found elsewhere in the Amazon: the vulture is allowed to rot (that is, arrive at a state of exaggerated rawness) before being burned (an exaggerated form of cooking). The shift from superraw to supercooked corresponds to the transformation of the vulture from a bird attracted to dead animals to a plant that attracts living animals.

What can this account tell us about the power of game grabbers? First, the Aguaruna are convinced that there are substances with a diffuse power to attract living things. These attracting substances reveal their power by appearing in unexpected places; indeed, their ability to be where they should not be is proof of their power. Through fasting, attention to dreams, and elaborate testing procedures, a hunter gives form and direction to the diffuse power of attracting substances.

Hunting Failure: Causes and Cures

One of the first things one notices about Aguaruna hunters is that they are frequently vague when discussing the time and place of their next hunting trip. A man passing through the village equipped with shotgun or blowgun, obviously on his way to hunt, states laconically that he is "going walking." He avoids a more detailed declaration because the act of talking about his hunting plans may "turn over his luck," as one Spanish-speaking Aguaruna explained to me early in my fieldwork. Similarly, it may spoil a man's hunting if someone comes to his house to visit him while he is away hunting. The hunter's family is likely to tell a visitor who arrives under these circumstances that the man has "gone to the forest," which explains his absence without explicitly stating the nature of his activities. Finally, it is considered bad form for a person to express a desire for a specific kind of meat in the presence of a man who is about to embark on a hunting trip. Children tend to do this more than adults, and when they do they are reprimanded by their parents. Any of these behaviors can cause a hunter to be afflicted by *shimpankámu*, the inability to find game.

These avoidances make sense in Aguaruna terms because statements about an intention to hunt, or one's desire for specific animal species, unmask the true uncertainty of hunting as a subsistence activity. One of the primary objects of hunting magic is to create an intimate relationship between animals and people approximating the closeness that existed in mythical times. In the context of this imagery, the coming together of people and game is perfectly natural, unlike the everyday world in which game may be elusive. When people inquire about the activities of a hunter or express a longing for certain kinds of meat, they call attention to the true nature of hunting. The fiction of intimacy is publicly exposed, replaced instead by an implicit assumption of scarcity. Such idle comments can only confound the hunter in his attempt to find game. In a more general sense, too, the Aguaruna are uncomfortable with the thought that others are discussing their success in subsistence activities. As we shall see, women make use of procedures to prevent precisely this sort of talk with respect to their horticultural pursuits, since they consider it potentially destructive to their gardens.

The most stringent avoidances associated with hunting are those related to the distribution and disposal of meat and bones. The Aguaruna are careful to see that all game animal bones, including those swept up when cleaning the house, are collected and wrapped in banana leaves so as to form a small packet. This packet of bones is later thrown into the nearest river or buried away from the house. The reason for this care is to prevent domestic animals from eating the bones and members of the household from inadvertantly urinating or defecating on them. Contact between the bones and domestic animals (especially pigs and chickens) or human excreta may cause the hunter who killed the animal to lose his ability to find game—that is, he will be afflicted with *shimpankámu*. Another precaution related to the proper disposal of animal remains is that all people who partake of the meat should wash their hands over the fireplace after the meal rather than doing it near the inner walls of the house, as is the usual custom. This practice makes it even more unlikely that minute portions of the animal will be exposed to pollution. The most fastidious hunters go so far as to insist that meat be cooked in a pot that has never been used to cook other kinds of food. Indeed, I was told that each animal *species* should have its own pot so that the meat is not mixed with that of other animals. (When elderly women inventory their clay pots, they often identify some pots as "paca cookers," "spider monkey cookers," and so forth.) One man claimed that his son lost his ability to find game "because his wife used the same pot to cook palm fruit, plantain broth, and meat."

When a hunting dog has been used to kill a particular game animal, the dog's owner observes a still more elaborate set of precautions. Meat taken with the assistance of a dog is never allowed to leave the house once it has been brought in. This means that portions of the animal are not sent to neighboring households as gifts. Animals killed with dogs are carefully butchered, and the meat is then wrapped in leaves and hung in a basket so that it will be out of the reach of domestic animals. When the meat is cooked, the pot containing it is not allowed to boil over, lest some of the meat or broth fall on the ground. When people drink the broth, they are supposed to scoop it out of the serving bowl with their hands or drink it directly by lifting the bowl; clam shells or metal spoons should not be used as eating utensils. Children who cry while the meat is being eaten or who complain that they haven't enough to eat are removed from the house. Failure to take these precautions will cause *shimpankámu* for both the hunting dog and its owner. One informant remarked that these rules are not always respected, citing the case of some Huambisa who made it a practice to sell meat taken with the aid of hunting dogs to mestizo settlers. They were able to get away with this breach of taboo only by constantly feeding their dogs powerful medicines that counteracted its effect.

The logic of these taboos is based on two related lines of thought. First, the Aguaruna recognize an enduring connection between an organism and its exuviae. Unlike the members of many other societies, however, the Aguaruna seem less concerned with the possibility that human exuviae might be used for purposes of witchcraft than that some accidental defilement of the castoff material will bring harm to the person from whom the material comes. When trimming hair, for example, people see to it that none of the hair is swept outside of the house where it might be urinated upon, since this kind of polluting contact will prevent their hair from growing in the future. Similarly, an infant's afterbirth is buried inside the house for fear that if it were buried in the forest it could become cold and wet, thus causing the infant to fall ill.[8] Based on this same logic, animal bones are thought to retain an enduring link to the species that produced them.[9] Defilement of the bones through careless handling contradicts the attraction and intimacy central to the ideal relationship between hunter and quarry.

The taboos also reflect concern with the relations between man and dog. When a dog provides meat through its hunting skill, in a sense it fills the role of a person and must be treated with appropriate respect. Thus the broth of the meat is drunk with cupped hands or by tipping the bowl, since the use of an eating utensil would formally mark the eaters as different from and superior to the dog. The rules against sending meat out of the house and putting up with the complaints of children may also be seen as ways of showing respect to the dog in return for its services. I wish to stress, however, that the latter interpretations are mine alone. The Aguaruna themselves were primarily concerned with preventing the dog from being "ruined" and offered no more detailed explanation of how these rules protect the luck of hunter and dog.

An important effect of this system of prohibitions is that people are disinclined to make gifts of raw meat between households, since one cannot be sure that members of another household will be as careful as they ought to be in disposing of the bones.[10] In both communities in which I lived for extended periods, gifts of raw meat were rare. On the other hand, dinner invitations in which a hunter asked several neighbors to eat meat in his own house were very common. During these visits, the host and his guests usually managed to consume most of the animal. Although mandated by a system of taboos, meal invitations are consonant with the prevailing system by which men acquire personal prestige. Communal meals permit the hunter to be the center of attention in his multiple roles as provider of protein, gracious and attentive host, and teller of tales. This could not be so easily accomplished through a gift of raw meat. The few exceptions to this pattern of meal invitations usually occurred when there had been a major kill of the increasingly rare collared peccary. In this case, a single household might acquire more meat than it could consume or preserve by smoking and salting, so gifts of meat were sent to households that had none. Restrictions on interhousehold sharing do not apply to foods such as wild fruits, fish, or garden produce, which are freely distributed in unprepared form.

When a man sees that he is consistently unable to find animals in the forest, he begins to suspect that in some way he or a member of his household has broken one of the rules that prevent *shimpankámu*. From my own observations, a hunter is less concerned with determining the cause of his *shimpankámu* than in finding the fastest possible remedy. There is, however, no single infallible way to do this. Men first try to acquire one or more of the hunting charms mentioned earlier, either a *yuka* stone, a "game bird fly," or a powerful variety of one of the herbs that attract game. If acquisition of a new hunting charm does not remedy the situation, they resort to more drastic cures. One consists of grabbing the trunk of the *tagkán* tree (probably *Triplaris* sp.), which is inhabited by a stinging ant of the same name. The hunter holds on until the stings of the ants become unbearable, an act that may result in a fever of one or two days' duration. He will subsequently discover that his ability to find game has returned. Alternatively, a man can cure *shimpankámu* by shooting off a branch of the same tree with a blast of his shotgun.

In a case of prolonged *shimpankámu*, men drink infusions of the powerful hallucinogenic nightshade *bikut* (*Brugmansia* sp.) with the hope of obtaining the type of vision known as *niimagbau*. This vision, which emphasizes material prosperity and hunting success, is usually sufficient to restore their ability to find and kill game. People in the Alto Mayo say that regardless of how one remedies *shimpankámu*, after it has been cured the hunter will find all the animals that eluded him during the period of his affliction. Old men are wont to complain that no cure is possible for their *shimpankámu* because their households have become so large that there are always women and children polluting the remains of game animals. "My father used to say that when he got old he couldn't find game any more," one elderly man told me wistfully. "Now the same has happened to me. Now I find nothing. My wives and children have given me *shimpankámu* through their carelessness."

Another condition that can afflict a hunter is the sudden loss of marksmanship ability. This is commonly called *beséjatjamu*, a word that is related to *besémat*, "to be ruined, to receive a bad omen." *Beséjatjamu* occurs when one man "dreams" another, that is, has a dream in which a second man plays a prominent role. The Aguaruna describe these dreams as being quite ordinary. In the most frequently cited example, a man dreams that an acquaintance has killed many animals and is carrying them back to his house. Despite the favorable imagery of the dream, it has the effect of spoiling the marksmanship of the dreamed person when he uses either a blowgun or firearms. It may also leave him feeling constantly drowsy.

If the dreamer and the dreamed enjoy friendly relations, the former will immediately tell the latter about the dream and propose a cure. The cure is very simple: the dreamer squeezes a small quantity of tobacco juice into the dreamed man's eyes while repeating the phrase "I throw out the *beséjatjamu*."

It was, and still is, baffling to me why the act of dreaming about another man's hunting exploits would cause the dreamed person to lose his marksmanship ability. This belief may be related to the Aguaruna concern with dreams that cause "soul killing" (*wakaní mantuámu*). A warrior or shaman who dreams that he is killing a game animal—an armadillo, an agouti, or whatever—may in fact be killing the soul of one of his young children who happens to be sleeping near him on the sleeping platform. A child whose soul has been killed soon falls victim to fatal illness. To prevent this, a woman sleeps between her husband and her child when they share the same bed. Men may also have dreams in which they kill an enemy's soul, which in turn makes the enemy's body more vulnerable to attack. (A common refrain in the songs of men who seek killing visions through the use of hallucinogens is "I dream my enemy," which implies that they will acquire the power to assassinate their rivals.) The dreams of men are thus perceived as competitive and, in some cases, damaging to the well-being of the person dreamed.

A second set of circumstances in which a hunter's marksmanship may be unfavorably affected was described to me by Miguel Daicháp:

> When a man has intercourse with his wife while hunting spider monkeys, his blowgun sometimes becomes jealous. The blowgun says, "You have committed adultery with my wife." Then it won't shoot straight.

To cure this, the man must give the blowgun to his wife to carry for awhile. The blowgun then says, "Everything's fine because I have had sexual relations with my wife." After that, the blowgun shoots straight and the man can kill monkeys.

This idiosyncratic account provoked much appreciative laughter among the other people who heard it, and I initially suspected that Miguel may have invented it to enhance his already considerable reputation as a storyteller. Nevertheless, it does fit rather well with some of the beliefs mentioned earlier in this chapter. I recorded two poorly remembered segments of songs directed to the blowgun in which it was addressed personally and told: "Wake up, wake up. Your enemy the spider monkey is coming." When a man offers his wife to the jealous blowgun so that it will shoot straight, his behavior echoes A.3, a song that draws attention to a woman's charms in order to attract game.

Sexual symbolism thus pervades hunting magic, and as we shall see in a later chapter, the symbolism of the hunt figures prominently in the magic of sexual attraction. Hunting, like sexuality, is fundamental to the perpetuation of the Aguaruna way of life. Its importance to the Aguaruna dictates an attentiveness to thoughts, utterances, contacts—conceptual connections of all kinds—that goes far beyond the confines of technology.

CHAPTER 4

The Garden's Children

It seemed to me that the dew-damp garden surrounding the house was infinitely saturated with invisible people . . . secretive, busy, and multiform in other dimensions of time.

J. L. Borges,
The Garden of Forking Paths

Amazonian peoples commonly contrast the danger and disorder of the forest with the security of the garden, a segment of space that has, for a time at least, come under the control of human beings. But the Aguaruna see things differently. For them the garden, like the forest, is a spiritually charged realm that poses dangers to the unwary or imprudent. They are deeply concerned with garden productivity, something that seems to be taken for granted in most other Amazonian societies. To a scientific observer, the Aguaruna horticultural system is remarkably productive and resistant to the climatic fluctuations, plant diseases, and pests that make plant cultivation so risky in the temperate zones. Not so for the Aguaruna gardener, who feels that without magical intervention the success of her crops is always in doubt.

The contradiction between garden productivity and the apparent anxiety of the producers is mystifying as long as we envision economic or botanical facts as being separate from culturally constituted emotions, understandings, and strategies of production. In this chapter, I present an outline of Aguaruna horticulture that calls attention to the links between practical activity, magic, cosmology, and the continuous realization of feminine identity. As we shall see, the production of crops and the production of meaning are interrelated processes.

Aguaruna Horticulture

The Aguaruna practice a complex form of shifting horticulture based on the cultivation of more than eighty species of plants (Berlin and Berlin 1976:10). Most of these are true cultigens—species not found outside of cultivation—while a few are useful wild species planted in gardens to be more readily available when needed.

Aguaruna horticulture is principally oriented to the production of the root crops manioc (by far the single most important cultivated plant), yams, cocoyams, sweet potatoes, taro, and arrowroot. The prominence of root crops is explained, among other things, by their lack of seasonality. They can be harvested throughout the year, eliminating the problems of harvesting and storage associated with seasonal crops. Some nontuberous crops, including plantains, bananas, maize, peanuts, and various fruits, do make a significant contribution to the diet, however. Rice, which is cultivated for sale rather than consumption, has also become an important horticultural product in some of the communities of the Alto Mayo. An inventory of the food crops of the Alto Mayo will be found in Table 5.

Plants are cultivated in slash-and-burn gardens, or swiddens (aja), located as near as possible to each house site. When a new house is constructed, people customarily plant manioc, plantains, and other crops immediately around the house. As production in the gardens adjacent to the house begins to decline, new gardens are established at suitable sites farther away, though part of the original garden near the house is usually maintained as a sort of kitchen garden for the cultivation of plants important in technology, ritual, and health maintenance. (See Figure 4.) Houses that have been occupied for a few years thus have a kitchen garden, one new root crop garden that is beginning to produce, and one or more old gardens (asáuk) whose production is in decline. Combined data from the communities of Huascayacu and Alto Naranjillo indicate that each household has an average of 1.1 hectares of land under cultivation in traditional crops, plus additional land planted in cash crops. After five to eight years of continuous occupation, most of the cultivable land within convenient walking distance of a house has been used up. People then begin to think of establishing a new house in areas of mature forest where potential garden sites are more readily available.[1]

Although the composition of swiddens varies somewhat among households, they are always prepared using the same procedures. First, the male household head, in consultation with his wife, se-

---

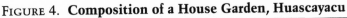

FIGURE 4. **Composition of a House Garden, Huascayacu**

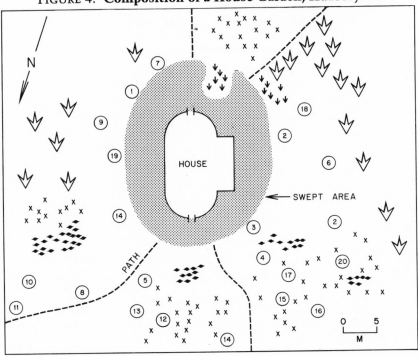

PLANTAIN (<u>MUSA</u> SPP.)

x MANIOC (<u>MANIHOT ESCULENTA</u>)

SWEET POTATO (<u>IPOMOEA BATATAS</u>)

FISH POISON (<u>CLIBADIUM</u> SP.)

Other plants:
1. achiote (*Bixa orellana*)
2. papaya (*Carica papaya*)
3. *chi* (unidentified cucurbit)
4. ginger (*Zingiber officinale*)
5. *pijipíg* (*Carex* sp./*Cyperus* sp.)
6. *tsuak* (*Brugmansia* sp.)
7. sapote (*Pouteria* sp.)
8. *shiwágkush* (*Solanum stramonifolium*)
9. cotton (*Gossipium* sp.)
10. squash (*Cucurbita maxima*)
11. tobacco (*Nicotiana tabacum*)
12. air potato (*Dioscorea bulbifera*)
13. *kumpia* (*Renealmia alpinia*)
14. achira (*Canna* sp.)
15. *kampának* (*Eleuthrine bulbosa*)
16. taro (*Colocasia esculenta*)
17. *manchúp* (*Colocasia* sp.?)
18. sugar cane (*Saccharum officinarum*)
19. *yujágmis* (*Physalis* sp.)
20. cocoyam (*Xanthosoma* sp.)

lects an appropriate garden site. People prefer to cultivate high, well-drained land away from marshes and frequently flooded river-banks. After choosing a site, a man invites his kinsmen to partici-pate in a communal work party (*ipáamamu*) to clear the low-growing vegetation and small trees with machetes. Later, he fells the large trees with an axe. (Some economically useful trees, such

Table 5
Principal Food Crops of the Alto Mayo Aguaruna

Common name	Aguaruna name(s)	Scientific name
Manioc	*mama*	*Manihot esculenta*
Plantain	*paampa*	*Musa balbisiana* x *M. acuminata*
Yam	*kegke*	*Dioscorea trifida*
Sweet potato	*kamút, idáuk, inchi*	*Ipomoea batatas*
Cocoyam	*sagku*	*Xanthosoma* spp.
Taro	*pituk*	*Colocasia esculenta*
Peanut	*duse*	*Arachis hypogaea*
Maize	*shaa*	*Zea mays*
Rice	*ajus*	*Oryza sativa*
Jícama	*nabáu*	*Pachyrrhizus tuberosus*
Arrowroot	*chiki*	*Maranta ruiziana*
Squash	*yuwí*	*Cucurbita maxima*
Secana	*namúk*	*Sicana odorifera*
Achira	*tuju*	*Canna* sp.
Achira del monte	*kumpia*	*Renealmia alpinia*
Pigeon pea	*biik*	*Cajanus bicolor*
Bean	*kistián biik*	*Phaseolus vulgaris*
Air potato	*papa*	*Dioscorea bulbifera*
Cocona	*kukúch*	*Solanum* spp.
—	*shiwágkush*	*Solanum stramonifolium*

as palms, are left standing.) The garden dries for several weeks until it is ready to be burned. After the garden is burned and some of the slash removed, it can be planted. Garden preparation may occur at any time of year in the Alto Mayo, although there is a tendency to avoid initiating this task in the period from January to April, the months of greatest rainfall.

The Alto Mayo Aguaruna follow several alternative planting strategies in their gardens. Most commonly, they plant manioc, sweet potatoes, yams, and other tuberous crops in the center of the garden and plantains on the perimeter. Sometimes a section of the garden is set aside for maize or peanuts; manioc and other tubers are planted after these are harvested. Old manioc gardens near houses are frequently cleared and replanted in large stands of plan-

Tsewa's Gift

Table 5 continued

Common name	Aguaruna name(s)	Scientific name
Chili	*jima*	*Capsicum* spp.
Sugar cane	*pagáat*	*Saccharum officinarum*
Papaya	*papí*	*Carica papaya*
Peach palm	*uyái*	*Guilielma gasipaes*
—	*pina*	*Calathea* sp.
Sorghum?	*shapna*	?*Sorghum vulgare*?
Yarina	*chapi*	*Phytelephas* sp.
Pineapple	*pina*	*Annanas comosas*
Sapote	*pau*	*Pouteria* sp.
Cacao	*bakáu*	*Theobroma cacao*
Macambillo	*akágnum*	*Theobroma bicolor*
Passion fruit	*kistián munchi*	*Passiflora* sp.
Breadfruit	*pitu*	*Artocarpus atilis*
Inga	*wampa*	*Inga edulis*
Turmeric	*kisatúra*	*Curcuma zeodara*
Star apple	*yaas*	*Chrysophyllum cainito*
Guava	*shawi*	*Psidium guayava*

Principal Source of Species Determinations: Berlin and Berlin 1977:22–25.

Note: In preparing this table, numerous cultivars of minor dietary importance have been deleted. See Berlin and Berlin 1977:22–25 for a more comprehensive list of Aguaruna cultivars. Specialists will note that some of the plants listed above (e.g., plantains, bananas, rice) are not native to the New World.

tains. Increasingly, the Aguaruna also plant pure stands of rice and other cash crops for sale to non-Indians.

A garden begins to produce mature manioc tubers about six to eight months after planting and continues to provide tubers for two to three years. Declining tuber production and the ever-increasing number of weeds seem to be the main factors that lead to garden abandonment. Even after a garden has ceased to be used on a daily basis, however, it continues to provide some food products (e.g., plantains, papayas, sweet potatoes) that people harvest sporadically.

The degree of sophistication of traditional Aguaruna horticulture is most obvious in connection with the cultivation of sweet manioc. Manioc is the most important garden crop, both nutritionally and symbolically; one of the words (*yujúmak*) denoting manioc tubers also means "food" in the most general sense. Most Aguaruna gardeners have from ten to twenty-five distinct, named varieties of manioc in their gardens, and the total number of varieties known to the Aguaruna may exceed one hundred (Boster 1983:61).[2] Varieties are distinguished according to several characteristics, particularly the shape and color of the leaves. People prefer to eat some varieties boiled or roasted, while others are more suitable for the preparation of beer. Women acquire new varieties of manioc from other women in the same community or from kinswomen in distant communities.

If the botanical knowledge underlying manioc cultivation is complex, its technology is extremely simple. Pieces of manioc stems are placed in the ground after a new garden has been prepared. When the stems have taken root and the plants have grown to a height of approximately 1.5 meters, a woman begins to travel daily to the garden to harvest as many tubers as she needs. After harvesting a mature plant, she cuts off a section of stem and replants it in the spot vacated by the harvested plant. Thus, like the harvest, replanting is continuous. The only implements used in the cultivation of manioc are the machete and a pointed digging stick (wai) made of palm wood.

One of the reasons why manioc is so important is that it can be converted into manioc beer (nijamánch), a dietary mainstay and the major lubricant of Aguaruna social life. To make beer, women boil the tubers, mash them to a pulplike consistency with a wooden pestle, chew the pulp to soften it further, and then place the mash in a large pot to ferment. When mixed with water, the fermented mash becomes a nutritious and intoxicating beverage. Beer is consumed daily, and most Aguaruna consider it to be an essential— even the most essential—part of their diet.[3]

Brent and Elois Ann Berlin (1977:13) calculate that during its productive life an average quarter-hectare garden supplies enough manioc to maintain a family of ten persons. Because the average household size is considerably less than this (five persons per household in the area studied by Berlin and Berlin, 7.4 persons per household in the Alto Mayo), they are forced to conclude that "the Aguaruna produce—or have the potential to produce—much more than they actually need" (1977:13). During my own fieldwork, I never heard of a catastrophic garden failure, nor did any household suffer from a substantial shortage of manioc unless serious illness or relocation to a new village prevented a woman from pursuing her horticultural tasks.

Horticultural tasks are sharply divided along gender lines. Men take charge of choosing a garden site, cutting the brush, felling trees, and burning the slash. They may also plant and harvest those few crops that are considered "male": maize, plantains, and rice. All activities involving tuberous crops, however, are performed by women. These tasks include planting, weeding, harvesting, washing the tubers, and cooking. Because Aguaruna horticulture is primarily oriented to the production of tuberous crops, gardening is thought of as a feminine activity. Women consider themselves to be the owners of most gardens, except those devoted to male cash crops.

A woman's success in horticulture has a direct relation to her social standing in the household and the community. The hospitality that a man can extend to visitors is in no small measure determined by his wife's skill in cultivating manioc and turning it into manioc beer; frequent shortages of beer in the household may kindle a husband's wrath. A man who is a mediocre hunter may have other socially valued skills that compensate for his inadequacy. Women, however, have few other avenues in which to excel if they lack horticultural prowess. A woman's social identity is thus closely tied to the productivity of her swidden garden.

The Swidden as Symbolic Space

The garden is an area of space rich in symbolic associations. Women and their children spend several hours there nearly every day. A woman puts her baby in a tiny hammock hung in some shady spot, and her other children play quietly nearby while she goes about her tasks. Sometimes women help each other in the garden—mother and daughter, for example, or a woman and her unmarried sister—and when one walks near the swidden their laughter can be heard through the tangle of manioc stems. Here, in the relative privacy of this space, women discuss intimate matters related to their daily lives. They may also use this time together to exchange magical songs that encourage the growth of their plants or renew the affection of their wayward husbands.

In mythical times, the garden was the scene of romantic liaisons between women and animals in human form. When the ancestors did not know how to give birth without cutting open a woman's womb, they were taught proper childbirth by *katíp*, the mouse, in a garden (Jordana Laguna 1974:107–10).

The garden is also the principal point of contact between women and a variety of powerful beings. The most important of

PLATE 5. *Wampurái Peas plants manioc cuttings in a recently burned swidden.*

these is Nugkui, who lives in the soil and gives life to cultivated plants. Nightly, Nugkui comes to dance in the garden, and she is particularly fond of attractive, well-weeded swiddens (Harner 1972:71). Women usually cannot see Nugkui, but they may see her messenger, the nighthawk *sukuyá* (*Nyctidromus albicollis*), who comforts manioc plants when they complain of mistreatment.

Nugkui is by no means the only being of consequence in the garden; several species of cultivated plants have souls that must be reckoned with. As one would expect, the souls of manioc plants are the ones with which Aguaruna women are most immediately concerned. How people came to know that manioc plants have souls was explained to me as follows:

> Long ago people did not make gardens as we do today. Instead of waiting until the entire garden was cleared of brush and large trees, women began to plant manioc as soon as a small part of the garden was cleared. [Presumably, this was because forest clearance was much slower before the introduction of steel tools.] Thus the manioc was sometimes mature in some parts of the garden before the entire garden had been cleared.
>
> One day a man who was clearing a garden said to his wife, "If I cut down this big tree, it might fall on the manioc that is already growing. Shall I leave it standing or cut it down?" He decided to cut it down and instructed his wife to make manioc beer so that he could invite his kinsmen to help him.
>
> A few days later the men came, and after drinking manioc beer they began to chop down the large tree. Suddenly the souls of the manioc plants arose; they were people, lots of people. The manioc people said, "We will help cut the tree so that it won't fall in our direction." When the manioc people arose, all of the men fell asleep.
>
> Some of the manioc people began to pull a vine growing on the tree, while others cut the tree with axes. They pulled the tree so that it would fall away from them. As they pulled, the old manioc people sang, "Sons, pull hard so that the tree won't crush our children. When we're done we'll eat the head of a spider monkey."
>
> When the tree had been felled, the manioc people disappeared. Among the sleeping men, the man who had called the work party could hear the songs of the manioc people in his sleep. Because of this, we know that manioc has a soul, that it has people.

Although Karsten (1935:123) reports that the Shuar regard the soul of manioc as being female, Alto Mayo women reason that since manioc plants are "people," there must be both male and female plants, as well as adults and children. The belief that manioc plants are sentient gives rise to a number of practices intended to maintain good relations between a gardener and her crop, and thereby to promote a good harvest. First, when women harvest manioc they always leave a few of the very largest plants unharvested so that these will "call" new plants to replace the ones just uprooted. One women explained this in a slightly different way. "The large plants," she said, "sing to the replanted stems to make them grow well." Of the plants that are harvested, not even the tiniest tuber should be left behind lest this "baby" begin to cry because it has been abandoned:

> The other manioc plants come to console the baby tuber saying, "Why did our mother leave you behind? If she does this, how will the manioc grow so that she can make beer for our father?" To avoid this, you must always collect every tuber when digging up a manioc plant.

The souls of manioc plants are extremely dangerous during the first few months after planting. The young plants become thirsty, and if this thirst is not quenched by the appropriate means they may "drink the blood" of people passing through the garden. The drinking of blood is also called "soul eating," and as far as I could determine the two expressions are used interchangeably. Both soul eating and blood drinking denote a tapping of a person's life force such that he or she becomes weak, pale, and unable to resist death in the form of illness or snakebite. To avoid this danger, children are discouraged from playing by themselves in recently planted manioc gardens (cf. Harner 1972:75).

While manioc is the cultigen most consistently attributed a soul, other plants of lesser importance—e.g., arrowroot, cocoyam, and achira—also have "people" with whom gardeners interact. One of the goals of a gardener is to encourage the plant "people" to assist manioc in its growth and development. So far as I know, nontuberous crops such as plantains, maize, and rice are never attributed souls, nor do they receive any ritual attention.

A few women spoke of a being whom they called the "manioc mother" (*mama dukují*) or "manioc master" (*mama muunji*). While I could obtain little information on this being—there was no consensus of opinion even on whether it exists—those women who mentioned it clearly distinguished it from Nugkui. They also suggested that it resides in the largest manioc plant in the garden. The manioc mother sometimes moves around in the garden while a woman is at work:

> When you hear a twig snap on the edge of the garden, you shouldn't look in that direction because it's the manioc mother. If you look at her, she gets angry and shits weeds. The whole garden fills with weeds. If you don't look at her, she is happy. She shits manioc and the plants grow quickly.

Clearly, the garden is a complex arena of human activity, one that requires a broader range of instrumental procedures than is usually implied by the term "technology." Apart from strictly botanical knowledge of the growth properties of manioc and other cultigens, gardening lore includes magical songs, beliefs and practices related to magical gardening stones (*nantag*), techniques for cultivating manioc with other plants believed to render it more productive, and miscellaneous avoidances that prevent horticultural failure.

Gardening Songs

Gardening songs, like the songs used by men during the hunt, are attributed an ancient origin. Some women claim that gardening songs come directly from Nugkui, but a more common belief in the Alto Mayo is that they were first sung by Yampan, the senior wife of Etsa, the sun. Yampan, a myth explains, had wonderful horticultural powers that she used to produce food for her family. When she tried to teach her food-producing magic to Etsa's other wives, however, they invariably made disastrous blunders. Tired of their incompetence, Yampan went to live in the sky after first teaching her daughters the secrets of gardening songs. In memory of the skill of Yampan, women sing "I am a Yampan woman" as they mash manioc tubers to make beer. This makes the beer sweet and strong, as Yampan's beer was reputed to be.

Every phase of the horticultural cycle, from clearing a garden to harvesting tubers, has its appropriate magical songs. The intent of the songs varies slightly according to the context, but their general purpose is to make the crops grow faster and more abundantly. One informant said simply, "If you plant a stem of manioc next to the stem of a forest plant, the manioc will always grow faster because songs help it grow." Specific gardening songs may also control weeds and pests, ward off influences that impede plant growth, and restrain the propensity of the manioc plants to drink human blood. Each type of song is performed during the activity with which it is associated. As is the case with all magical songs, singing may be done aloud or in the thoughts alone.

Aguaruna theories of how the songs affect plant growth vary substantially. Some people stress the mediating role of Nugkui, who is pleased by the songs and translates her pleasure into a lush garden. Others argue that the songs are heard directly by the plants, by the bird *sukuyá* (a Nugkui messenger), by the manioc mother, or by all of these. In the examples that follow, however, it is evident that while some of the songs are formally addressed to Nugkui and other powerful beings, many are simply descriptive or imperative statements: "Sweet potatoes are falling / yams are falling," "Let the manioc grow like the *wampu* tree," and so on. In this respect, gardening songs share much in common with the hunting songs discussed in the previous chapter.

Women think of gardening songs as valuable personal possessions that should be accumulated and hoarded rather than shared freely with their peers. Indeed, comments made during interviews and the contents of gardening songs themselves suggest that women see their relationship to other gardeners as potentially competitive, even hostile. They are secretive about their songs and magical gardening stones. They fear envious comments made by other women about their gardens, since these can have a negative effect on plant growth, and they occasionally use songs to curse women who surreptitiously enter their swiddens. Because a woman's personal prestige and her desirability as a wife are at least partly determined by her horticultural productivity, the magical knowledge that ensures this productivity is a jealously guarded commodity.

The following are some examples of gardening songs known to women of the Alto Río Mayo. In choosing examples for analysis, I have used songs whose translation I am satisfied with and which are fairly representative of their class as a whole.

Songs for Selecting and Clearing a Garden Site
As was noted earlier, the responsibility for choosing a garden site usually falls on a woman's husband. However, women believe that certain songs create favorable conditions for garden site selection. The following song, A.7, is sung by a woman as she accompanies her husband on his search:

A.7 The soil of the ancients he will find
   Manioc that does not spoil he will find
   Yams that grow fat he will find
   Peanuts that grow fat he will find
   The soil of the ancients he will find
   Being a Nugkui woman,
   I come without bringing misfortune
   Shakáim man, lead the way

   Others say that I make a garden
   They themselves work poor soil
   [In] mine, [in] mine
   The soil of the ancients he will find
   Yams that grow fat he will find
   Manioc that does not spoil he will find

The Aguaruna word that I have glossed as "the ancients" in the first line of A.7 is *ajútap*, which also denotes the spirit that comes to vision-seekers. All of the people whom I consulted insisted that in this context *ajútap* refers not to the spirit but to "ancestors" or "old ones" in general. Nevertheless, the word inevitably has resonances of spiritual power. The gardener seeks soil that is as fertile as that of ancient women such as Yampan and as untouched by human activity as a remote, ancestral forest. Thus establishing the fertility of the soil, the song proceeds to describe the flourishing crops that will grow there, and in doing so the actors are metaphorically telescoped into a highly favorable future. Allusions to Nugkui and Shakáim, which have already been noted in hunting songs, appear again: "Being a Nugkui woman / I come without bringing misfortune / Shakáim man, lead the way." The singer and her husband fulfill traditional and complementary roles, and like the mythical beings who established these roles they can expect only good fortune to come as a result.

The work of felling trees and clearing underbrush at garden sites is both arduous and risky. Falling trees sometimes cause injury or death, and men cutting brush are frequently exposed to the dangers of snakebite. A knowledgeable wife sings songs that protect her husband from these threats to his well-being. These songs may, for example, equate her husband with the coati (*Nasua rufa*), an animal that reportedly is unafraid of snakes and skillful at dodging their attacks. The woman also goes frequently to the garden to serve beer to her husband and the other men working there. During these visits, she is exposed to sights and sounds believed to exert a baneful influence on her gardening ability—the whistling and joking of the men as they work, the crack of falling trees, the sight of leaves fluttering to the forest floor. It is the fate of men to destroy plants so that their wives can give plants life, and a woman's contact with this male activity diminishes her growth-promoting powers. To protect herself from these harmful influences, a woman sings songs such as the following:

A.8 Large, ugly demon's eye [the look
         of her husband as he turns to drink beer]
     Bringing misfortune with your look
     Bringing misfortune with your whistle
     I never fail, I never fail
     A Nugkui woman cannot fail

A.9 Doves, doves [i.e., the falling leaves of felled trees]
     Manioc is falling

It is not leaves that fall
Sweet potatoes are falling
Yams are falling
I am a little woman of Nugkui
I cannot fail

A.8 acknowledges the damaging influence of the sights and sounds of men's work (the "demon's eye" of the husband, the shrill whistles of the men as they encourage each other while chopping large trees), but states that, being a Nugkui woman, the gardener will not suffer misfortune. I find A.9 to be a particularly elegant song because it metaphorically converts the falling leaves—the sight of which can be harmful to a woman's ability to cultivate— into falling tubers, an auspicious and beneficial image.

In songs A.7, 8, and 9, the name of Nugkui is invoked not in a supplicative way but rather as a symbol of gardening skills with which the singer strongly identifies. A.10, in contrast, consists of a direct plea for Nugkui's help:

A.10 In worn-out soil I make a garden
In the thicket of the bird *chuchumpiú*
I make a garden
Mother Nugkui, mother Nugkui
Let me know your manioc
I am an orphan among enemies
Almost dying I live
In worn-out soil I make a garden
In the thicket of the bird *chuchumpiú*
I make a garden
Mother Nugkui, mother Nugkui
The children of others cry like birds' offspring
"Chianana" they cry, suffering
My child does not do this
Mother Nugkui, mother Nugkui
Let me know your manioc

A.10 hyperbolically describes the misery of the gardener and the sterility of her garden to almost the same extent that earlier songs extolled her infallibility and good fortune. Emphasis on the suffering of the singer seems to be a characteristic shared by many supplicatory songs known to the Aguaruna, including those sung by men when they anxiously await a vision of an *ajútap* spirit. One vision-seeker's song, for example, laments: "I am so sad / weeping I leave my shelter / with my little tobacco bowl / how can I have a vision?" Both the songs used to attract an *ajútap* and to recruit

Nugkui's assistance in the garden attempt to manipulate powerful beings by stressing the wretchedness of the supplicant.

Planting and Cultivation Songs
Planting is the most critical phase of the horticultural cycle from the Aguaruna point of view, and there is a substantial inventory of songs used to ensure that all will go well. To plant manioc, a woman first goes to her old garden and cuts short sections of manioc stems. While leaving the old garden with the stem cuttings, she sings:

A.11 I go, I go
    I leave the old soil
    The soil of the deer [deer are associated with abandoned gardens]
    You are old
    I go, I go
    On the edge of the garden
    The stems are rotten
    You shout "chiya"
    Calling my children

The woman who sang A.11 explained that it is directed to the below-ground part of the stem (*nantuji*), which is thrown to the edge of the garden when manioc is harvested. The song depicts these old, castoff parts of manioc plants calling tubers ("my children") to the new garden site.

A.12 is a passage from a longer song performed while preparing the soil with a digging stick:

A.12 Digging stick of palm wood
    Sounding "tuh tuh tuh" on Nugkui's back
    Because it sounds thus
    Because it kills [when in the form of a palm wood lance]
    A Nugkui woman never fails

Though brief, A.12 elaborates a complex and expressive metaphor. The song equates the percussion of the digging stick with drumming, which (as will be discussed shortly) has life-giving connotations in Aguaruna mythology. Unlike the sounds made by men when clearing a garden, the sound of a digging stick is an auditory expression of a woman's proper activity and therefore exerts a favorable influence on her labor. The song also plays on the similarity between the traditional palm wood lance and the digging stick; the lancelike stick kills weeds as the woman turns the soil. On a more abstract level, the allusion to lances is appropriate because a real lance draws blood, and one of the obligations of a gardener is to see that her manioc is given symbolic blood to satisfy its dangerous thirst.

When the young plants begin to develop, various songs are employed to ensure that their tubers become large and flavorful. A.13, an example of this kind of song, equates the tubers with objects of great thickness—the cayman's tail, the plant *seekemu* (which has a large root similar in appearance to a manioc tuber), a pig, and so on:

A.13 The tail of the cayman is lying there
    The root of *seekemu* is lying there
    The pig is lying there
    On the other side of the garden
    Let there be *wampu* [a large tree, *Ficus* sp.] on the other side
    The root of *seekemu* is lying there
    The pig is lying there
    On the other side of the garden

Ideally, a woman should sing gardening songs day and night during the first three to six months of a garden's life, when the manioc plants are considered most vulnerable to drought and other harmful influences. A.14, directed to the manioc plants, expresses a woman's concern for their welfare and her unremitting efforts to help them grow through the use of song:

A.14 I don't sleep, I don't sleep [i.e., neglect singing]
    As you [the manioc] sleep
    You become as large as *mente*
        [a large tree in the family Bombacaceae]
    I don't sleep
    You grow like the branches of *wampúsh*
        [a large tree, possibly *Ceiba* sp.]
    "My mother sleeps" you say
    Why do you say it?
    I don't sleep

A garden that grows conspicuously well invites the envious comments of other women. Even favorable comments can have a negative influence on a garden's growth, in much the same way that public comments on hunting can bring bad luck to a hunter. To prevent this sort of discussion from occurring, a woman sings:

A.15 "What person is this
    What person is this
    That she has so much manioc?"
    Thus they say to me
    "Your manioc plants abound"

A Nugkui woman cannot fail
A Nugkui woman cannot fail
They say I have much manioc
"Your manioc plants abound"
Who is saying this?
"That, that is *tsanímtsanim* [a weed resembling manioc]
The branches of *mamántug* look immature"
This they should say

Central to the meaning of A.15 is an ethnobotanical pun based on the morphological and linguistic similarity between the weed *tsanímtsanim* (*Manihot* sp.) and *tsaním*, cultivated manioc (*Manihot esculenta*). The identification of the second plant, *mamántug*, is in doubt, but at least one informant described it as a weedy aroid bearing some similarity to such cultivated aroids as cocoyam and taro. Both plants mentioned in the song, then, are weeds that strongly resemble cultivated species. The obvious intent of A.15 is to cause people to mistake the garden plants for weeds, thus diminishing the garden in their eyes and heading off envious comments.[4]

Harvesting Songs
The following is the only reasonably complete harvesting song that I was able to record in the Alto Mayo. The woman who sang it remarked that it is appropriately performed while digging up and washing manioc tubers:

A.16 Basket, basket, basket
    Taking it on my back
    I will walk
    With the demon's fire [probably refers to coals
        brought to the garden to burn weeds]
    I will walk
    Carrying
    In the trail
    Step by step
    I will walk
    In the trail

    With the water of Atsut
    I will wash [the manioc]
    With the urine of the stars
    I will wash
    With the hands of Atsut
    I will move [the manioc in the water]
    With the urine of the stars
    I will move
    Petsa, petsa [duckweed, *Lemna sp.*]

I will put in the basket
Petsa, petsa
I will move

This song uses several metaphors and mythological allusions to construct its imagery of horticultural abundance. The first stanza evidently describes a woman's morning journey from house to swidden. She carries a basket and some coals from the fireplace, the latter to be used for kindling a small fire to burn weeds. Returning with a full basket, she stops to wash the tubers in a stream or river. "With the water of Atsut," begins the second stanza, "I will wash / with the urine of the stars / I will wash." The allusion to Atsut is based on a myth (a variant of which is found in Jordana Laguna 1974:39–44) that identifies Atsut as a person or group of people who receives the souls of the dead as they ascend into the sky. In an Alto Mayo version of this myth, Atsut places the dead in a drum-like container and restores them to life by beating on it. Later on in the same tale, Atsut and the souls of the dead change themselves into fruits and tubers when they are frightened by an attack of ants whom they mistake for warriors. Atsut thus has at least two qualities that lend themselves to the representation of fertility: (1) the power to change into edible plants, and (2) the ability to impart life through rhythmic pounding, just as the gardener brings life to her swidden by beating on the ground with her digging stick.

The succeeding phrase, "With the urine of the stars / I wash," is more difficult to interpret. Some people contend that the urine of the stars is simply dew, and that the phrase means that the woman washes the tubers with hands as cool as dew rather than with hot hands that can harm the manioc. Star urine, however, is given a different identity in a myth about a man who marries a star that comes to earth in the form of a woman (Jordana Laguna 1974:132–36). The star-woman urinates small, colored beads (*shauk*) instead of ordinary urine. The sensible properties of beads include their abundance—it takes many beads to fill a small volume—and attractiveness; they are the most highly valued ornaments owned by Aguaruna women. The phrase "With the urine of the stars / I wash" can thus also be construed to suggest that the woman brings the tubers into contact with numerous beads. This image leads naturally to the next metaphor, which turns on the properties of the plant *petsa*. *Petsa* is a diminutive but extremely prolific aquatic plant, *Lemna* sp. or duckweed. The name *petsa* is related etymologically to the verb *petsat*, "to lay eggs"; apparently the plant is fed to chickens to increase their egg production. The song substitutes *petsa*, a fertility-inducing, prolific, abundant plant, for the manioc tubers that the woman washes. The principal idea behind this and the preceding star-urine metaphors is that the tubers should be as numerous, fecund, and attractive as beads or *petsa* plants.[5]

As A.16 demonstrates, many of the symbols and images of gardening songs originate in mythology. The examples already adduced allude to Nugkui, Yampan, Shakáim, and Atsut. Another myth figure frequently mentioned in gardening songs is Uwancháu, a being who is identified in this grisly tale:

> Long ago, a woman whose newborn child had recently died came upon an infant in the forest. It had been brought by the wind. The baby cried "uwá, uwá." Because of this it was called Uwancháu. It had very fat lips. The woman took Uwancháu home and began to nurse it. It sucked and sucked until the woman had no more milk. Then it kept on sucking until it drank all of her blood and the woman died. Her husband killed the baby Uwancháu with his machete. The baby was full of blood.

Gardening songs often end with the couplet, "I am a Nugkui woman / I am an Uwancháu woman." The persuasive intent of the identification of the gardener with Nugkui is obvious, but why the comparison to the ghoulish infant Uwancháu? I feel that this usage has a twofold significance. First, by saying that she is like Uwancháu a woman establishes an affinity with her "children," the manioc plants, which are also beings capable of sucking blood. Second, a woman who is full of blood like Uwancháu has demonstrated that she is able to control the dangerous thirst of her manioc plants by using the appropriate songs and rituals. That is, she has retained her blood because her manioc plants have been unable or unwilling to take it from her owing to her ritual knowledge. By invoking the image of Uwancháu in this context, the gardener implies that she is close to her plants and that, like a mother controlling her children, she prevents them from misbehaving.

Gardening Stones

> Long ago gardens did not grow well. A young man married a girl and came to live at her father's house. The girl said to her mother, "Are there no plantains to serve?" Her mother went to the garden to get plantains, while the girl stayed behind. As the woman walked she cried with shame because her garden did not produce fine harvests of manioc and other crops. Then in the trail she saw an *ajútap* spirit in the form of a jaguar. It was small, like a cat, but it had a terrifying voice. The woman was so sad that she passed the *ajútap* saying, "Let it eat me."

The Garden's Children 115

When she came to her garden, the jaguar was lying across a log with a stone in its mouth. The woman took the stone and put it in her own mouth. The jaguar, now grown large, arose and knocked her over. It urinated all over her and said, "You will have good fortune with the plants in your garden." Then it disappeared.

The woman cut some plantains and returned to her house, where the others had begun to worry about her delay. She told her daughter to cook the plantains. She changed her clothes, bathed, and went to a small shelter in the forest. She drank tobacco water. That night the jaguar *ajútap* appeared in a vision and spoke to her. It said, "I am going to leave gardening stones (*nantag*) in a special place. You will use them to plant manioc." It disappeared.

She got the stones and returned to her house. Her daughter's husband gave her meat to cook and eat. She told her husband and son-in-law to make her a new garden. She planted manioc using the stones. Soon the garden was full of manioc with huge tubers. She made a new beer urn and a great quantity of manioc beer. They got drunk, and when the woman danced with her husband she sang "*Juj, juj.*" This is the call of the jaguar. Thus it was. Because of this, all women want gardening stones.

This myth about a woman's visionary experience and the jaguar's gift is typical of narratives related to a category of magical stones called *nantag*. Women use *nantag* stones to increase the productivity of manioc and other tuberous crops. Because the acquisition and use of *nantag* are considered essential to horticultural production, these stones are a woman's most closely guarded personal possessions.

Aguaruna women conventionally describe *nantag* as shiny, red pebbles, a claim that is consonant with Harner's statement that similar stones used by the Shuar are "chips of unworked red jasper" (Harner 1972:72). However, from my own observations and those of Margaret Van Bolt, the *nantag* used by Alto Mayo women actually resemble riverbottom pebbles of two to ten centimeters in diameter and of various colors (Brown and Van Bolt 1980). A few women state that the color of the *nantag* indicates the cultigen with which it is primarily associated—e.g., red stones are for manioc, black stones are for yams, and so on—but this opinion is not widely held. Most women feel that the actual color of the stone does not affect its powers, though as we shall see it is significant that the archetypal color of *nantag* is red.

Although it was difficult to penetrate the secrecy surrounding *nantag* use, I was able to determine that most, if not all, adult women own several of them that they have obtained in various ways. The most powerful *nantag* are those that a woman inherits from her mother or some other older kinswoman because these stones have been used for a generation or more and in some cases may go back to the time of ancestors. During the course of her life, a woman also accumulates new *nantag* to which she is guided in dreams or finds accidentally in the course of daily activities. A woman describes how a dream led to the discovery of one of her many *nantag*:

> This stone is the tapir's *nantag*. Long ago my husband found a tapir's trail. He followed the trail and came upon a curassow sitting in a tree. He shot the curassow and returned home. That night he had a dream in which a person came to him saying: "Where you were yesterday, in the tapir's path, there is a log that crosses the trail. There I am going to leave a stone. Tomorrow you should go there and get it. This is a stone for manioc and yams. I never suffer from hunger [i.e., because the stone is powerful]. Don't neglect the stone. Give it achiote to drink, because it killed my sister. Take care of it." The next morning, he went to the spot and found the *nantag* stone on the log across the tapir's trail.

While this account is somewhat unusual in that the woman's husband is the one who dreams of the stone, in other respects it is typical of many such experiences described by Alto Mayo women. The person who appears in the dream is sometimes said to be Nugkui. In other cases, the speaker is the nighthawk *sukuyá*, an *ajútap*, or an animal spirit.

Women occasionally stumble across *nantag* in a totally unexpected manner. A shiny stone found in the nest of a bird or rodent, or in the entrails of certain fish, is often suspected of being a *nantag*. Women say that a stone may catch their eye by "moving by itself" on the riverbottom; this, too, is a sign that the stone is a *nantag*. My co-worker, Margaret Van Bolt, once witnessed the discovery of a possible *nantag* while helping a woman harvest manioc. The woman, Wampurái Peas, found a pebble next to the tuber she was digging, an unmistakable sign that the pebble was associated with manioc growth. After cleaning the stone and examining it carefully, Wampurái wrapped it in a rag and commented that she would later test it to see whether it had the power of a *nantag*. One tests a suspected *nantag* by bringing it into contact with stem cuttings during planting and then looking for evidence of unusual growth. Stones that have no visible effect on plant growth are simply discarded.

Opinions vary as to the ultimate origin of *nantag* stones. A common belief is that Nugkui created the stones to help women

---

with the arduous work of gardening. A different though not necessarily contradictory account was given to me as follows:

> Our ancestors in the Alto Marañón had *nantag* just after the earth was made, but they threw them away. The nighthawk [*sukuyá*] collected the best ones and has them now. The great tinamou [*waga, Tinamus major*] also has them. So do the crab and the honeybee.

Still another explanation is that the stones originally belonged to the night bird *tugkuíjau* (unidentified). This bird cared for the stones as if they were its eggs, until they were stolen by human beings.

Women use *nantag* to encourage the growth of cultivated plants by bringing the stones into contact with cuttings of manioc and other cultigens just before they are planted.[6] This is accomplished in a brief ritual performed privately in the garden.

Before planting a new garden, a woman collects stem cuttings of manioc as well as tubers or cuttings of other root crops—taro, yams, cocoyams, achira, and sweet potato. Peanuts are sometimes also included. When she is ready to plant a section of the garden, she rises early in the morning, carefully washes her hands, and goes to the garden without eating. She takes with her the tubers and manioc stem cuttings in a basket, her *nantag* stones wrapped in a piece of cloth, an old ceramic or metal pot, enough water to fill the pot, and a number of pods of red-staining achiote (*Bixa orellana*). She may also bring one or more of the following plant substances: the roots of *wampúsh* and *mente* (both of which are trees), the root of the herb *seekemu* (source of a native soap), and the roots or bulbs of the medicinal herbs *pijipíg* and *kampának*. (See Table 6.) In some cases, the bowl, water, *nantag* stones, or plant substances are stored in a small shelter in the garden in preparation for the planting ritual.

Upon arriving in the garden, the woman crushes a pod of achiote and uses the red pulp to paint lines on her cheekbones and on those of other people who may be accompanying her, e.g., her children. This is done because the *nantag* stones (and the manioc plants, if some have already been planted) are potentially dangerous, and it is important that the woman and her companions identify themselves as friends by being painted.

The woman unwraps the *nantag* from their cloth and puts them in a bowl. Then she mashes the rest of the achiote pods and puts the red seed pulp in the bowl, mixing it with water to form a red liquid. If the other plant materials mentioned earlier have been collected, they are now mashed and mixed with the liquid in the bowl.

Tsewa's Gift

TABLE 6
Plants Used in Manioc Planting Ritual

Aguaruna name(s)	Scientific name	Part used in ritual	Key attributes
ipák, shampu, pisu	Bixa orellana	fruit, seeds	Source of red dye.
wampúsh	Ceiba sp.?	root	Large, fast-growing tree of great girth.
mente	Unidentified member of Bombacaceae	root	Large tree; repository of shamanistic powers.
seekemu	Unidentified	root	Has a thick root, similar to manioc tuber; also used as a soap which produces foam similar to that of manioc beer.
pijipíg	Cyperus/Carex sp.	root	Has diverse magical/medicinal powers
kampának	Eleuthrine bulbosa	bulb	Medicinal powers?

Principal Source of Species Determinations:
Berlin and Berlin 1977:22–25.

The root of the soap plant *seekemu* is cut up with a machete and the pieces rubbed together in the red liquid to form a sudsy mixture. All the ingredients are then stirred with a manioc stem. Although Aguaruna women handle *nantag* freely in other contexts, they say that when stirring them with other ingredients one must not touch them or the stones might lose their power.

In one of the planting rite performances that was recorded, the gardener sang the following song while stirring the red mixture of stones, water, and plant substances:

A.17 My child has hair cut in bangs
    My child has blood
    The enemy's child has an oval face
    Drink his blood

My child has blood
Drink, drink the blood of the paca
   [a large rodent, *Cuniculus paca*]
Drink, drink the blood of the agouti
   [a large rodent, *Dasyprocta aguti*]
Don't drink the blood of my child
Let the manioc of my enemies come to me
Come, come

The red liquid is then poured over the manioc stem cuttings and other tubers that are to be planted. While pouring, the woman is careful not to pour out the stones and mashed plant substances. To give themselves luck in planting, the woman and her daughters may wash their hands in the red liquid as it pours out of the pot onto the pile of cuttings and tubers. Then the manioc stem sections are planted by lifting the soil with a palm wood spade and inserting the stem in the ground. If manioc planted on previous days is already growing in the garden, the woman reserves some of the red liquid and later sprinkles it over the young plants, saying "Drink, drink." After the entire garden has been planted, a process that may take several days, the *nantag* are placed in a covered pot and hidden somewhere in the garden, usually at the base of a large tree. This is done so that the stones will be close to the developing plants but invisible to potential thieves.[7]

The principal purpose of this ritual, from the Aguaruna point of view, is to convey the growth-promoting powers of the *nantag* stones to the manioc stem cuttings and other cultigens. The medium for this transfer is the red liquid made of achiote and water in which the stones are immersed. Aguaruna women state that the red liquid satisfies the dangerous thirst of the manioc plants; some women explicitly refer to the liquid as "blood." The plant substances added to the "blood" further increase its power by transferring their desirable qualities to the liquid and, through the liquid, to the manioc. The root of *wampúsh*, for example, is mixed with the liquid "so that the manioc will be thick like the trunk of the *wampúsh* tree," and so on. These plants and the attributes that relate them to the planting ritual are listed in Table 6.

While the primary purpose of the planting procedure is to encourage the growth of crops, it has a secondary function of a defensive nature. The Aguaruna state emphatically that *nantag* stones, like manioc plants, have a propensity to "drink the blood" or "eat the soul" of people who pass through the garden. If anything, the stones are more dangerous than young manioc—so dangerous, in fact, that they are classified as *yukágtin*, "things that eat us," a distinction that they share with the jaguar and the anaconda. Women occasionally find human hair wrapped around their *nantag*, almost like a nest. This is a sign that the stones have eaten the soul of the hair's owner. A woman told me this tale of soul-killing by *nantag*:

> One day a woman left her *nantag* in the garden. Her son came there alone to take cocona fruits. That night she had a dream in which the *nantag*, in the form of a person, sang to her, "Mother, mother, I have eaten." The woman awoke and thought, "Why did she speak to me like that?" She went to her garden to look at her stones. On top of the stones was a bunch of human hair. She asked her children, "Who went to the garden?" Her son said, "I went hunting, and on the way home I was hungry and ate cocona fruits." He soon died of snakebite. The *nantag* had eaten his soul.

The planting ritual and its songs protect the gardener and her family from the *nantag* by slaking their dangerous thirst. The ritual is not the only context in which the stones are fed; a prudent woman immerses her *nantag* in achiote and water "blood" about once a month to keep them satisfied. Said one woman: "Each month the *nantag* must drink achiote. If they are not fed, they can eat us." When the stones become thirsty, the owner may have a dream in which a young girl tells her, "Mother, I am suffering from thirst. Please give me something to drink." To feed the stones, a woman takes them from the cloth in which they are wrapped and leaves them in a bowl of achiote and water for several hours or overnight. The stones are then removed from the liquid, dried off, rewrapped in cloth, and returned to their hiding place.

Besides having the propensity to drink blood or eat souls and the ability to assume human form in dreams, *nantag* stones also move by themselves as if alive. A woman who fails to keep her stones well fed and securely wrapped in cloth will someday find that the stones have "run away." I was told by one woman that as a young girl she went to a woman's garden and came upon a bowl full of *nantag* immersed in water and achiote, which had evidently been left there by the garden's owner. She stole two of the stones—they were, she said, "so pretty that it was impossible to resist taking them"—and later gave them to her mother, who was very pleased. That same night the girl dreamed that a child was saying to her, "I don't like it here. I miss my mother." The next day, the two stolen *nantag* had disappeared from their hiding place. They had undone the cloth and "escaped" by themselves.

Many Alto Mayo women distinguish between two categories of *nantag* stones, "true" (*dekás*) *nantag* and "false" (*wainak*) *nantag*.

True *nantag* are those that have the greatest power to assist plant growth; they are also the ones most likely to harm human beings. Stones known to have been used for many generations are likely to be classified as true *nantag*. False *nantag* are the stones that a woman acquires in her own lifetime. They have less power to promote plant development but offer the advantage of being less threatening to people. As far as I was able to determine, most Alto Mayo women have a mixture of the two kinds of *nantag*. Women who feel insecure about their ability to control true *nantag*—perhaps because their knowledge of magical songs is deficient—have been known to trade or sell them to other women, keeping only the false *nantag* that pose no immediate danger to anyone.

Aguaruna women seem almost obsessed by the fear that other women will steal their *nantag*, although I heard of few cases in which this actually occurred. Gardeners keep their stones hidden at all times when not in use; they are either buried in a covered bowl at the base of a tree stump in the garden or stored with a woman's valuables in the house. I recorded one song that reportedly is used to curse a woman who comes to one's garden with the intention of stealing *nantag*. The song is supposed to make the thief fall down in the garden—an action that in other contexts is interpreted as a sign that one's soul is being eaten—and then lose her ability to cultivate:

A. 18 Tai tai, tai tai [a shout, cry]
   The one who annihilated us [i.e., an ancient enemy]
   You knock down
   Her face is pallid
   Let her be ruined
   Tai tai, tai tai
   Let her be ruined
   The one who annihilated us

The singer added, "When the woman falls, she is crushed by the worm *baga* (a garden-dwelling worm or caterpillar often described as an evil being in myths). Her entire body is crushed. She will always suffer for lack of manioc." If a woman must go through someone else's garden, she protects herself by tearing off some manioc leaves and putting them in her armpit, while saying softly, "Manioc, don't eat me. I am your owner, the one who planted you."[8]

Growth-Promoting Plants

Aguaruna women cultivate several kinds of plants that are believed to help their gardens develop rapidly. The most important of these growth-promoting species are the cultigens arrowroot, cocoyam, and achira. Besides being plants that produce edible tubers considered desirable in their own right, arrowroot, cocoyam, and achira have souls or "people" who bring water to the thirsty manioc plants in the garden:

> Arrowroot [chiki] is a woman adorned with a snail-shell dance belt. She carries water to the manioc. Cocoyam [sagku] brings even more water because she has big leaves to carry the water in. Achira [tuju] has a twisted arm [an allusion to the bent leaves of this plant?] and when she brings the water it sloshes out as her arm hits branches, but she always arrives with a little water. If a woman doesn't have these plants in her garden, manioc won't grow there.[9]

The belief that manioc will thrive only when planted with other cultigens provides a culturally compelling reason to maintain a mixed planting strategy in the garden. It also expresses the degree to which women see the relations of the plants in the garden as approximating human social relations. Many of the plants are "people," with husbands, wives, and children. The gardener is their "mother," who cares for them while maintaining order in their relations. By creating and maintaining a harmonious environment for plant growth, a gardener becomes the "Nugkui woman" so frequently mentioned in magical songs.

I was able to gather fragmentary information on two other plants used to promote manioc growth: an unnamed variety of pijipíg and a papayalike plant called tsampáunum (possibly Carica microcarpa).

Earlier I mentioned the importance of pijipíg in such diverse fields as shamanism, fertility control, and hunting magic. The reported ability of pijipíg to encourage manioc growth appears to be an extension of the diffuse and wide-ranging magical powers attributed to it by the Aguaruna. In other contexts, people say that pijipíg attracts rain—indeed, Stirling (1938:116) goes so far as to identify "Piribri" as a Jívaro rain god—so it may be that through its association with rainfall the plant protects the manioc from thirst.[10] However, no one interviewed during my fieldwork offered an explicit account of how pijipíg promotes the growth of manioc and other cultivated plants.

Tsampáunum is planted so that it grows intertwined with one or two manioc plants in each garden. It produces bright red fruits that the Aguaruna consider poisonous, although non-Indians of the region reportedly eat them. Here again, people offered no clear statement of how the plant helps manioc. Some informants remarked that the fruits are "just like *nantag* stones," leading me to suspect that it is the fruits' color, through its chromatic associations with blood and *nantag* stones, that links this plant to garden productivity in Aguaruna thought.

Finally, a few Alto Mayo women mentioned the existence of a special variety of manioc, called *yapáu mama* (literally, "bitter manioc"), that women plant at the edge of the garden to promote growth and to poison garden pests such as the paca and agouti. They said that few Aguaruna women have this variety, and that it is most commonly found among the Chayahuita Indians, with whom Alto Mayo people have occasional contact. Presumably, the plant they are referring to is true bitter manioc, that is, one of the manioc varieties that must be processed before consumption because of its high prussic acid content. As far as I know, no Alto Mayo women cultivate bitter manioc (nor do ethnographic sources mention bitter manioc cultivation among other Jivaroan groups), but it is interesting that gardeners have heard of it and attribute it unusual powers.

Gardening Avoidances

Certain juxtapositions of objects or acts are detrimental to plant growth and therefore to be avoided, especially during planting and the first few months of a garden's life. Gardeners avoid sexual relations immediately before, during, and after planting days because the pollution of intercourse can have a negative effect on highly vulnerable manioc cuttings. (Contact with sexual pollution also destroys the power of *nantag* stones; this in turn prevents the full development of the garden.) Women apparently avoid newly planted gardens during their menstrual periods, since the smell of menstrual blood "burns" the plants, causing them to turn yellow and sickly. The smell of newborn infants is similarly dangerous, presumably because of neonates' association with placental blood.

I collected from various women a heterogeneous list of less important avoidances:

- During manioc planting, women should not eat the feet of any game bird or domestic fowl, "so that the manioc will not be thin." One informant added a prescriptive dimension to this belief by commenting that it is good for a woman to eat the foot of the tapir because this makes the manioc grow well.

- On planting days, a woman should not wash her lower legs when bathing lest her manioc "stay as thin as our calves."
- Women do not comb their hair in the garden because this prevents the manioc stems from growing well.
- Manioc is not roasted in the coals on planting days "because the heat of our hands [acquired when a woman removes the roasted manioc from the coals] would burn the plants."
- Sometimes when planting a swidden, a woman digs more planting holes than she has manioc cuttings to insert. Instead of leaving the holes empty until more cuttings can be collected, the gardener "plants" twigs of any available tree until they can be replaced with manioc stems. "If a hole were left empty," said one woman, "a deer might put its hoof in it and spoil the garden." The deer is one of the forms taken by demonic souls, and its contact with the new garden would be harmful to the growing plants.
- When planting, women never drink plain water when they are thirsty; manioc beer is always drunk instead. Opinion varies as to why this is important. Some women say that drinking plain water simply stunts the crop, while others take the view that avoiding water prevents the tubers from becoming hard and unpalatable.

The diverse avoidances are clearly intended to prevent bringing together things or activities whose salient qualities might be transferred to the garden with disastrous results. A woman who eats birds' feet on planting days, for example, juxtaposes the feet, which are outstandingly scrawny, with her manioc, which she wants to be outstandingly thick. The manioc might then assume the character of the feet, to the detriment of the garden. The taboo against drinking plain water has a similar logic. Water is a liquid drunk by the Aguaruna only when manioc beer is unavailable, that is, when they are in a state of temporary poverty. The gardener, therefore, avoids plain water lest the poverty it represents be transferred to her plants.

The Structure of Garden Magic

Here it would do us well to step out of this thicket of ethnographic details and try to look for a general pattern by which we can better understand horticultural practices and beliefs. What, if anything, do *anen, nantag* stones, and avoidances have in common? How is garden magic connected with notions of feminine identity?

The avoidances just described are testimony to the concern with juxtaposition that runs through all of the procedures intended to increase garden productivity. I have noted that while gardening songs differ in their intended aims, all of them are alike in that they pile up images of fertility, thickness, or unusual growth in a metaphorically dense verbal format. This juxtaposition of images in the context of practical activity is reinforced by the juxtaposition of objects (for example, the plant substances used in the planting ritual) similarly noted for their rapid growth or some other desirable characteristic. *Nantag* stones, palpable sources of spiritual power, are also brought into direct contact with the plants of the garden. Finally, gardening taboos guarantee that unfavorable juxtapositions—by which I mean the bringing together of objects or actions whose symbolic qualities are antagonistic to productivity—do not occur. By manipulating imagery, acts, and objects, a gardener consciously creates a new order in the swidden; she informs nature, restructuring it to serve her own ends. In this restructuring process, two symbolic themes or patterns of imagery are especially prominent: (1) the complementarity of men and women, and (2) blood and blood taking.

Subsistence tasks and other pursuits are, as I have noted, distinguished according to gender. Men perform the activities of highest prestige, hunting and warfare, as well as such additional tasks as woodworking, weaving, and basketmaking. Women labor in the swidden, tend domestic animals, and manufacture pottery. The attribution of highest prestige to male activities corresponds to a pervasive masculine bias that is also reflected in marital relations, politics, and religion.[11]

As is so often the case, the sexual division of labor lays the groundwork for a dialectical symbolism in which male activities, qualities, objects, and spirits are paired with and opposed to female activities, objects, and so forth. Some of the more obvious oppositions are listed in Table 7, but this twinned litany could be expanded to include additional cultural elements ad infinitum.

In their lucid analysis of sexual symbolism in a remarkably similar culture, that of the Ilongot of Northern Luzon, Michelle Rosaldo and J. M. Atkinson (1975:43) argue that "the opposition between life-giving and life-taking illuminates symbolic definitions of the sexes." The Ilongot, like the Aguaruna, are former headhunters who associate warfare and hunting with men and horticulture with women. Rosaldo and Atkinson suggest that the pervasive life-giving versus life-taking opposition ultimately boils down to one of nature (female) versus culture (male), since homicide is a willful

TABLE 7
Aguaruna Symbolic Oppositions Based on Gender

Male	Female
warfare	childbearing
hunting	gardening
forest	swidden
above-ground crops (maize, plantain, tobacco)	below-ground crops (manioc, sweet potato, etc.)
woodworking	pottery manufacture
Etsa (Shakáim)	Nugkui

cultural act while childbearing is the involuntary result of natural processes. Here, I think, the similarity to the Aguaruna case ends, for the Aguaruna do not elaborate the culture/nature theme as consistently as one might think at first glance. Women have certain traits that put them on the "culture" side of the equation: they sing better than men and are therefore more adept at using magical songs; they work in the garden, which is more culturalized than the forest domain in which men seek game. Even the elemental contrast between warfare and childbearing is not quite what it seems. Headhunting certainly requires the taking of life, but the rituals celebrating the acquisition of trophy heads confer life-giving powers on warriors and the women of their households (Karsten 1935). And as we have seen, the procedures used by women to promote plant growth may be life-threatening if not often life-taking.

Rather than being concerned with sexual opposition per se, Aguaruna myth, ritual, and song consistently emphasize the interdependence of men and women, and the mutual benefit that accrues as a consequence of male-female collaboration in all fields of endeavor. This concern is consciously expressed in a variety of situations, including the formal speeches that men give to their families in the early hours of the morning (cf. Harner 1972:104–5). Men gain prestige by extending hospitality in the form of manioc beer, the abundance of which depends on the horticultural skill of their wives. Women, of course, are equally dependent on men, since it is men who obtain meat, prepare a garden for planting, and defend the household against attack. Men and women bring separate understandings and, by extension, separate powers to subsistence activities. Women convey their knowledge of Nugkui and the swidden domain obtained through the instruction of childhood, the visionary experiences of adolescence, and adult years at work in the garden. Men bring their own knowledge, based on visionary insights obtained through their more extensive experience with hallucinogens and their long apprenticeship to the craft of reading the subtle signs of the forest.

The magical practices associated with hunting and horticulture share this concern with sexual complementarity. Many of the metaphors of hunting songs derive their meaning from the fact that attraction between men and women creates conditions favorable to the attraction of game. Equally fruitful results may come when a woman, singing *anen*, accompanies her husband during his search for a new garden site. Some songs call attention to the special dangers that come with the bringing together of opposing qualities. When a woman intrudes on the male task of felling trees, her future productivity may be put in jeopardy unless she protects herself by singing songs such as A.5. Once the garden is planted, it is the man's well-being that is threatened—in this case by the blood-thirsty manioc plants and *nantag* stones—so a woman takes precautions to defend him. A man who takes his wife hunting must magically reassure the game animals that she poses them no danger. Her presence then becomes an attracting force rather than a repelling one.

Because the ideal, balanced union of man and woman in subsistence tasks cannot always be realized, magical songs construct it through the appropriate imagery. Songs create and safeguard the beneficial complementarity of the sexes at the same time they celebrate it in an expressive medium.

The second pattern of imagery prominent in garden magic is related to blood and blood taking. Why should blood imagery be important in so bloodless an activity as gardening, when it scarcely figures at all in hunting, a pursuit that entails contact with real blood?

The question is not an easy one to answer, nor did the Aguaruna themselves shed much light on it in their comments. In common with people in many other societies, the Aguaruna think of blood as a life-giving substance intimately related to human vitality. Harner (1972:149) says that the Shuar see blood as a manifestation of the "true" soul, that is, the soul that people have from birth to death. Although this does not accord precisely with soul beliefs in the Alto Mayo, it does underline the connection between blood and life in Jivaroan thought and helps to explain why "blood drinking" and "soul eating" are often used as equivalent metaphors. We have already seen that hunting and horticulture, the quintessential subsistence activities of men and women, stand as paired opposites.

Within the logic of this opposition, men take blood in the course of killing animals while women give blood (either voluntarily, in the form of achiote and water, or involuntarily, as soul substance) to impart life to plants.

More than an abstract symbol of vitality, blood is a sign of women's fertility. Many Aguaruna women say that menstrual blood appears "because a woman is going to get pregnant," in other words, because postpartum amenorrhea has ceased and a woman is again ready to conceive (Margaret Van Bolt, personal communication). Menstrual blood is a manifestation of the mythical being Etse (not to be confused with Etsa, the sun), whom myths describe as an extremely seductive woman with a scent so magnetic that men cannot resist having intercourse with her (Akuts Nugkai et al. 1977, I:281–83). Alto Mayo women say that they menstruate because "Etse cuts their wombs," causing them to bleed and thus restoring their capacity to conceive. Some accounts describe Etse as an essence or quality present in all women. Men who wish to avoid polluting contacts while on the vision quest must not look at any women they meet lest they "see Etse" and thus lose the chance of having a powerful vision. Etse, then, is more than a mythical being—she is a female essence, at once attractive, fecund, and dangerous to men. All of these qualities are reified in menstrual blood. Women attempt to control their menstruation through an elaborate technology of fertility regulation (E. A. Berlin 1977). The sanguinary themes so prominent in Aguaruna garden magic are part of the feminine concern with regulating reproductive power through the control of blood.

Another property of blood is that it is the medium by which thought is conveyed within the body. As it is used in the planting procedure, the achiote and water "blood" gives palpable evidence of the transfer of thought (in the form of gardening songs) that is taking place between the gardener and her plants.

The chromatic correlate of recurrent blood imagery is found in the prevalence of the color red in garden magic. Women apply red face paint before entering the garden on planting days; the red dye achiote is used to make the "blood" poured on the manioc cuttings; nantag stones are described as red, even though they often aren't; gardeners cultivate the plant tsampáunum, which has prominent red fruits, to promote the growth of their manioc. There is an obvious connection between blood and the color red, but beyond this it is hard to see how the prominence of red in garden magic fits into a broader pattern of color symbolism such as that which Victor Turner (1967) found among the Ndembu. The importance of colors for the Ndembu is relational: red, white, and black each have fairly fixed meanings, but it is their incorporation in dyadic and triadic relationships (red vs. white; red and white vs. black) that generates movement in the symbolic representations of ritual. In the Aguaruna case, though, I never observed a circumstance in which red was opposed to any other color. Moreover, most Aguaruna recognize five basic color categories (Berlin and Berlin 1975), which necessarily makes the relations between colors more complex than those observed among the Ndembu, who have a three-term system. Other ethnographic sources on the Jívaro have little to say about color symbolism, and Norman Whitten's interesting observations on the meaning of specific colors among the closely related Quichua (Whitten 1976, 1978b) are the only evidence that there might be more to this subject than met my eye in the Alto Mayo.

Manioc Horticulture as Practical Signification

Facing the sheer density of Aguaruna manioc symbolism, it is easy to think of gardening lore as being somehow independent of the more strictly technical aspects of horticulture. When talking to a woman in her swidden, however, one is reminded at every turn that these beliefs are not just quaint and expressive ideological tidbits but important calls to action.

Earlier I noted that women customarily plant cocoyam, arrowroot, and achira in their gardens so that these plants will "bring water" to the young manioc cuttings, thus helping the manioc grow quickly without eating the souls of human cultivators. The practice registers an effect that is eminently material—the intercropping of cultivars in the swidden. A cultural materialist might argue that the beliefs behind this practice are caused by and epiphenomenal to its "real" purpose, which is to maintain (through magical belief) a system of polyculture that helps the Aguaruna adapt to their tropical ecosystem. This reductionist approach, which is probably unprovable even on its own terms, founders on the principle of parsimony: why should such a belief, and the elaborate theory of manioc growth on which it is predicated, be needed to ensure the maintenance of a practice as simple as polyculture? Symbolists fare no better here. They would see the practice as a symbolic statement that addresses existential problems and gives voice to the cultivator's concern about her crop.

If one sets aside the action/meaning distinction implicit in both of these formulations, it is evident that the practice is situated within a "meaning-full milieu" (Chevalier 1982:43)—a manioc production system predicated on the idea that key cultigens possess human characteristics and needs. Certain cultigens have special qualities relative to others just as, in society, some people are gifted with unique skills. Both the manioc cultivation practices that we consider technical (varietal selection, planting, weeding) and those that seem magical (singing *anen*, using *nantag*) address the perceived needs of the sentient manioc plants. All aspects of garden work are equally part of meaningful horticultural practice.

A different instance of the process of practical signification is found in the manner by which new manioc varieties are introduced into cultivation. Despite some statements to the contrary (e.g., Sauer 1969:46), recent research has shown that many cultivated varieties of manioc retain an ability to produce flowers and fruits with viable seeds. They may cross freely with other varieties of cultivated manioc or with different species of the genus *Manihot*. In their definitive taxonomic study of the genus, David Rogers and S. G. Appan (1973:34) remark:

> Wherever the species [*Manihot esculenta*] occurs (or has been transported by man), there is evidence (putative) that the plants have hybridized with other locally-occurring wild species, thus changing the genetic composition of the cultigen in such ways that the hybrid produced becomes a cultigen essentially unique to the region where the hybridization occurred.

Most ethnographic descriptions of Amazonian manioc cultivation have nothing to say about the role of seed-grown manioc varieties, yet it is difficult to see how so many cultivars of manioc could have come into use if the plant were propagated only vegetatively, a procedure that is in fact a kind of cloning.

That manioc plants produce viable seeds is no mystery to Aguaruna women. They do not commonly plant manioc seeds for the simple reason that their growth takes longer than plants propagated by cuttings. From time to time, however, knowledgeable women find seed-grown plants in recently abandoned gardens. They say that these plants (called *tsapak mama*, "grown manioc") have the potential to be highly productive varieties.[12] Women therefore take cuttings from promising-looking plants and cultivate them under controlled conditions, which from the Aguaruna perspective include the use of garden magic. New varieties that respond well to these procedures are incorporated into the garden inventory and propagated like any other of the many manioc varieties that each woman has in her swidden.

Young women ask older kinswomen for cuttings of these new varieties because an older woman has accumulated more gardening expertise and is therefore more likely to have treated the plant in such a way that it will produce well. In taking inventories of manioc variety names, it was not unusual to come across varieties named after the woman who originally discovered and propagated it (e.g., *Urucínta mama*, "Rosinda's manioc"). Young women could look for new varieties in their own abandoned gardens, and to some extent they probably do, but they prefer to get them from older women whose expertise in magic is widely recognized. James Boster (1980:41) discovered an identical movement of new cultivars during his research with the Aguaruna of the Alto Marañón:

> Some of the older women took a special pride in their knowledge and ownership of a range of different cultivars of manioc. The gardens of these women served as a source of rare cultivars for other women in the community. Younger women tended to cultivate only the core of the most common cultivars and I suspect would be likely to treat a manioc volunteer as just another weed.

The movement of new varieties between women even ties into the network of regional trade. The Aguaruna of the Alto Mayo say that the Aguaruna of the Alto Marañón have greater knowledge of magic, especially garden magic. In their contacts with kinswomen from tributaries of the Marañón, Alto Mayo women try to obtain (by purchase or trade) new varieties of medicinal and food plants, including manioc, in part because they believe that the Marañón women's superior magic inevitably produces better plants. Varieties from the Chayahuita Indians, a distant Cahuapana-speaking group, are still more highly valued.

From the Aguaruna perspective, then, new varieties of manioc are found by women of acknowledged expertise in magic and eventually make their way into the gardens of less knowledgeable women. From the analyst's point of view, new varieties of manioc originate through cross-pollination in abandoned gardens, are selected by women with superior technical proficiency, and are then disseminated to other households and eventually to other regions. The system of expertise in magic that underlies this pattern contributes to the continual assimilation of new genetic material into the garden, with obvious adaptive benefits. While this fact does not in any sense account for the existence of garden magic, it does demonstrate the degree to which the interpenetration of magic and technology constitutes a meaningful and successful form of food production.

CHAPTER 5

A Technology of Sentiment

Relations between the sexes leave little room for
gestures of affection. When the [Jívaro] husband
feels sexual desire he points out to his wife the
path to the river and follows her there. . . .
His wives accept favors and brutality with equal
indifference; they are the two alternatives
inalterably inherent in their condition.

Bertrand Flornoy,
*Jívaro: Among the Headhunters
of the Amazon*

The mute and priapic male whom Bertrand Flornoy claims to
have seen among the Jívaro is notably absent from the accounts
of more reliable witnesses. Both Rafael Karsten (1935) and Michael
J. Harner (1972), for example, found the concept of romantic love
and its corresponding social conventions to be highly developed
among the Shuar. Much the same can be said for the Aguaruna. One
expression of this concern with romantic matters is the elaboration
of a complex technology by which people secretly manipulate the
feelings of others.

In the preceding chapters, I described how the Aguaruna assert
control over animal behavior and the growth of cultivated plants.

Covert intervention in the psychological states of people is not, as it might seem at first, a radical departure from this pattern. After all, the Aguaruna see the world of plants and animals as an eminently social domain. The extension of control from this realm to the human one is probably inevitable. The Aguaruna technology of sentiment differs from the other forms of magic that I have discussed in one important respect—its moral ambiguity. Successful hunting or gardening benefits the community even as it rewards the hunter or cultivator; covert manipulation of people, particularly where sexual matters are concerned, can threaten the foundations of social life and take the actor perilously close to the frontiers of sorcery.

Male-Female Relations

To understand the secret manipulation of sentiments, we must first consider Aguaruna attitudes toward courtship, sexuality, and marriage—areas rife with contradictions. From one perspective, it is undeniable that traditional lore stresses the threat that sexual activity can pose to the well-being of men and, to a lesser extent, of women. Young men anxious to obtain a vision from an *ajútap* spirit are enjoined to observe the strictest sexual purity, since the taint of sexual pollution is anathema to the spirits. A myth explains that long ago a certain man who failed to remain chaste actually became pregnant. He was forced to endure the mockery of the entire village until an *ajútap* removed the fetus (which, the myth implies, was not a true child but a reified form of pollution) and granted him a powerful vision. Other myths recount cases of men losing special skills or powers when they succumbed to feminine charms. Today the Aguaruna continue to insist that for both sexes abstinence from intercourse is essential for recovery from a serious illness.

Despite this current of thought emphasizing the dangers of sexuality, the Aguaruna regard sexual adventures as exciting and highly desirable. In private conversations men often joke about their hidden paramours (*japa ampúya*, "little deer") in other communities, and during parties they freely sing joking songs of an overtly sexual nature. This kind of humor is not unlike the proverbial locker room conversation of American males, except that the Aguaruna are more imaginative in their use of metaphor. Though typically more reserved than men, women also share a ribald sense of humor that is given fullest expression during drinking parties. When talking about sexual relations in general terms, then, both men and women express the view that sex is enjoyable and relatively harmless if pursued in the proper manner.

This laissez-faire attitude toward sex in the abstract tends to evaporate when the Aguaruna confront concrete cases. Sexual liaisons often lead to social conflict when they become public knowledge. Incest and adulterous relations with the spouses of close kin cause the greatest uproar, but even unions considered proper—say, between unmarried people who are classified as opposite sex cross-cousins—may provoke discord. I suspect that this stems in part from the conflict between the desire of men to dispose of their daughters in marriage as they see fit and the desire of daughters to marry whom they please. The secrecy in which affairs must be conducted thus requires that meetings between lovers be brief and sporadic, taking place at night or in some secluded spot during daylight hours.

Kayáp Jiukám, my closest confidant in Huascayacu, took it upon himself one evening to tutor me in the art of seducing women. He assumed, no doubt, that after five months of celibate life in the village I was sorely in need of feminine company. Kayap set out to teach me the proper manner of approaching Soledad, a young widow who at that time was considered the most desirable unattached woman in the community:

Listen, Mayak, I'll explain how you make her your sweetheart. First you should go to her house during the day when nobody else is around. You just start to talk. "Sister, are you home? Can I come in for a while? Will you serve me beer?" [Here Kayáp's voice dropped from the forceful style typical of men's public speech to an ingratiating, almost wheedling tone.] You talk for a while like that, and if she smiles and seems friendly you say something like "Woman, I think about you all the time." You can give her a small present, too, maybe a ring, some beads, or a little bit of money. If she doesn't get mad or leave the house, you know that she likes you.

Now here's the tricky part. You ask her to let you into the house late at night or before dawn, when everyone's asleep, so that you can talk some more. Then you slip into the house and speak to her quietly on her bed. If she wants you, she'll offer to come outside to meet you in some quiet spot, maybe in her garden. If anyone asks her where she's going, she'll say she's got to urinate. So you make love, then get home before people wake up. Now she's your *paki*, your girlfriend. It's easy.

As Kayáp's lesson suggests, men are expected to take the initiative in amorous affairs, but women sometimes become openly flirtatious during parties, and they make themselves more alluring by wearing strands of aromatic seeds and scented packets fashioned from vanilla pods.

Although the ideal manner of contracting a marriage is for a man (sometimes represented by an intermediary) to approach a woman's father and ask formally for her hand, many first marriages in the Alto Mayo now begin with elopement. By eloping, the couple hopes to circumvent objections to the marriage by presenting it as a fait accompli. Parents raise objections to marriages for one or more of the following reasons: (1) the partners are very young and still partially dependent on their older kinsmen, (2) they are not in a marriageable relation to one another, (3) their families do not enjoy good relations, (4) either partner is considered lazy or dissolute by the other's family, or (5) the father of the bride wants his daughter to wed another man more to his liking. An eloping couple spends several days hiding in the forest, in a mestizo town, or in the home of sympathetic kinsmen in another community. Eventually, they return to the woman's home, and a meeting is called to reconcile the differences among the concerned parties. Lovers always claim that they eloped because of their strong affection for one another; the woman may threaten to commit suicide if she is forced to separate from her new husband. After considerable debate, they are usually allowed to cohabit in the home of the wife's father, and from then on they are considered married. Only in the case of an irregular marriage between parallel cousins or some other prohibited category of relatives is there continued pressure for them to separate. In time, even this pressure may diminish.

The Aguaruna say that marriage is best contracted between bilateral cross-cousins (children of one's father's sister or mother's brother), although people with no established genealogical connection are also free to marry. Data that I gathered in the Alto Mayo show that the cross-cousin marriage ideal is frequently realized in practice: 70 percent of all marriages are between people of the category *antsúg*, "opposite sex cross-cousin." Of these, approximately 17 percent are true cross-cousins, while the rest are more distantly related in genealogical terms. A surprising 22 percent of the marriages that I recorded were between people of prohibited categories, usually real or classificatory parallel-cousins. I don't know whether this high incidence of incorrect marriages is typical of all Jivaroan populations or the result of the scarcity of acceptable marriage partners in the demographically isolated Alto Mayo region.[1]

First marriages between people in their teens are highly volatile regardless of previous genealogical connection. Nearly half end in separation after a few months. Marriages tend to stabilize after the birth of a child; the divorce rate for couples whose marriages survive the first year of marriage drops to about 15 to 20 percent.

Tsewa's Gift

There are marked disparities in the freedoms granted to men and women within the institution of marriage. Men can have more than one wife—about 15 percent actually do—and, as an unstated corollary to this, married men are relatively free to engage in discreet extramarital philandering as long as they avoid having affairs with married women. The wives of these men, however, enjoy no such license. They are expected to dedicate themselves to their domestic tasks while avoiding even the hint of scandal. Men sometimes punish their wives for "visiting too much" or even "laughing too much," since visiting and flirtatious laughter are interpreted as signs that a woman wants to attract the attention of other men. Only elderly women—in particular, elderly widows—can socialize as freely as men.

While custom dictates that men have the right to form polygynous marriages, in practice arranging them is a delicate matter. A woman rarely welcomes the addition of a second wife to the household. She may respond to the arrival of a new wife by attacking her physically (cf. Harner 1972:95) or, more commonly, by threatening or actually attempting suicide. Sororal polygyny is common (62 percent of all polygynous marriages) because a woman is more likely to accept her sister as a co-wife than an unrelated woman. Even when plural unions are successfully established, relations between co-wives often remain chilly. A prudent husband divides his time equally between his wives to avoid domestic friction.

Besides the freedom to form plural marriages, men have much more leverage than women in ending marriages. Many divorces occur when a husband rejects his wife because of her barrenness, sloth, or even simple old age. Women, on the other hand, find it difficult to separate from their husbands when they are dissatisfied with their domestic situation. If a woman leaves her husband, he may simply ask her family to return her; they usually agree to do this unless he has treated her with the most extravagant brutality. About the only way that a woman can end an unsatisfactory marriage is to run off with a man from another, usually distant, community. The Aguaruna consider this a serious crime, and both the woman and her lover are severely punished if caught by the pursuing husband and his kinsmen. An astonishing number of adult female deaths in the Alto Mayo occur as a result of suicide, usually following a domestic argument.[2] The restrictions and insecurity of the woman's role in marriage undoubtedly contribute to this high suicide rate.

I hope it is clear from this brief summary that the area of courtship and marriage is a turbulent one for the Aguaruna. There is an obvious double standard at work: men look forward to their own amorous affairs but express great moral outrage when their sisters, daughters, or wives are implicated in similar affairs. That the Aguaruna themselves recognize the disruptive nature of sexuality is evident in a set of written statutes—the first attempt at written laws in the Alto Mayo—prepared by the residents of the community of Shimpiyacu in 1978. There are eleven laws in the Shimpiyacu document, nine of which concern the regulation of sexual conduct. The remaining two statutes treat such crimes as fighting and shirking communal work. Theft is not even considered significant enough to be mentioned in the community laws. Only witchcraft accusations have as great a role as sexual pecadillos in disrupting village life.

The Aguaruna thus see sexual activity as having some formidable dangers—metaphysical, physical, and social—but also as being inherently desirable. Courtship is characterized by a strong notion of sentimental attachment and an atmosphere of intense secrecy. Marriage is a volatile institution within which men are permitted greater freedom of action than women. Married women are in an insecure position because they may be rejected by their husbands in favor of a younger spouse, and they have few avenues of escape should they suffer from mistreatment.

Magical practices related to courtship and marriage reflect these conditions. Men are primarily concerned with soliciting the affection and sexual favors of women. Women are more preoccupied with maintaining the affection of their husbands and preventing them from philandering with younger rivals. Both men and women want to avoid gossip that might implicate them in adulterous affairs; if their adultery is discovered, they are anxious to escape punishment. For each of these concerns, there are techniques that secretly produce the desired end.

Songs That Direct Human Emotion

When the Aguaruna speak of *anen*, the first songs they mention are likely to be those that manipulate other people's emotions. For the sake of convenience, I shall call this vast corpus of *anen* "romantic songs," but it should be understood that not all of these songs are concerned with romantic relations per se, and some are designed to quell affection rather than kindle it.

People learn romantic songs in much the same way that they learn other *anen*: the receiver of the song memorizes the words and melody after first inhaling tobacco juice prepared with the saliva of the song's teacher. A newly acquired song is ready to be used after a period of fasting and sexual abstinence. Romantic songs have their greatest effect when performed at sunset, the time of day when people's reflections are said to take a melancholy turn toward loneliness and longing, desire and desperation. The singer seeks a private place, takes a bit of tobacco juice through the nasal passages, and softly sings the *anen* that will catch his or her beloved at this vulnerable moment. "When you sing a love song at sunset," say the Aguaruna, "the person to whom you are singing suddenly sighs and feels a sadness that won't go away." The songs, of course, are not heard in a literal sense because the singer may be many miles away from the one to whom they are directed. Rather, the thoughts and emotions of the recipient suddenly change to conform to those suggested by the words of the song.

There is general agreement that women are much more skilled at singing romantic songs than men, "because their voices are better." Men, however, can play their songs on the bamboo flute or, better yet, on a mouth bow called *tumág*. The mouth bow, made from a thin, springy branch strung with a palm fiber cord, has an ingratiating sound that is supposed to have a profound effect on the emotions of the woman to whom the song is directed, despite the fact that she doesn't hear it in a conventional way. When men play love songs on the flute or mouth bow, it is sufficient for them to think the words rather than to sing them aloud.

I was unable to collect any stories explaining the origin of romantic songs, but various ethnographic sources stress their link to Tsugki, the water spirit. Stirling (1938:109), for example, mentions that Shuar men sing special songs directly asking Tsugki for help in love affairs. Romantic songs collected by Pellizzaro (1977) and Tsamaraint et al. (1977) support Stirling's observation. As we shall presently see, many substances used in love magic come from aquatic animals thought to be manifestations of Tsugki.

I found that it was generally easier to persuade people to record romantic *anen* than other categories of magical songs. Love songs are thought to be more benign than other forms of amorous manipulation. The Aguaruna also consider them intrinsically beautiful and therefore worthy of public performance. The openness with which people share songs of love does not, however, extend to those songs intended to extinguish affection, which are among the most secret that I was able to obtain.

The most straightforward romantic songs are those that cause a member of the opposite sex to be attracted to, or to fall in love with, the singer. These sort themselves into two general categories: songs that are used outside of marriage (i.e., in courtship or in pursuing extramarital affairs) and those used within marriage to strengthen the bond of affection between spouses. As far as I could determine, the first kind of song is better known to men, while the second kind is almost exclusively known to, and presumably used by, women.[3]

A.19 is an example of the kind of song that men use to make women more receptive to their amorous advances:

A.19 Look where the sun hides itself
　　Woman, woman
　　Look where it hides itself
　　Its rays red, they strike
　　Your little face
　　The last rays striking your face
　　Sit with pain in your heart
　　If you are thinking of another
　　Think of me

　　Woman, woman
　　If you are thinking of your husband
　　If you are thinking of another
　　If you are thinking of your food
　　Think of me
　　"I feel that I cannot remain happy here"
　　Think thus
　　Woman, woman
　　Think of me

This song requires little interpretive commentary. It evokes the image of the setting sun, which marks the time of day when the woman is most inclined to think of the singer. The words seek to create in her a feeling of sadness and profound agitation that can only be remedied by meeting with her lover. If the woman knows the singer but slightly, she will find that when they next meet she will be inexplicably attracted to him.

The fervid words of A.19 seem bland by comparison to those of the songs used by women to keep their husbands' affection from wandering, or to effect their early return from extended journeys during which they might be tempted to have affairs with other women. The following two *anen* hurry a woman's husband home from a trip:

A.20 Husband, husband
　　Husband, husband
　　Like the palm grub *datúnch*
　　You will fast [i.e., be unable to eat from sadness]
　　Let your stomach rumble "jachachaka"

Let your stomach rumble "jachachaka"
Thinking of me
Let your stomach rumble "jachachaka"
Let it throb
Little heart
Little heart
Let it move like a tethered animal
Let it move like a tethered animal

"Oh dear! What am I doing? [the husband says]
Is my wife still alive?
I shall return
Thus I think
Are my children suffering
While I travel like this?
Thus I think
Rapidly I shall arrive"
Do you think this?
Let your stomach rumble "jachachaka"
Little heart
Let it move like a tethered animal

Let your feet run "tu tu tu ra"
Let your feet run "tu tu tu ra"
On the little pointed hill
On the little pointed hill
You walk, appearing suddenly
Let the dogs whine
Let the dogs bark [i.e., announcing his arrival]
Passing over little thorns
Feeling nothing
Let your feet run "tu tu tu ra"

You will be lonely
"I do not eat"
Are you thinking this?
Let you be in my heart
Sitting with a thud on the ground [like dog with his master]
Let the dogs bark
Let the dogs whine
Little heart
Let it move like a tethered animal
Let it whine
Fill my heart
Are you thinking as my heart thinks?
Let it whine
Let it shake with emotion

A.21 Frog *bukún*, frog *bukún*
  After it has rained

Among the clouds
Where the rains are perpetual
Frog *bukún*
Wet with dew, you sit
Your eyes, also damp
Where my husband sleeps
At my husband's head
With fast little steps
Sing "wara wara"
Sing "wara wara"

"Oh dear, oh dear! [the husband says]
At the blue hill
I let my wife go
My wife thus
My wife remaining
Oh dear! Ay!
While I wander here
Will my wife leave me?
Where she walks
I will not see her [i.e., she may commit suicide from loneliness]"

Let him say these words
"Oh dear, oh dear!
I have a wife
Others have wives
If I wander for nothing
I may regret it
I shall return swiftly
When the sun reaches the horizon
I shall go"

Husband, husband
Be not with other women
I am your little wife
I incline toward you
When the sun reaches the horizon
When the sun reaches the horizon
"Oh dear, oh dear"
Frog *bukún*, frog *bukún*
Sing "wara wara"
Sing "wara wara"

Both A.20 and A.21 exploit fully the conventions of Aguaruna romantic imagery. The husband is depicted wandering in some lonely, inhospitable place, torn with worry about his wife and children, missing the comfort of his own house and his wife's meals. The songs sketch the man's anxious thoughts in considerable detail (e.g., "Oh dear! What am I doing? / Is my wife still alive?" and so on) to add to the vividness of the imagery. From my own observations, men do worry about such things when they are away from home. Husbands of young and attractive women are particularly restless on extended journeys because they fear that their wives may be taking advantage of their absence to commit adultery. On several occasions, I saw young men suddenly abandon a journey and return to their own community, saying that they were "worried about their family." The men who continued on were wont to remark sarcastically that their departed colleague was "worried about turtle heads," that is, other men's penises. These songs, then, play on the very real fears and discomforts suffered by men when they are traveling without their wives.

Song A.21 begins by addressing the frog *bukún*, which in the original text is labeled with the esoteric term *ukaráip*. The woman who recorded this song commented:

> The woman singing this song says to the frog *bukún*: "Change yourself into me. Take my tobacco. Become my soul. Go to my husband in a dream." The man will be unable to sleep. His thoughts will turn constantly to his wife. He will think, "Perhaps she has died. I should return home right away." He is filled with such desperation that he will turn around and return quickly to his home.

These observations illustrate the commonly voiced belief that romantic songs act on people's emotions by secretly influencing their souls. A woman who takes tobacco juice uses her intoxication to enter the visionary world of souls and manipulate her husband's soul through the power of the song. His soul "hears" the song unconsciously, or perhaps in a dream, and this subtle influence alters his thoughts to conform to his wife's desires. In the case of A.21, the woman's message is conveyed through the mournful croaking of the frog at sunset, which turns the man's meditations to thoughts of home.[4]

Some wives know even more powerful songs that prevent their husbands from dallying with other women. I was told that the following *anen*, a particularly expressive example of this genre, is very effective in keeping a man tied sentimentally and sexually to his wife:

A.22 The untamed agouti
   Tying with the vine *yais*
   I fasten tightly
   In my vagina
   "Tu tu tu" I domesticate it

   The untamed mouse
   In my vagina

Tying with the vine *yais*
I fasten tightly

The paper of the mestizos
Rolled up
With new branches [i.e., legs]
I fasten tightly

Here the agouti, the mouse, and the rolled-up "paper of the mestizos" serve as metaphors for the man's penis, which the woman "fastens tightly" so that it will not be inclined to wander to other women. The domestication theme is especially apt because women are in charge of taming wild animals that their husbands bring back from hunting trips. The song illustrates yet another reversal of the equation culture/nature :: man/woman, since here it is the man (metonymically represented by his penis) who is controlled and brought into the regulated domestic sphere by the woman. Indeed, in contrast to the myths stressing the danger that female sexuality poses to society, the romantic songs of women operate under the assumption that it is the promiscuity of men that most threatens normal domestic life.

Thus far I have discussed songs that magically influence a person's feelings toward the singer, but there is also a genre of songs that attempt to manipulate feelings toward a third person, usually a potential or actual co-wife. The Aguaruna say that a woman who knows such songs can successfully prevent her husband from establishing a polygynous marriage; he suddenly loses interest in his new love and contents himself with his first wife alone. The imagery of these anti-love songs is quite malevolent, the prospective co-wife being equated with a dangerous viper, a flea-ridden dog, a demon, or some other undesirable creature.

I had considerable difficulty in obtaining recordings of these songs of loathing, apparently because women feared that I might bring their knowledge to public attention. The woman who sang A.23, for example, had a daughter who was one of the three wives of her community's bilingual teacher. She was at first unwilling to record the songs for fear that I might play the tape for other villagers who, she said, would then leap to the conclusion that she must be teaching them to her daughter for use against her co-wives. If the husband subsequently rejected one of the wives, the family of the rejected woman would have cause for grievance against the singer and her daughter. Only by promising never to play the tape in her own village could I prevail upon her to make the recording. Another cause for secrecy is that a woman's husband might beat her severely if he thought that she were using *anen* to control his actions and emotions. These factors conspire to make songs of rejection among the most closely guarded *anen* known to the Aguaruna.[5]

A.23 You, you
    Say, "I will marry a woman"
    Her, her
    You marry a mangy dog
    "I will marry a woman" you say
    "Later, the day after tomorrow"

    That bed
    "It is my wife's" you say
    That bed
    Is nettlesome, like the skin of the fruit *kukúch*
    Oh! don't sleep, don't sleep!
    A death shroud will wrap you
    Oh! don't sleep, don't sleep!

    My little bed
    Is the armadillo's nest [i.e., warm and cozy]
    Is the armadillo's nest
    In mine, mine
    You sleep warm

    Your other wife
    Day after day
    You will beat like a signal drum
    Day after day
    You will beat like a signal drum

    You, you
    "When she gives me beer, I drink"
    You say, you say
    Beer of human brains
    She gives you, she gives you
    Thus you drink

    "She gives me food" you say
    She, she
    She gives you dog's excrement
    Served in a bowl
    [The bowl] filled, you eat
    Oh! don't eat, don't eat!

    You are wrapped in a death shroud
    Don't sleep!
    "I give you food" she says
    Don't eat, don't eat!
    She will give you human flesh
    At your side will be a mangy dog
    Oh! don't sleep, don't sleep!

My back
Makes your hand fly away
Your other wife
Her back
Day after day
You will beat like a signal drum
My back
Makes your hand sleepy
Your other wife
Her back
Makes your hand light [i.e., it is easy to strike her]

A.24 Oh, don't look!
You say that she is your wife?
She is not your wife
She is a vulture who eats the dead
Belching noisomely
She will harm you

You say that she is your wife
She is a fierce boa
She traps those who approach
To devour them
Oh, don't look!

I am your wife, not she
She is a viper
She will strike you
She is a scrawny dog
With mucous-filled eyes
Curled in the ashes of the fireplace
Barking, she opens her mouth
Full of yellow teeth
Oh, don't look!

Since when is she your wife?
She is like a chicken house
Uncleaned, it has a foul odor
Oh, don't look!

The tropes used in A.23 and 24 are bluntly self-explanatory. The songs take major symbols of happy domestic life—a warm bed, well-prepared food and beer, and so on—and imply that these things will be perverted or lost if the man is foolish enough to marry the singer's rival, who is likened to a series of repulsive animals. The Aguaruna insist that these songs, when performed correctly, can create an almost instant revulsion in a man with respect to his potential spouse.

Because men are aware that their wives may be using this sort of magical strategy to prevent the establishment of a polygynous marriage, they sing *anen* of their own that are supposed to reconcile their wives to the addition of a new woman to the household. Samuel Wajajái, who in 1977 had two wives, recorded several brief examples, which I shall render as if they were part of a single song:

A.25 *Waníg, waníg* [an insect]
 Waníg that does not anger
 Waníg, waníg
 The little women
 Let them join
 Waníg, waníg

 Chiág, chiág [a plant, *Renealmia* sp.]
 Chiág, chiág
 Chiág that does not separate
 Chiág that grabs
 The stems
 Chiág that grabs
 Not angering
 Chiág, chiág

 Puush, puush [a wood-quail, *Odontophorus* sp.]
 Puush, puush
 Puush that does not anger
 With their husbands
 The *puush* join together
 The *puush* following
 Their husbands
 The *puush* following
 Behind, the *puush*
 Their food
 The *puush* eating together
 Puush, puush

The three organisms mentioned in this song share the characteristic of living in close and harmonious association with their fellows, a trait that a man wishes to transfer to his wife so that she will accept the addition of a co-wife to the household. The unidentified insect *waníg* is described as being like a waterstrider; it lives in holes in tree trunks and, as Samuel explained it, "Many *waníg* live together without fighting." *Chiág* is a plant in the ginger family that has parallel stems growing together in clumps, hence the allusion to "*chiág* that grabs." The species of wood-quail called *puush* is said to travel in groups, with a male in the lead and the females following obediently behind him. A man sings this kind of song before bringing home a new wife in hopes of preventing a violent outburst on the part of his first wife.

When a person becomes entangled in an adulterous affair, he or she may use certain *anen* to silence the gossip that can lead to public exposure:

A.26 Lies lies [i.e., the gossip]
    I am a bird's egg
    I burst and disappear
    Lies, lies
    I burst, I fly
    Lies, lies
    I leave the lie
    Next to the bed of another woman
    I am innocent
    There is no gossip about me
    Lies, lies
    I am not from this place
    Lies, lies

Here the prominent metaphor of bursting seems to be used in two senses: first, that like an egg the singer is different from her outward appearance and therefore innocent of the charges that would seem to indict her; second, that the woman will "burst and disappear" from the arena of gossip in which she is currently enmired. A similar metaphor is exploited in A.27, which was recorded by a man who explained that it is sung to dissipate another man's anger when one has been caught philandering with his wife:

A.27 "Te te" [sound of stick hitting ground]
    It is erased
    "Te te" it is erased
    The red worm
    The red worm
    The red worm
    Your anger
    In the heart of the earth is erased
    It remains erased in the heart of the earth
    It remains erased
    In the heart of the earth it is erased
    "Te te" it is erased
    You say your anger is new
    In the heart of the earth it is erased
    "Te te" it is erased
    The center of the papaya
    "Pak!" bursting

Put inside
Scattered, it is erased
Let it erase anger
New anger is impossible
It is difficult to anger
Your anger
The red worm
Taking into the earth, erases
"Te te" it is erased

A unique aspect of A.27 is that the singer, again Samuel Wajajái, described a set of actions to accompany it. To use this song, he said, one chews a wad of tobacco, digs a shallow hole, and then pounds the tobacco into the hole with a stick while singing, this last action being echoed in the song by the onomatopoeic refrain "te te." Samuel added that the tobacco "becomes the anger" of the aggrieved party; this anger is then pulled into the earth by the "red worm" (*kapá nampich*) and thus neutralized. The "new anger" mentioned in the song is an allusion to the belief that recent anger is more rancorous than anger that is "old" or partially forgotten. The song's second stanza asserts that the cuckolded husband's anger will burst and disappear just as the seeds of the papaya scatter when the fruit falls to the ground.

When caught in an adulterous situation, people rarely have time to perform the sort of acts associated with A.27, or even to sing anger-dissipating *anen* aloud after taking tobacco in the forest. It is more likely that a man or woman will, by dint of circumstance, only have time to sing songs hurriedly in his or her thoughts before facing those whom they have angered. Most of the songs that are believed to lessen anger follow one of two metaphorical lines. Some emphasize the singer's ferocity, the terrible powers at his or her command, with the idea of inspiring fear in the aggrieved parties, thereby inducing them to be satisfied with mild punishment. Other songs take the opposite approach—they equate the singer with some abject creature that is at once too pitiable and too beloved to deserve severe sanctions. The following song, A.28, illustrates the first of these two approaches:

A.28 Peccary, peccary
    That throws out anger
    I come enraged, I come enraged
    "A bad woman" they will say
    But with my glances
    I silence them
    When I enter

A Technology of Sentiment   149

Anger departs
I am a peccary woman
I come enraged, I come enraged

This song vividly conveys an image of a furious peccary, hackles raised, casting its intimidating glances over a crowd of people. At the same time, it metaphorically reverses the relationship of the singer to the people who will mete out punishment. In reality, the woman returns contrite while her husband and his kinsmen are angry, but in the song the enraged woman returns to silence her critics. A.29 is somewhat less forceful than A.28 but follows a similar line in that it equates the singer with Nugkui (who of course cannot be harmed by ordinary mortals) and unspecified ancestors who could make the earth tremble:

A.29 Being a Nugkui woman I say [three times]
      I don't bleed easily [three times]
      Husband, husband
      Husband, husband
      If you speak with harsh words
      The ancestors
      Dividing the land
      Destroyed, it is said
      I will do this to you
      I will do this to you

      It is not easy to bruise me
      Being a Nugkui woman I say
      Being a Nugkui woman I say
      I, I
      Being a Nugkui woman I say
      Being a Nugkui woman I say
      Don't speak with harsh words
      Don't speak with harsh words

      "Returning above [i.e., dying]
      My wife did thus
      Because I spoke harshly"
      You will say this
      Your little hands
      Breaking you will remain [i.e., clapping them with grief]

The traditional punishment for adulterers is to slash their scalps with a machete or knife. The phrase "I don't bleed easily," then, suggests that the singer is immune to such punishment. The next lines assert that, like the ancestors who were able to part the earth, the woman can use her Nugkui-given powers to destroy her husband. The final stanza describes the grief the husband would feel if the woman were to commit suicide after being beaten. The husband, concludes the song, will break his hands as he mourns for his dead wife, an image that is based on the handclapping that accompanies demonstrations of profound sorrow among the Aguaruna.

A.30, which is sung by men, achieves the same end by focusing attention on the imposing demeanor of the singer:

A.30 I, the *wirakocha*, am coming
　　I, the *wirakocha*, am coming
　　Wearing red shoes
　　Sounding "tak tak" I come
　　Wearing a red belt
　　Don't stare at me
　　With *señoras* I couple
　　I come, I come
　　If you stare at me
　　If you stare at me
　　I shall go far away
　　The ancestors, the ancestors
　　Annihilated [their enemies] it is said
　　I shall do the same
　　I shall do the same
　　Don't stare at me

　　Making the earth boil
　　The ancestors, the ancestors
　　Annihilated, it is said
　　I shall do the same
　　With my pistol I shall annihilate
　　With a *cushma* [a garment] to my feet, I come
　　With a *cushma* to my feet, I come
　　I, Waisukuan [a personal name?], come
　　Don't stare at me
　　Making the earth boil
　　I shall annihilate
　　Don't stare at me
　　I come, I come
　　I come, I come

The principal rhetorical means of self-aggrandizement used in A.30 is the repeated association of the singer with the trappings of non-Indian culture. Thus the singer claims to be a *wiracocha* (*wiakuch* in Aguaruna), a wealthy person of European ancestry, who consorts with *señoras*. He wears articles of European dress—a red belt, red shoes—plus a *cushma*, a long garment indicative of authority. He also carries a pistol, a firearm that the Aguaruna associate with mestizo landowners and policemen. The words for these objects are all borrowed from Spanish and therefore have a slightly esoteric ring in the context of the song. The song develops images of authority, self-possession, and extraordinary power that have the effect of cowing the singer's antagonists.

The last song that I shall present illustrates the opposing strategy for dissipating anger:

A.31 Brother, brother
The lost dog [i.e., which strayed in the forest]
The lost dog
It comes, it comes
After such a long time, it comes
The lost dog
It comes

Brother, brother
Give the word of food [i.e., ask that it be fed]
The lost dog
Its little ears flapping, flapping
It comes
Give the word of food
Give the word of food
Feed it

Don't speak of anger
To the lost dog
When dogs became lost like this
The ancestors
Spoke not with harsh words
It is said

The lost one
It comes
After such a long time, it comes
Give these words
Brother, brother
Give the word of food
Don't give words of anger

Here the adulterer—man or woman, since either can sing this song—is equated with a dog that has strayed from the path and returned days later to its owner. Instead of words of admonition, the singer seeks the friendly reception symbolized by "the word of food," that is, hospitality as opposed to hostility. The intent of the song is to replace indignation with a reaction of sympathy and pity.

Puságki: Agents of Demented Attraction

Without fail, on the night before I planned to leave my field site for a trip to a large jungle town such as Iquitos or Tarapoto, at least one of my male neighbors would stop by to visit, seemingly to engage in casual conversation. Once he was sure that no one else was within earshot, he would say softly, "Brother, in town they sell dolphin teeth. If you see one, buy it for me and I'll repay you when you return." "Why do you want a dolphin tooth?" I would ask, to which the reply was simply, "Because it's a *puságki*. It attracts women."

The term *puság* or *puságki* covers a variety of substances used in courtship to attract members of the opposite sex.[6] As a consequence of this attraction, *puságki* make the person on whom they are acting more receptive to sexual advances. "My friend Mantu knew all about these things," one man told me. "He had bad skin— a case of *pinta*—but he always found sweethearts. That's because he had *puságki*."

Although *puságki* have a generalized ability to attract members of the opposite sex, the Aguaruna associate their acquisition and use primarily with men. People claim that no woman would want to use a love charm and that it would be highly improper if she did. I cannot say for sure that women never use charms to attract men, but if they do the fact is shrouded in a secrecy that I was unable to penetrate.

The Aguaruna prepare love charms from several animal, vegetable, and mineral substances. Different kinds of *puságki* substances may be used separately or combined to form powerful mixtures. As is the case with all charms, the intrinsic power of the substance is intensified by the fasting and sexual abstinence of the person who has obtained it. A typical fast reportedly lasts from seven to ten days, after which the owner tests the *puságki* by rubbing it with his hands and then touching a neighbor's dog. If the dog suddenly becomes friendly and playful, it is a sign that the *puságki* is effective. The efficacy of the *puságki* may also be substantiated by dreams in which the owner enjoys the attention of many attractive women.

A man uses a *puságki* by contriving to bring it into contact with the woman he desires. Usually this contact is indirect. The man may, for example, store the *puságki* substance next to or mixed in with a quantity of red face paint and then use the paint to decorate himself before going on a social visit. He touches the paint before drinking beer served by a woman who interests him, and when she receives the bowl after he has finished drinking she is necessarily

PLATE 6. *Men and women dance during a drinking party in Shimpiyacu. Men reportedly take advantage of such occasions to seduce women with love magic.*

brought into contact with a minute portion of the paint and its attracting power. Sometimes a man touches a woman directly with a *puságki* while she is dancing at a party. Generally, though, direct contact is considered too dangerous because it exposes the woman to the full effect of the charm and may cause her to become literally mad with desire. The great drawback of *puságki* is that it is impossible to predict their effects on different people. A woman who has been exposed to an overdose of *puságki* power is likely to throw herself into a river and drown, or commit suicide in some other manner, if she is not able to satisfy immediately her passion for her lover. Even the owner of the charm is not immune to its unhinging effects. If he gets drunk while carrying the *puságki*, he is inclined to fight with his kinsmen (an action that the Aguaruna associate with an inability to think right or "straight"), and he also becomes more prone to accidental drowning. The following two incidents illustrate ways in which the use or alleged use of *puságki* can produce tragic results:

Case 1. A young man making an extended visit to the community of some kinsmen reportedly used an exceptionally strong charm (called *wawágki*) to secure the affection of a girl he was courting. The man eventually returned to his own village, which caused the girl to become "crazy" with grief. She died after drinking poison, but not before telling her family about the charm, the existence of which she had somehow divined. Her family held the man responsible for the suicide. There was serious talk of a vengeance raid, but the principals later resolved the dispute through a cash payment by the man to the girl's father.

Case 2. A man was accused of having loaned a *puságki* to a younger brother-in-law who subsequently shot himself. The dead man's father argued that the power of the charm had deranged his son and thereby caused his suicide. The accused denied that he had either owned or loaned a love charm. At a public gathering, he produced a hunting charm that he owned but insisted that it had no effect on women. Because the accusers could not establish that a love charm had been involved, there was no definitive resolution of the dispute.

In both instances a *puságki* was held responsible for suicidal behavior, in the first case by a woman who had been the object of the charm's power and in the second by a man who had simply possessed one. Another effect of the deranging power of *puságki* is that they arouse passion in a woman with whom a charm's owner cannot legitimately have sexual relations (e.g., a real or classificatory sister) if she should accidently come into contact with it. The fact that love charms are thus associated with incest, suicide, and social conflict leads most Aguaruna to state publicly that their possession and use are "bad" or "stupid." Nevertheless, self-interest apparently lures men into acquiring them despite the risk.

Puságki *of Zoological Origin*

Residents of the Alto Mayo consider a tooth of the Amazonian dolphin (*Inia* sp.) to be the most powerful kind of love charm. Interestingly enough, few Alto Mayo people have ever even seen live dolphins, since they are only found far downstream in the larger Amazonian tributaries. The teeth are thus obtained by trade either from Aguaruna who live near the Río Marañón or mestizo merchants who traffic in resources from downriver. The price of a single tooth is said to be high; in 1976–78 the cost was about fifteen hundred soles each, the equivalent of ten days' wages.

As Lévi-Strauss (1973:200–201) points out, many Amazonian cultures associate dolphins with sexuality. Although the Alto Mayo Aguaruna have had few firsthand encounters with this animal, they hold at least two dolphin-related beliefs that shed light on the sexual power attributed to dolphin teeth. First, people say that it is dangerous for a pregnant woman to travel by canoe on large rivers because male dolphins may tip the canoe "to deliver the woman and the fetus to the dolphin's father, the anaconda." Here the dolphin is clearly seen as an agent of the anaconda, which in turn is the principal manifestation of the water spirit Tsugki. A second belief is that the genitalia of the female dolphin are identical to, and more desirable than, those of human females. People tell of men who have tried to copulate with dolphins and found it so pleasurable that they were unable to stop. A dolphin, caution the Aguaruna, will take all of a man's semen and then all of his blood until the man dies.[7] Cetaceans symbolize the arousal of sexual desire beyond the limits of prudence, a quality that is further emphasized by their link to Tsugki. Tsugki once appeared in the form of a beautiful woman to lure an Aguaruna man into the depths of the river in spite of his legitimate fear of the anacondas that lurked there. As the mythical first shaman, Tsugki also represents the ultimate source of the powers used to manipulate human sentiments and physical well-being. The dolphin is thus the nexus of several distinct properties: excessive sexual desire, unreasonable attraction, and shamanistic power.

The teeth of the otter (*Lutra* sp.) are sometimes mentioned as potential *puságki*, though they are considered less powerful than dolphin teeth. The otter, like the dolphin, is conceptually linked to Tsugki because of its aquatic habitat. Lévi-Strauss (1973:200) notes that in the mythology of the Americas the otter is often identified as an "aquatic seducer," but I cannot confirm that the Aguaruna share this view.

One man stated that the teeth of snakes (species not indicated) may serve a similar purpose. More commonly, the attracting power of snakes is concentrated in special stones called *yuka*.

Informants listed the internal organs of two birds as possible components of love potions: the heart, eye, tongue, and brain of the *bijágchichi* (unidentified) and the heart, liver, eye, and brain of the *bichíkuat* (*Monasa* sp.). I obtained no direct explanation of why the entrails of these birds should have an attracting power, nor did I find any evidence linking them to the prevailing pattern of aquatic symbolism.[8]

Puságki *of Mineral Origin*

An extremely potent charm is a liquid called *wawágki* or *wakágki* (cf. Chevalier 1982:385). Reportedly, people can acquire this liquid only in remote escarpments near the Alto Río Marañón, where it drips slowly within rock crevices. To obtain the liquid, one must scale the cliffs and collect the drops in a tiny vessel. Once collected, *wawágki* liquid can be carried in a small bottle by itself or mixed with other charms to form a potion.

I have few clues at hand that can explain why this liquid is thought to have remarkable powers. Water, of course, is linked symbolically to Tsugki, but in this case the source of the liquid seems to be far removed from the rivers in which the water spirit resides. Quite possibly, there is an underlying association between the liquid and the demons that inhabit such remote, rocky places. These demons have formidable shamanistic powers that they sometimes use to attract and imprison women who become separated from their husbands while traveling near the demons' dwelling place.

Yuka stones, mentioned earlier in connection with strategies for attracting game, can also be used to attract women. A speaker who wishes to distinguish one type of *yuka* from the other sometimes calls one "game grabber" and the other "woman grabber." A person who discovers a pebble that he suspects of being a *yuka* establishes the nature of its power by trial and error, as well as by attending to dreams and omens. The accounts I recorded in the Alto Mayo indicate that "woman grabber" *yuka* are most commonly found in snakes, fish, and aquatic mammals. One man, for example, stated that people encounter such stones in the entrails of the otter, while others named the dolphin, various fish, or an animal called *wagkánim* (possibly a kind of nutria), which is said to live in or near the water. The following narrative, recorded by a woman, is typical:

> *Yuka* are found inside the fish *mamayák* or in the "nose" [mouth?] of the fish *nayúm* [*Pterygoplichthys gibbiceps*]. If the stone is found in a *nayúm*, the fish is not killed or eaten. One must take the stone and put the fish back in the water. The stone is white. If a man dreams of women after finding the stone, this means that it is a *yuka* or *puságki* for attracting women. If a woman finds the stone and dreams of men, she should give it to her unmarried brother. She shouldn't keep it, because it's bad.

Some knowledgeable men describe a technique for obtaining a very potent kind of *yuka* found in the mouth of a snake. One account went as follows:

> A man who wants a strong *yuka* should kill a snake [species not identified] and bury it in the forest. After a while, another snake will come to the place because it is attracted to the dead snake. The man must kill this one, too, and bury it in the same spot.
>
> Later another snake will come, an enormous snake with a glowing stone in its mouth. The man quickly pins the snake's head to the

ground with a forked stick, then pries the stone out of its mouth. He runs away. He does not kill the snake, because when it dies the stone is ruined. This stone is called *yuka*. It attracts women.

After acquiring the stone, the man continued, one puts it in a closed vessel with a small quantity of red face paint. The new owner will soon have a dream in which a person tells him, "I give you the *yuka*. Take it and enjoy many women, so long as you don't use it to attract your sisters."

The question of why snakes—and though the narrator does not name the species, it appears that he speaks of poisonous snakes—carry a stone with attracting powers was not clarified to my satisfaction, despite my many queries. One man did say cryptically, "Snakes easily have sexual relations with women because they attract them with these stones." Yet I collected no tales of sexual contact between women and snakes, nor do other ethnographic sources stress such unions.[9] Poisonous snakes are connected with shamanism in many accounts, however, since shamans may take the form of vipers to bring death to their victims. There is also a prevalent notion that snakes are drawn to human beings in a way that resembles the attraction of vultures to carrion. In chapter 2, I noted that when a person is bitten by a poisonous snake, an important part of the usual treatment strategy is to isolate the patient in a shelter surrounded by four campfires in order to frighten off other snakes that are inevitably drawn to the victim. Note that a similar sequence of elements is described in the account of how one steals the snake's *yuka*: one snake is killed and others are mysteriously attracted to its place of burial. Snakes thus symbolize the kind of uncanny attraction that a man wishes to exploit through the use of a love charm.

Like *nantag* stones, *yuka* may "run away" from their owners if they are not properly cared for:

> My brother-in-law once found a stone in the mouth of a snake. It was red. He put it in a gourd and hid the gourd in a pot where he stored cotton thread. But the stone broke through the gourd, ate the lid of the pot, and ran away. He never found it.

Puságki *of Botanical Origin*

People commonly cite two herbs, *pijipíg* and *tsumáik*, as sources of love charms. Varieties of the sedge *pijipíg*, it will be recalled, figure prominently in hunting and gardening magic as well as in the treatment of diverse illnesses. In contrast, the uses of *tsumáik* (a folk taxon that includes species of the genera *Justicia* and *Alternanthera*) seem to be limited to hunting and love magic.[10] Men often acquire varieties of these herbs suitable for making love charms from kinsmen who have previously established the plants' efficacy in their own love affairs. Powerful plants command a high price in cash or an equivalent amount of trade goods. When a man obtains a cutting of one of these species, he plants it in a sheltered spot and sees that it remains undefiled by animals or through contact with people who have recently engaged in sexual intercourse. Once the cutting has established itself, its owner is free to take part of the plant (leaves, stems, and roots in the case of *tsumáik*; rhizomes in the case of *pijipíg*) and put it in a pomade of face paint which, after a period of fasting and abstinence, he can use like any other *puságki*.

Many men are familiar with complex procedures by which varieties of *pijipíg* and *tsumáik* can be obtained from animals. Manta Tsajupút, an elderly man from the Alto Marañón who had recently immigrated to the Alto Mayo, explained:

My father Wejin told me how to get *pijipíg* from the woodpecker *tatasham* [*Coephloeus lineatus*]. First you need to find a woodpecker's hole with chicks inside, crying, waiting to be fed. You plug the hole with a piece of wood, then wait for the woodpecker to come to feed its young. It comes with worms or grubs in its mouth, but it can't get through the hole. The bird leaves then returns, leaves then returns, each time with food for the chicks. You wait, hidden at the bottom of the tree, until sunset. At about that time, the woodpecker brings a stalk of *pijipíg* to open the hole. You must jump out of hiding just at this moment so that the bird will be frightened and drop the plant. After you grab the plant, you must climb the tree to unplug the hole.

This *pijipíg* is planted. It's used to attract either game birds or women.

Another man described a way to obtain *tsumáik* from vultures:

A kind of *tsumáik* that attracts women is found in the vulture *chuág* [either *Cathartes aura* or *Coragyps atratus*]. A man must kill the vulture, then burn it where it falls to the ground. He leaves the ashes. After a few days, three *tsumáik* plants grow from the ashes. The vulture carries *tsumáik* in three places: in the back of the neck, in the shoulder, and in the chest. The man should collect the plants and hide them in his house. He takes one of the plants to his bed when he sleeps that night. He dreams of many snakes—angry, dangerous snakes. This means that this *tsumáik* attracts snakes. The next night he takes another plant to his bed. He dreams of the anaconda. This *tsumáik* is for anacondas. He tries the third plant and dreams of women, beautiful women. This is *tsumáik* for women. It is mixed with face paint, and he uses it after fasting. When he touches a woman with this *puságki*, she cries for no reason at sunset. She desires him very much.[11]

One informant closed his version of an identical account by saying, "This plant has its power. Who can bear to kiss a vulture? It eats rotten things. No one will go near it. Yet it has this plant that everyone wants."

Aside from its obvious sexual symbolism (the woodpecker brings an herb that can unblock a closed cavity), the first of these two recipes remains obscure. Why is a woodpecker an appropriate source of *tsumáik*? What is the connection of this *tsumáik* to sexual attraction? The second recipe is, I think, more amenable to analysis. It is obviously a variant of the account presented in chapter 3 that explains how people obtain a charm (in this case identified as a variety of *pijipíg*) that brings game birds to the vicinity of the hunter.[12] Despite its repulsiveness, the vulture is a symbol par excellence of attraction because it is drawn to carrion from great distances. A difference between the attraction symbolized by the vulture and that sought through love magic is that the vulture is attracted to carrion for the purpose of eating it, whereas a man with a love charm seeks to become the attractor, filling the structural role of carrion while remaining the predator with respect to the woman he attracts. The shift from attractee to attractor is accomplished by transforming the vulture to carrion or ashes, or both. The herbal charms that result from this transformation give the bearer the same attracting power that carrion has vis-a-vis vultures.

Love Magic, Hunting Magic, and the Limits of Affinity

Aguaruna love magic and hunting magic exhibit striking similarities. A single term denotes the stones used to attract game and women; the same herbs figure prominently in both kinds of magic. The Aguaruna often say that hunting charms "make game fall in love with a man" in the same way that love charms make people fall in love with one another. Furthermore, hunting songs exploit metaphors of sexual union to reorder the relationship of men and animals to one of affinity. In both arenas men try to arouse a demented attraction—demented because game animals and women are made to lose their normal attitude of caution or suspicion. Descriptions of the effects of hunting charms stress their stupefying power, which causes birds to sit tranquilly as their fellows are shot one by one with darts, or monkeys to abandon their usual wariness and approach a hunter. The effects of love charms are less stupefying than arousing, but the result is that women lose all sense of propriety, even to the point of desiring incestuous unions. The bearer of the love charm is similarly affected and easily descends to behavior (e.g., fighting, incest, adultery) that prudent and straight-thinking men regard with contempt.

The Aguaruna note two other negative effects of love charms that express the danger they pose to the social order. First, when charms are used to secure a wife rather than a casual lover, the resulting marriage is certain to end in discord. People point out that the effect of the charm eventually wears off, causing the woman to lose affection for her husband. She is then drawn into adulterous affairs with other men. Second, a wife obtained through the use of a love charm will never be able to raise domestic animals with success.[13] Clearly, the reason why the use of love charms is inimical to domestic tranquility is that to fulfill properly and happily their domestic roles men and women must "think straight," something that they learn to do through the accumulation of visionary experience. When a man uses a *puságki* to acquire a wife, he prevents her from thinking correctly by bringing to bear deranging powers ultimately derived from Tsugki, the water spirit. The resulting chaos prevents the establishment of the harmonious order that the Aguaruna seek, but so rarely find, in their domestic lives.

CHAPTER 6

Working Metaphors

> Human beings are not simply actors following
> a written script, or entities in a field of forces.
> They are self-conscious beings who must
> conceptualize and comprehend their
> environment in the face of the ambiguous, the
> anomalous, and the evocative. . . . In this
> process humans are constantly becoming.
>
> Janet W. D. Dougherty and James Fernandez,
> *American Ethnologist*

Social scientists of all theoretical persuasions have traditionally shared the assumption that there are patterns twilled into the rough fabric of happenstance. It is a measure of the skepticism, or perhaps pessimism, of the 1980s that this search for order is being called into question, at least where symbolic representations are concerned. In a review critical of a recent collection of essays by Clifford Geertz, for example, Jonathan Lieberson (1984) argues that the way Geertz (and by implication, other symbolic anthropologists) uses the term "symbol system" is meaningless because Geertz fails to provide a clear definition of what he means by "symbol" and consistently misuses the word "system." The elements of symbolic representation, Lieberson says, are neither as specific nor as interdependent as the term "system" implies. Dan Sperber (1982:162) states the case even more emphatically when he claims that "anthropological evidence does not warrant . . . the assumption that particular beliefs are integrated into coherent, all-embracing, culturally transmitted world views." Relativists who insist on understanding a given culture in terms of its underlying assumptions about reality are waggishly dismissed by Sperber as members of a "hermeneutico-psychedelic subculture" (ibid.:154).

Such criticisms reflect a growing impatience with the sterile formalism of some styles of symbolic analysis. Beliefs are rarely as consistent and formally elegant as many analysts of "symbol systems" would have us believe. Yet even if beliefs, convictions, or symbolic representations do not constitute a system in any strict sense, they nonetheless derive their existence from the considerable degree of shared understanding found among members of a society. Shared (or in the current parlance, "intersubjective") knowledge provides the mental forestructures that allow people to interpret experiences in ways that are distinctive to their own culture. At the same time, cultural knowledge is not static. Symbolic representations can and do respond to changing environments and to the personal interests of social actors.

In the preceding chapters, I have described a heterogeneous array of practices by which the Aguaruna act upon their world. I presented the techniques more or less as the Aguaruna themselves speak of them: according to the practical sphere in which they are applied. Now I shall seek a different vantage point, one that distances us slightly from the ethnographic particulars so that their underlying form may be discerned. To understand Aguaruna magic in any comprehensive sense, some loss of the "experience-near" perspective is inevitable. Magic is not, after all, a "problem" for the Aguaruna. They feel no compulsion to explain it. Nor did I encounter a gifted native exegete—an Alto Mayo equivalent of Ogotemmêlli, Muchona, or Don Juan—who could provide me with an insider's reading of the total "system." My goal is to make explicit the implicit assumptions that underlie Aguaruna magic while avoiding the temptation to explain too much or exaggerate the coherence of magical strategies. As Rodney Needham (1983:90) notes, anthropologists tend to use overly mechanistic metaphors to describe local theories of ritual causality, models that imply a "rigidity of outlook which is quite inappropriate to the subtle interplay of ideas" characteristic of ritual. Aguaruna magic is not lacking in systematic features, but it also has its share of loose ends and ambiguities.

In the introduction, I briefly raised the question of whether "magic" is an appropriate label for the phenomena I have set out to analyze. Jeanne Favret-Saada (1980:195) takes anthropologists to task for employing a negative definition of magic, that is, identifying it in terms of what it *isn't* rather than in terms of what it *is*. An explicit, positive definition of magic is, however, difficult to develop for the Aguaruna case. There is little evidence that the Aguaruna see magic as a discrete category of behavior. It is true that certain aspects of magic, such as *anen* or *yuka*, constitute separable objects or fields of expertise. Other magical techniques are less distinct. Most of the avoidances I recorded came to my attention through casual references or observations rather than because "taboos" exist as a marked category of acts.[1] As John Skorupski (1976:158–59) argues, to assert that people see magic as a technique separate from technology we must either demonstrate that there exists a generic term roughly congruent with the Western notion of magic or, at the very least, show that those who use the rites find something "distinctive, problematic, and bizarre" in them. Let us therefore investigate the nature of magical efficacy to clarify whether magic embodies principles that are, from the Aguaruna perspective, qualitatively different and substantially more "problematic" than other ways of acting on the world.

The Question of Agency

A perennial issue in the analysis of magic—in fact, the pivotal issue in the fruitless debate over whether specific practices are "religious" or "magical" or "practical"—is the matter of agency. The Aguaruna, like many other peoples, call upon several kinds of agency when asked to explain the power of magic. Some people account for the efficacy of *anen* in terms of soul manipulation. By entering into a trancelike state with the aid of tobacco, they say, one can "speak to" and thereby influence the soul of the plant, animal, or person to whom the song is directed. A related idea, though one apparently restricted to the realm of the garden, is that *anen* please Nugkui, who then grants the singer's wishes by causing manioc to produce in abundance (Chumap Lucía and García-Rendueles 1979:755). Very occasionally, the influence of magical substances is explained in animistic terms: they have souls or "people" who effect the desired result. In the Alto Mayo, none of these explanations is universally accepted.

That the power of magic is perceived as being primarily derived from supernatural beings can, I contend, be ruled out. Only a portion of *anen* refer to powerful beings, and this is usually to allude to the being's legendary prowess in the task rather than to ask directly for help. Some of the beings prominent in the lyrics of *anen* no longer intervene directly in people's lives, except perhaps through the effects of their mythical deeds. Finally, all powerful beings are classified as *aents*, "people," which means that despite their unusual powers they are ultimately as subject to magical manipulation as ordinary humans.

The major role of powerful beings such as Nugkui, Tsugki, and Etsa in Aguaruna magic is cognitive: they provide reference points around which disparate associations are organized into meaningful patterns, which then provide blueprints for action. Here the work of Norman E. Whitten, Jr. (1976, 1978b) among the Quichua provides some instructive parallels. Whitten notes that the concept of the earth spirit Nugkui, the water spirit Tsugki, and a male forest spirit named Amasanga[2] are integrated by the Quichua into a system of "paradigmatic imagery." The relations among the three beings and their various transformations provide a cognitive template by means of which the Quichua understand and act upon the world. This system of paradigms, concludes Whitten, is used to "heighten the interpretive possibilities of discrete observations by providing multiple transformational, associational, allegorical, and indexical avenues" (1978b:848).

Much of Whitten's analysis is applicable to the Aguaruna in both form and content. The Quichua and the Aguaruna share the

TABLE 8
A Sample of Cultural Elements
Ordered by Powerful Beings

	Nugkui	**Etsa**	**Tsugki**
Gender	female	male	ambiguous
Terrestrial locus	garden	forest	river
Cosmographic locus	earth	sun	rainbow
Subsistence activity	horticulture, animal husbandry	hunting	—
Crafts, skills	ceramics	woodworking	shamanism
Animal transformations	nighthawk	spider monkey	anaconda, dolphin, otter
Lithic manifestations	*nantag*	*yuka* (hunting)	*yuka* (love magic)

concepts of Nugkui and Tsugki. The role of the forest spirit Amasanga is to some degree filled by Etsa, the sun, although there are
differences between the two. Each being is the nexus of diverse associations, ranging from the concrete and everyday (subsistence activities, for instance) to cosmographic features and abstract propo-
sitions of Aguaruna world view (for example, the notion that
celestial bodies were once human beings). These relationships provide direction for practical activity as well as for the interpretation
of experience at a more abstract level.

Having ruled out the supposed intervention of powerful beings
as a major cause of magical efficacy, we are still left with several
other contradictory explanations, none of which is adequate to the
task of explaining magic comprehensively or reconciling the observed differences of opinion. Clearly, we must probe deeper into
local notions of how human beings cause things to happen in the
world. Jivaroan ethnography suggests that the idea of visions may
hold the key to underlying premises about the nature of goal-
directed action. The Aguaruna consider visions to be a vital means
of elaborating a sense of self and developing ways by which the self
can influence the world at large. What can visions tell us about
Aguaruna notions of causality in the most general sense?

Visionary Experience and the Direction of Events

People understand perfectly well that a shotgun blast or a well-
aimed lance is the proximal cause of an enemy's death. Nevertheless, when the Aguaruna were still engaged in warfare it was considered foolhardy to enter into battle without having "dreamed" one's
foe beforehand. The killing vision is a distant cause that makes the
proximal cause possible. Life-giving (niimagbau) visions have a
similar role with respect to domestic accomplishments.

The question of how visions exert this effect introduces a vex-
ing issue of interpretation. Michael Harner's description of Shuar
killing visions states that the ability to prevail in combat comes
from the acquisition of the soul of an arutam (ajútap in Aguaruna)
during the vision (Harner 1972:134–45). The presence of this soul
confers upon the dreamer a formidable killing power. The Aguaruna
case demands a different interpretation. People in the Alto Mayo
insist that the vision itself—the experience of controlling one's terror, facing the fearsome ajútap, and finally receiving its account of
future triumphs—becomes part of the dreamer. Indeed, the dreamer
is thereafter known as a kajintin, "dream-owner." My informants

emphatically denied that this dream is a soul, however. It attains soul status only when the dream-owner dies, leaving his body with a terrible detonation on the night of his death. The newly created soul then joins the ranks of the *ajútap* and subsequently appears to other vision-seekers in their dreams.[3]

Alto Mayo narratives about killing visions emphasize not a migration of soul from *ajútap* to dreamer but rather a transfer of words or images. The *ajútap* presents a detailed description of the dreamer's role in a future battle. Dream-seekers sing songs that ask the *ajútap* to "bring your little words," that is, declarations of victory. Immediately before a battle, men performed a ritual declaration called *kaja tigbau,* "dream telling," which seems to have had the function of renewing the imagery of the dream so that its power could be brought to a fever pitch.[4] The efficacy of the dream comes from suffering the deprivations required of the dream-seeker, standing up to the terrifying *ajútap,* and securing a verbal description of future triumphs. The *ajútap* is instrumental in the process insofar as it provides a test of courage that the dreamer has to pass; it also acts as the vehicle through which the future is expressed. But it is primarily the actions of the man, not those of spirit, that determine his fate.

By seeing killing visions in this light, we are better able to understand *niimagbau* or life-giving visions, which involve no direct contact with powerful beings. What life-giving and killing visions have in common is an unveiling of the future in the form of words or images. Visions are thus the culmination of a campaign to enter the dangerous realm of the unseen world and, through immense personal effort, extract from it a specific kind of knowledge-bearing experience. The disciplined actions of the vision-seeker ultimately produce images of the future, creating order where there had previously been uncertainty.

The ways that visionary knowledge can be used to manipulate material things are expressed in ideas about psychotropic plants. The Aguaruna consider the intoxicating power of the plants to be only partially innate. It is given fullest expression through proper cultivation techniques. Moreover, as a man acquires ever more powerful visions (hence greater knowledge), the plants he uses increase their potency, so they are sought after by others (Brown 1978). Victor Turner's description of the relations between human knowledge and the medicinal power of plants among the Ndembu of Zambia brilliantly condenses an attitude toward man-plant exchange quite similar to that of the Aguaruna:

> Knowledge among the Ndembu is far more literally "power" than it is with us. . . . In whatever way such knowledge may have been obtained, it confers some kind of mystical power on its possessor, gives him or her an affinity with the materia medica used, and enables the herbalist to activate the latent virtues of the herbs he uses (Turner 1967:350).

The "activation of latent virtues" is more than a process of using culture to inform nature. It is also an exploratory procedure through which the human actor learns about the world and acquires knowledge that can subsequently be put to use for practical ends.

The premises that support the vision also apply to ordinary daily activities. Physical acts are, of course, generally necessary and sometimes sufficient to get things done. Nevertheless, the repertoire of techniques used to accomplish common tasks usually includes a series of steps for creating a more demanding, pervasive, comprehensive, and multidimensional order than that which can be created by technology alone. All of the major elements of Aguaruna magic—songs, medicines, power objects, and avoidances—contribute in their own way to the construction of this compelling order.

Creating Order

Anen originated in a time when the order that prevails today in the world was created by mythical heroes. Tsewa, the primordial spider monkey, was the source of hunting technology and hunting *anen*. Garden *anen* came from Yampan, the wife of Etsa, or from Nugkui herself. Both had prodigious knowledge of plant cultivation. When people perform *anen* today, they participate in a creative process that was inaugurated by these mythical personages.

Anen are ideally sung without improvisation in melody, rhythm, or lyrics, which places them among the most formalized genres of speech known to the Aguaruna. Maurice Bloch (1974) identifies ritual songs performed by rote as an extreme case of formalized language, one possessing great directive power owing to its disengagement from the give-and-take of ordinary discourse. To perform *anen* is to focus one's thoughts, to impose a pattern on the free associations that characterize ordinary mental activity. All *anen* make extensive use of metaphor and simile, assembling images that are meaningfully related to one another and to the activity being manipulated. *Anen* are not characterized by directive speech. Few commands are to be found in them. Instead, they consist primarily of descriptive statements about the singer or the future state of things after the singer's actions have taken effect. A.24, for instance, juxtaposes vultures, boas, vipers, and mangy dogs to cause a man to feel disgust toward a potential second wife. A.13, a gardening song, brings together images of objects that suggest great thickness—the cayman's tail, the root of the plant *seekemu*, a pig, the *wampu* tree—to promote the development of manioc tubers. Through *anen*, a singer makes connections among diverse things in the world and reorganizes the sensible properties of these things in a way that favors the accomplishment of a concrete task.[5] There is no question that the special language of *anen* is thought to have some sort of sui generis power. This reflects the Aguaruna belief that words can activate the things to which they refer. I was told that upon encountering a jaguar or an anaconda in the forest, I should never utter the creature's true name lest this make it feel ferocious and therefore inclined to attack. It is better, I was instructed, to address the animal as *pasún*, a term that denotes something vaguely menacing rather than truly life-threatening. The jaguar, alternatively, can be called *yawáa*, "domestic dog," an obvious diminution of its proper name, *ikám yawáa*, "forest dog." People avoid calling magical stones by their true names (*yuka, nantag*, etc.) because too frequent use of the names may diminish the stones' power. Have the Aguaruna then fallen prey to what C. R. Hallpike (1979:409) refers to as "nominal realism," the illusion that names have a special connection to the things they denote?

To some extent, they probably have. But *anen* are clearly more than just a vehicle for the utterance of powerful words. The songs consist of vivid images, sets of reticulated connotations that link mythology, cosmology, and lived experience. Magical words undoubtedly contribute to the efficacy of *anen*, but they cannot explain the songs in any comprehensive sense. On balance, the evidence suggests that the power attributed to *anen* has less to do with words per se than it does with words as indices of powerfully structured thoughts. The myth of the origin of cultivated plants explains that Nugkui's daughter was able to "call" the plants into the garden. She did this not with special words, but with ordinary commands—backed by the knowledge (*yachamu*) that gave the words special force (Chumap Lucía and García-Rendueles 1979:380).[6]

The manipulative quality of *anen* shares much in common with the power of visions. Both are constituted by evocative imagery that illuminates a desired future state. Consumption of psychotropic substances figures in the performance of *anen* and the search for visions. Although both are essentially private experiences, they place the actor in direct contact with ancient sources of knowledge, thus projecting past and present into the future. Visions and *anen* are attributed a palpable quality that distinguishes them from other phenomena: they are both reified, referred to as "things" that have a life of their own. This reification underscores the degree to which the performer of an *anen* sees himself or herself as engaging in a real operational procedure rather than as performing a purely symbolic act.

The role of material things, including charms, in the magical manipulation of practical activity parallels that of verbal imagery. Each object embodies one or more qualities that the magician uses to help create favorable conditions. Hunters, for example, find that *yuka* stones have an unusual affinity for certain species of game animals. By carrying the stones while hunting (or using face paint in which the stones have been immersed), a man juxtaposes the attracting power of the stones with his own.

Analogical thinking plays a central role in the selection of many magical substances. The roots of *wampúsh* and *mente*, both conspicuously large trees, are added to the mixture that women pour on manioc cuttings to encourage their growth. Men consume shavings of the penis bone of the monkey *yutapkiú* (*Cebus macrocephalus*) to cure impotence. As Robin Horton (1967) has pointed out, such analogies are not unique to magic but in fact figure prominently in all forms of thought.

The power attributed to some substances is based on conventional, culture-specific meanings rather than analogical thinking in the strict sense. A man who finds a stone in the entrails of a fish responds to the discovery by considering the following cultural facts: (1) stone is a rare substance that is attributed unusual powers, (2) this particular stone has shown itself to have special qualities by virtue of having made its way into the fish's gullet, (3) the fish comes from the river, the domain of Tsugki, and (4) Tsugki is conventionally regarded as the source of powers of sexual attraction. These facts lead almost inexorably to the conclusion that the stone might serve as a *puságki*—a conclusion that can, however, only be verified by preparing and then testing the stone in the proper manner.

What is perhaps most striking about the preparation of magical substances is the complexity of the recipes and testing procedures employed. Recalling the process by which a bird-stupefying herb is acquired (chapter 3), we see a step-by-step series of actions that includes close observation of the plant's effects. The rigorous, highly ordered procedure ultimately produces a substance that, when applied to a blowgun, imbues the hunting implement with new meaning. This meaning is powerful in terms of Aguaruna notions of causality because it expands the range of order surrounding the use of the blowgun.

When constructing a desirable order through the juxtaposition of objects and images, it is imperative that associations which might generate undesirable conditions be avoided—hence taboos. In this interpretation, I am in agreement with Frazer, who saw taboos as "negative magic," beliefs based on the notions of similarity and contagion but directed toward the avoidance of harmful effects.

The act of observing specific avoidances, of course, is in itself a form of ordering, since the actor brings an unusual degree of attention to his or her actions. Here the insights of Bloch (1974) are again pertinent. Avoidances impoverish behavior in much the same way that formalized utterances impoverish speech. By limiting the enterprises in which people can engage and the contacts they can make, avoidances remove the actors from the varied behavioral discourse of ordinary life. Thus reduced in the ability to respond to outside influences, their actions embody a kind of directedness that adds still another dimension to the ordering qualities of magical procedures.

Aguaruna strategies for creating order contradict two bits of received wisdom about magic: first, the idea that magic is employed where technology fails, and second, the claim that magic is conceived by its practitioners in mechanistic terms, as distinct from the personalistic quality of religious thought. Although the first assertion is usually credited to Malinowski, it survives in more recent analyses of magic. S. J. Tambiah (1973:226), for instance, resuscitates this idea when he says that

> many (but not all) magical rites were elaborated and utilized precisely in the circumstances where non-Western man has not achieved that special kind of "advanced" scientific knowledge which can control and act upon reality to an extent that reaches beyond the realm of his own practical knowledge.

Karl Rosengren (1976:674) casts the same idea in a slightly different form. "To the understanding observer," he writes, "[magic] is a constitutive act applied to an unconstitutable object when instrumental acts do not suffice to control reality." Rosengren uses "constitutive" in preference to the term "performative" as employed by Austin (1962) and Tambiah (1968, 1973). The problem with this argument lies less with the question of performativity, to which I shall return shortly, than with the issue of how one determines whether a given technology will, as Rosengren puts it, "suffice to control reality." Presumably, hunting is an example of a pursuit in which instrumental acts do not suffice to control reality, since hunters are often unsuccessful. Hunting magic is thus seen as a response to technological inadequacy. Yet how are we to deal with the fact that the Aguaruna have developed elaborate forms of garden magic even though their horticultural system is extraordinarily reliable? Love magic poses an equally knotty problem. Would Rosengren and Tambiah argue that the Aguaruna are less knowledgeable in the technology of seduction than, say, American adults, so that the former must use love magic while the latter needn't? The Aguaruna case exposes the speciousness of the "magic as last resort" thesis. Like such concepts as "carrying capacity" and "basic needs," "technological insufficiency" is a cultural construct, not an empirical condition.

Aguaruna notions of order-production are mechanistic in the sense that they advance the idea that the actor can direct events by controlling pertinent variables. But the Aguaruna are not guilty of the simplistic "if A then B" determinism that anthropologists customarily impute to magical thought. The Aguaruna world is defined by possibilities and probabilities rather than mechanistic certainties. Uncertainty arises because no one can ever possess enough knowledge to understand and control every factor that touches on a given situation. The magical universe is not passive but defined by a lively complexity. Even the most ordinary action—fetching water from the river, walking through a garden—may take a turn for the unexpected. Perhaps a strange being will present itself or a powerful omen change a person's understanding of his situation. Immutable facts often prove illusory: I collected numerous accounts of dead people who suddenly revived, and mourners frequently discuss the possibility of such a revival before a burial. In a world where such possibilities exist, people attribute to magic a strong but by no means infallible power of compulsion.

Is Aguaruna Magic Performative?

An important claim of some symbolist analyses of magic is that magical acts and utterances—and ritual in general—are, to quote Austin (1962), "performative." This position is argued by Tambiah in two influential essays (1968, 1973) and commented on, either favorably or unfavorably, in subsequent work by other scholars.

Briefly put, Austin labels "performatives" those utterances that not only describe an act but actually constitute it. Frequently mentioned examples of performative utterances include marriage ceremonies ("I now pronounce you man and wife") and christenings ("I baptize thee . . . "). The efficacy of performatives is not measured by their observable results—in most cases there aren't any—but by the "felicity" of their performance, that is, whether the person making the pronouncement was qualified to do so, whether the parties concerned were eligible to participate, and so on.

Drawing heavily on Malinowski's description of Trobriand magic, Tambiah asserts that spells are primarily performative in nature because "by virtue of being enacted [they] achieve a change of state, or do something effective" (1973:221). What they do, apparently, is "effect changes . . . in terms of convention and normative judgment, and as solutions of existential problems and intellectual puzzles" (1973:226). Tambiah's earlier essay on magic frames the goal of magic somewhat differently. Magic, he says, serves to "restructure and integrate the minds and emotions of the actors" (1968:202). Thus the effect of magic is more akin to that of myth than it is to technology. Given their performative nature, magical acts and utterances cannot appropriately be subjected to the same kinds of verification as ordinary instrumental acts, nor are they to be understood in terms of a logic of causation in a scientific sense (1973:223).

This is not the place to consider whether the concept of performativity can properly be applied to all classes of ritual, although there are strong arguments that it cannot (Gardner 1983). Insofar as magic is concerned, performativity is problematic in several respects. Social convention determines the "results" of truly performative acts. Through an African investiture ceremony, a man becomes a chief, provided that the proper forms are observed. The ceremony has "worked" regardless of whether that person turns out to be a good chief or a bad chief. An Aguaruna *puságki* charm, on the other hand, is ultimately evaluated in terms of the effect it produces in another person. If the loved one fails to respond to the *puságki*, the charm's owner wants to know why. Some of his questions may concern the "felicity" of the procedure by which the *puságki* was prepared (Were the correct steps taken? Did the *puságki's* owner observe the proper precautions?) whereas others are directed to the efficacy of the charm itself. The Aguaruna realize that sexual attraction is a complicated matter and that it may be difficult to explain why a woman resists a man's advances. This does not mean, however, that the contribution of the *puságki* to sexual conquest is any less verifiable from the Aguaruna point of view. Tambiah observes that the objectives of performative acts are "'persuasion,' 'conceptualization,' 'expansion of meaning' and the like" (1973:

219). As we have seen, these aspects of true performatives are evident in Aguaruna magic, though from the perspective of the actors they produce palpable, material results, not ones based solely on social convention.[7]

It is no accident that symbolist accounts devote more attention to speech acts than to procedures involving direct, physical intervention—for example, the use of medicinal plants. For if these medicines "really work" in a Western scientific sense, they present us with a riddle: if magical operations are strictly symbolic in character, how can we account for their material effects? To say that their material effects are merely fortuitous is to replace the intellectualist approach ("Magic is a flawed form of science") with something even worse—the implication that technological innovation is accidental rather than the direct result of acute observation and cogent thought. Throughout the long debate on whether the thought systems of tribal societies are "closed" or "open," it is scarcely noted that the most important inventions in human cultural history occurred within a "magical" milieu. There must therefore be critical links between the symbolic thought characteristic of magic and the kinds of thinking that produce technical advances.

Magic, Technology, and the Symbolic Power of the Ordinary

To move beyond an approach that imprisons magic in words and symbolic acts, thus artificially separating it from the material world in which it is so firmly fixed, we must rechart the conventional limits of symbolic analysis. There is evidence that this process is already under way, as scholars finally become alert to the symbolic implications of the ordinary activities often ignored precisely because they do not embody the exotic "differences" that are the usual stuff of ethnography (Ortner 1984:154). In these ordinary acts, the attentive ethnographer can find many of the exotic elements that were conventionally assumed to exist only in the symbolic domains of language and ritual. Language and ritual are losing their privileged status as the bearers of meaning.

From this perspective, apparently self-evident facts can be seen in a new light. Consider, for example, the Aguaruna's view of Western medicine. In the field, I was constantly confronted by the Aguaruna's high regard for modern pharmaceuticals. For many months, I took it for granted that their faith reflected the obvious superiority of Western medicines in treating common afflictions. Close examination of illness episodes, however, showed that this was quite wrong: pharmaceuticals as they were used by the Aguaruna pro-

duced cures only rarely. In the 1970s, few residents of the Alto
Mayo, Indian or non-Indian, could avail themselves of professional
medical care. They customarily purchased medicines on the rec-
ommendation of kinsmen, store owners, or, at best, pharmacists,
often resulting in the use of drugs that were inappropriate for the
complaint under treatment. Only infrequently did Aguaruna families have enough cash to be able to purchase a complete course of a
needed medicine. As is the case elsewhere in the developing world,
the drugs they were sold had often passed their expiration date by
many months.

The ironies of pharmaceutical use in the Alto Mayo were poign-
antly expressed in a funeral I attended in 1978. Next to the corpse
of the deceased, a man in his late thirties who had apparently succumbed to complications resulting from acute dysentary, was a
large pile of commercial drugs of every description—drugs purchased by relatives in a desperate attempt to save his life. There was
ample reason to suspect that this bewildering mixture of drugs may
have caused his death, or at least hastened it. Upon leaving the funeral, I happened upon a bereaved kinsman waiting for a truck that
might take him to the pharmacy in Rioja. There, he told me, he
would buy "sadness medicine" for the women so that they wouldn't
commit suicide in their grief.

What at first seemed obvious is no longer so clear. Why are
pharmaceuticals perceived as better than traditional medicines if
they are no more effective (and quite possibly more dangerous) in
real episodes of illness? Why do the Aguaruna have a higher opinion
of Western drugs than do the physicians who dispense them?

A myth explains, with droll ethnocentrism, that the fearsome
diseases associated with the arrival of non-Indians were originally
created by an Aguaruna shaman named Kushi, who unleashed them
on the kistián, "Christians" or mestizos, who had murdered his
son. After suffering terrible losses, the clever Christians captured
the diseases in bottles and invented remedies for each. Now Christians control both the diseases and their cures. The apparent resist-
ance of non-Indian children to the maladies that take so many Aguaruna lives confirms the Christians' monopoly on good health in
Aguaruna eyes. It is undoubtedly true that the efficacy of vaccinations, which the Aguaruna were quick to appreciate, contributes to
their sense of the power of Christian medicine.

Christians also introduced a powerful symbol of therapeutic intervention, the hypodermic needle. Injections mesmerize the Aguaruna. Hypodermic kits are found in every Alto Mayo village, where
they are used with appalling frequency. Traditional illness theories

PLATE 7. *Celestina Cahuaza, a community health-care worker, administers vaccinations in Bajo Naranjillo.*

link the intromission of substances into the body with sorcery and sudden death. Perhaps because injections so dramatically invert traditional knowledge (just as Christian norms invert Aguaruna customs in so many ways), they possess great symbolic force. *Kistián ampi*, "Christian medicine," is meant to be injected, and whenever possible it is. Injection instantiates its power. To use a syringe is to perform an act at once unquestionably instrumental and profoundly expressive. It is the meaning of *kistián ampi*, as much as its observable effects, that leads the Aguaruna to use it in preference to traditional remedies.

As the Aguaruna's use of pharmaceuticals should remind us, all cultural acts take place within a milieu charged with implicit meanings, and their efficacy is judged in those same terms. No actions, practical or otherwise, are free of the burden of signification. Signification is not epiphenomenal to technology but part of its very essence.

The Aguaruna's assertion of control in hunting, horticulture, and interpersonal relations requires an interpretation that rejects the artificial distinction between action and meaning implicit in both symbolist and cultural materialist formulations. "There is no such thing," writes Jacques Chevalier (1982:43), "as man-in-nature or nature-in-man which would exist in 'relative' independence of the meaning-full milieu in which men live and act, and which could be treated as a distinct object of social scientific analysis." I have tried to lay bare some of the connections between magical symbolism and practical thinking in the Aguaruna world. By focusing on the cognitive aspects of "magical" operations and their relation to local notions of practical causality, I have not intended to revive the tired debate about whether magic is closer to science than to religion. What I am proposing instead is that we ask different kinds of questions: What is the relationship between symbolic thought and encyclopedic knowledge? How can symbolic thought lead to discoveries? What influences do cultural meanings have on productive acts and vice versa? Is the relationship between symbol systems and cognition the same in all societies?

The operations I have described in the preceding chapters are neither expressions of an uncritical faith that shuns common sense nor manifestations of a technology wanting in symbolic power. They represent a thoughtful, creative exploration of possibilities—a careful bringing together of abstract cosmological concepts and encyclopedic practical knowledge to address real-world problems. The procedures we call "magic" are more than a system of signs, a form of social action, or a kind of rhetoric. Not only do they speak, they explain and explore.

Afterword

In Amazonia dust may be the most conspicuous product of economic development. Indians walk so lightly on the land that they stir up dust only in their houses and dance plazas. Real dust comes with roads, with town construction, with mechanized agriculture, with airplane propwash. It blooms behind double-axled Volvo trucks bearing names like "Our Lord of the Earthquakes" and "Two Beers and I'm On My Way."

Nuevo Cajamarca in 1981 is a study in dust. Dust in the streets, on canned goods in stores, on the screen of the television that casts its blue glow in a corner of a restaurant. There has not always been so much dust or so many places for it to settle. In 1976 Nuevo Cajamarca was a small collection of shabby houses occupied by colonists from the sierra, people who still wore wool clothing in the tropical heat. But its location on the highway to the coast and its proximity to new areas of rice production in the Alto Mayo made it an ideal site for a market town. A Sunday market was established, stores and restaurants constructed, electric wires strung, a generator put on line. All this took place in five years and scarcely ten kilometers from the boundary of the nearest Aguaruna community.

Similar changes are under way in nearby towns. Residents of Rioja, Moyobamba, and Tarapoto proudly note the "movement" around them—movement registered as increased traffic and cash flow. A new hotel is going up in Moyobamba. It boasts a collection of stuffed rain-forest birds and mammals, a sure sign that the jungle has been pushed back far enough to be romanticized. The taxidermist's craft speaks of domination: we are predator, the animals prey. For people who still live in the forest, the relationship is uncomfortably ambiguous.

The few available statistics record the Alto Mayo's transformation. The population of the provinces of Moyobamba and Rioja increased by 135 percent between 1972 and 1981, the result of unprecedented levels of immigration from the coast and sierra. A region sparsely inhabited in the early 1970s, the Alto Mayo has become an

PLATE 8. *An Aguaruna schoolteacher, Adolfo Juép, studies documents that have been sent to the community by authorities in Rioja.*

area where virtually all cultivable land is occupied. More than nine thousand hectares are now irrigated.

In June 1981 I sit across from Zacarí Yagkitai, who for some reason is commonly known as "Robinson" in his village. He is small but sturdily built. His hair is cut in the traditional Aguaruna style: straight bangs in front, reaching his shoulders in back. He wears a red tee-shirt and dark trousers. The strap of his *wampach* or palm fiber bag crosses his chest. A shotgun lies on his lap.

"Next time you come back," he says to me, "I want you to bring me some things."

"All right, what would you like?"

"I want a cassette tape recorder."

"What will you use it for?"

"To record songs and stories and public meetings . . . and I want you to bring me an airplane."

Slightly taken aback, I reply, "That could be hard. An airplane costs millions of *soles*."

Zacarí pulls an enormous wad of bills from his trousers pocket. "Look," he says, "I just sold my rice harvest. See how much money I have. It will be easy for me to buy an airplane." (Other people present speak up: "We have money too! How many millions will the airplane cost?")

"But there is no landing strip here in the community," I counter. "Where will the plane land?"

"That's no problem. I'll get the young men to clear a field away from the houses. We'll use axes and machetes to make a place for the airplane to land."

"But who will fly it here? I don't know how, and anyway my eyes are too bad. None of you knows how to fly an airplane."

"Mayak, your eyes are bad because you have looked at too many women's privates," Zacarí says, to everyone's amusement. "But don't gringos and Christians fly planes? If they can do it, so can I."

Zacarí's attitude toward airplanes is emblematic of the approach that many Aguaruna take to technology and relations with the developed world in general. Residents of some villages are aggressively trying to beat the colonists at their own economic game. The leader in this movement is the community of Bajo Naranjillo, which because of its location on the highway has had to bear the brunt of the contact with colonists and government officials. As if to refute the romantic "Indian-as-first-ecologist" stereotype so dear to anthropologists, Bajo Naranjillo has embarked on a frenetic campaign of deforestation and rice cultivation. Martha Works, a geographer who spent a year investigating agricultural change in the Alto

---

Mayo, reports that one Aguaruna household, with the help of numerous kinsmen as well as hired non-Indian laborers, cleared twenty-two hectares of forest for rice planting (Works 1984a:94). This reflects a desire to share in the economic boom of the region, but it is also a consciously elaborated defensive tactic. Community leaders feel that if they can demonstrate they are "using the land" in a way that is obvious to outsiders, their land titles are less likely to be put in jeopardy. One way they do this is by cutting fields right next to the highway so that they will be visible to the government functionaries who rarely leave the mobile shade of their jeeps.

Ironically, the agencies that fund development projects in the Mayo have advised the Aguaruna to follow a more conservative strategy. The World Bank–financed *Proyecto Especial Alto Mayo* has stated that it wishes to promote intermediate technology, watershed protection, and ecologically appropriate agriculture in the native communities. Many Aguaruna will have nothing to do with this. The community of Bajo Naranjillo took it upon itself to purchase a bulldozer, which it planned to use to clear forest and divert streams for an irrigation system—precisely the sort of capital-intensive and ecologically destructive scheme that has failed elsewhere in Amazonia. Though it is hard to be optimistic about the outcome of this strategy, one can at least admire the Aguaruna's determination to make their own decisions and, if need be, to live with their own mistakes.

Economic activity is not the only arena in which the Aguaruna are drawing upon the resources of the non-Indian world. After years of petitioning, the Alto Mayo communities secured funds for the establishment of a secondary school in Bajo Naranjillo. Aguaruna evangelists continue to proselytize in some villages. A few Aguaruna have converted to the Baha'i faith, and in 1982 the Baha'is sponsored a conference that brought Navajo Indians from the United States to the Alto Mayo to talk about their culture and their experience with Baha'i (Works 1982:15).

The Alto Mayo Aguaruna were touched indirectly by a strange series of events that took place in the Río Cenepa, Department of Amazonas, in 1979. The celebrated German New Wave film director Werner Herzog, whose movie credits include the Amazonian epic *Aguirre, the Wrath of God*, arrived in Aguaruna country to arrange the production of a second Amazonian film, *Fitzcarraldo*. Herzog planned construction of a movie set in the village of Wawáim, and apparently his initial negotiations with the community began on a cordial footing. But when the villagers realized the magnitude of the disruptions that the project would bring, some demanded that the filmmakers depart. Herzog also ran afoul of the newly organized Aguaruna-Huambisa Council, whose right to enter into the negotiations he reportedly refused to recognize. Precisely who was most at fault in the affair—Herzog, the obsessed foreign director, or Evaristo Nugkuág, the ambitious head of the Aguaruna-Huambisa Council—is disputed by the parties concerned. What is certain, though, is that Herzog misjudged the political situation in Wawáim and failed to respond to it properly. On December 1, 1979, an angry party of Aguaruna men burned the film set and sent Herzog's crew fleeing downriver to Iquitos, never to return. (For details of the Herzog incident see Kirchheimer 1979, IWGIA 1979, Chirif 1980, Brown 1982, and Goodwin 1982. The story of Herzog's completion of *Fitzcarraldo* after the Wawáim debacle is told in Les Blank's documentary film *Burden of Dreams*.)

This encounter took place far from the Alto Mayo, but its repercussions were felt in all Aguaruna communities. Owing to their easy access, several of the Alto Mayo communities are frequently visited by foreign experts of various descriptions—anthropologists, agronomists, biologists, health-care workers, journalists. The Herzog affair heightened the Aguaruna's suspicion of the motives of all outsiders. Fear of foreigners assumed mythic proportions in the appropriation by the Aguaruna of the Andean belief in *pishtacos*. *Pishtacos* are ghoulish killers, usually described as looking like gringos, who harvest Indians to render their corpses for the fat. This fat is used to grease the factories of North America or, in a recent version of the story, to fuel the rockets of the U.S. space program. Fear of *pishtacos* has moved down from the sierra, doggedly following development projects throughout the Peruvian jungle. A group of scientists involved in medical research among the Aguaruna were rumored to be taking blood samples to determine people's body-fat content. Similar stories circulated while Herzog's film was under way. One version had it that when the Europeans filmed battle scenes using Aguaruna actors, the Indians would be killed with real bullets. When I returned to the Alto Mayo in 1981, a friend confided to me that after my departure from the field in 1978 there had been some speculation that I might be such a *pishtaco*.

These contradictory currents—on one hand, a strong fear of outsiders, on the other, the enthusiastic acceptance of foreign religions and technology—illustrate the complexity of social change in the Alto Mayo. The Aguaruna case defies simplistic models of "acculturation." The Aguaruna continue to use their own language and interpret the world in their own way, though they are cosmopolitan enough to take advantage of new ideas when they seem advantageous. And through it all, they remain convinced of the superiority of their own culture. "All the 'Christians' want is money," the Aguaruna say "and they lie and steal to get it."

The fate of magic in the midst of such turmoil is uncertain. There has been a steadily growing demand for the services of Aguaruna *iwishín* or shamans among non-Indians. Colonists seeking relief from sorcery sent by envious neighbors travel considerable distances to be treated by shamans. For them, Aguaruna healers represent the diabolical yet potent healing forces of the jungle.

Other forms of Aguaruna ritual are not enjoying a similar renaissance. Visionary experiences, a crucial source of the personal knowledge that underlies magic, are remote from the lives of today's children. When they arrived in the 1970s, the bilingual teachers strongly discouraged the consumption of hallucinogens. And most people seemed to have agreed with this measure, for in their opinion visions are first linked to warfare—something they feel they have left behind.

What threatens magic is not a head-on collision with Western scientific ideas but a more oblique impact with different social and economic realities. The demands of school make it difficult for children to spend as much time with their parents as they could in the past. Young men pass their days in the rice fields or in town rather than in the forest tracking game. Women are more tenacious in their commitment to traditional knowledge, but if their subsistence skills decline in importance the value of their magical knowledge may dwindle as well. Still, it would be hasty to pronounce Aguaruna magic moribund. Scores of observers predicted that North American Indians would lose their traditional culture, and history has proved them wrong. Ideas that at one point seem atavistic have a way of reappearing in new forms appropriate to new conditions. The Aguaruna are firm in their sense of ethnic identity, even if they differ sharply among themselves about how best to defend it. Provided they are able to survive as a people amidst the predatory forces of the Amazonian frontier, the Aguaruna will continue to fashion their own distinctive view of the world.

When parents express their bewilderment about the behavior of youngsters today, someone will occasionally suggest that they prepare ayahuasca so that a new generation of adolescents can get its thinking in order through the search for life-giving visions. So far, the signal drums used to announce ayahuasca-drinking sessions lie forgotten and silent. The air vibrates instead with the sounds of distant traffic on the highway.

Sources of *Anen* Cited in Text

Anen	Singer	Community
A.1	Miguelina Pijúch Ampúsh	Shimpiyacu
A.2	Eladio Jiukám Wasúm	Huascayacu
A.3	Eladio Jiukám Wasúm	Huascayacu
A.4	Samuel Wajajái Kasép	Alto Naranjillo
A.5	Samuel Wajajái Kasép	Alto Naranjillo
A.6	Eladio Jiukám Wasúm	Huascayacu
A.7	Samuel Wajajái Kasép	Alto Naranjillo
A.8	Samuel Wajajái Kasép	Alto Naranjillo
A.9	Mariana Kasép Pijúch	Alto Naranjillo
A.10	Shimpu Tentéts Bashigkásh	Shimpiyacu
A.11	Inancia Bashigkásh Entsákua	Shimpiyacu
A.12	Rosinda Chijiáp Shajián	Alto Naranjillo
A.13	Inancia Bashigkásh Entsákua	Shimpiyacu
A.14	Kapari Wajajái Agkuash	Alto Naranjillo
A.15	Inancia Bashigkásh Entsákua	Shimpiyacu
A.16	Kapari Wajajái Agkuash	Alto Naranjillo
A.17	Wampurái Peas Tiwíp	Alto Naranjillo
A.18	Rosinda Chijiáp Shajián	Alto Naranjillo
A.19	Genaro Wajai Besént	Alto Naranjillo
A.20	Inancia Bashigkásh Entsákua	Shimpiyacu
A.21	———*	———
A.22	Ikanám Antún Pichík	Shimpiyacu
A.23	———*	———
A.24	———*	———
A.25	Samuel Wajajái Kasép	Alto Naranjillo
A.26	Miguelina Pijúch Ampúsh	Shimpiyacu

* Singer requested anonymity.

A.27	Samuel Wajajái Kasép	Alto Naranjillo
A.28	Miguelina Pijúch Ampúsh	Shimpiyacu
A.29	Inancia Bashigkásh Entsákua	Shimpiyacu
A.30	Cristobal Shimpu	Shampuyacu
A.31	Manúgka Tsapík Wajai	Huascayacu

APPENDIX 2.

Notes on the Collection, Transcription, and Translation of Aguaruna *Anen*

M y introduction to *anen* came during social gatherings, especially drinking parties, when people traded songs that they
considered beautiful or memorably witty. People in all of the villages I visited were delighted to hear their voices reproduced on my
tape recorder, and they enjoyed even more the opportunity to hear
(and in some cases criticize) the songs of kinsmen from other villages. Although most of the music I recorded was social music (i.e.,
nampét), on a few of these early recording sessions singers performed *anen*, usually songs intended to sway a loved one's feelings
about the singer. In these cases, the singer claimed to be "reproduc-
ing" or "imitating" the songs rather than "singing" them, the implication being that in this context they carried no manipulative
force. In retrospect, I think that it was when the *apu* of Huascayacu,
Eladio Jiukám, sang several hunting *anen* for me that I began to
understand that the songs were supposed to have material effects
when employed properly. This was confirmed by Margaret Van
Bolt's observations of manioc planting rituals, when *anen* were used
with *nantag* stones to encourage the development of manioc stem
cuttings.

Once it became clear that there were a host of *anen* considered
too important to sing in public, I began to press my informants for
details. Some people never cooperated; others contributed what
they knew, though often subject to certain conditions—for example, that I agree never to play the tapes for other people in the
same community. The social meaning of *anen*—the secrecy associated with their use, the moral ambivalence of *anen* that manipulate sentiments, and the prevailing notion that *anen* are a form of

187

private knowledge that need not be shared freely—posed powerful constraints as to when I could talk about them and with whom.

Recording the songs was only the first step in a long process. Transcribing the lyrics proved difficult, mostly because I had only limited help from bilingual assistants. Only one of my assistants had the patience to spend more than an hour a day on the grueling business of listening to the songs line by line, often many times in succession. Once a song was transcribed, I often had to return to the singer, or other knowledgeable people, for clarification. It was never enough to obtain a "literal" translation, for *anen* contain a wealth of onomatopoeic or ideophonic words rarely encountered in daily speech. I then had to develop a free translation that captured the essence of the lyrics without sacrificing interpretability.

I also discovered that because some of the vocabulary used in Aguaruna *anen* comes from Shuar, Spanish, and possibly other languages with which singers did not have great familiarity, there was not always a precise lexical meaning attached to each word or phrase. The word *shakáim*, for instance, was translated by one woman as "the little boy who works in the garden with the child Nugkui," by another as "paca," a large rodent that frequents manioc gardens. It was only later that I learned of the central role that Shakáim (a transformation of Etsa, the sun) has in Shuar myth; my Aguaruna informants had never heard of this mythical being. A similar problem arises with ideophonic words—that is, words that are meant to convey an impression of movement, sound, or smell. Since I rarely heard Aguaruna ideophones used in ordinary speech, I had to accept on faith the interpretations of the people I interviewed. It is entirely possible that other Aguaruna-speakers might interpret them differently. Despite the fuzziness of some of the lexical elements of *anen*, my native consultants always explained the words in terms of specific images associated with the song's intent. Thus from the point of view of the individual singer, the language of *anen* creates definite associations, though different interpreters might emphasize slightly different associations. I suspect, too, that more systematic collection and examination of *anen* performances would reveal that the songs are not as invariant as the Aguaruna claim. The presence of Spanish words in *anen* shows that performers do create new lyrics, the Aguaruna insistence to the contrary notwithstanding.

My field notes include the lyrics of 77 *anen*, ranging in length from three lines to several pages of text. These were recorded by 16 adults (8 men and 8 women, representing four communities) ranging in age from 18 to approximately 65. I have complete transcriptions of 53 of these, while the rest consist of Spanish glosses only. Some of these *anen* deal with themes not treated in this book: the search for powerful dreams during the vision quest, manipulation of the sentiments of enemies, success in animal husbandry, and the avoidance of dream visits by the souls of dead kinsmen.

Clearly, there is much more that could be done with *anen* in the hands of linguists and ethnomusicologists. When my fieldwork among the Aguaruna began, I had no idea that song would be a major focus of the research. Although I am an amateur musician with some basic training in music theory, I had no previous experience in interpreting non-Western musical forms. I particularly regret that I could not analyze the relation between the musical elements of these songs and their instrumental power.

Readers interested in Jivaroan music should consult the recent essay by William Belzner (1981) as well as the record *Music of the Jívaro of Ecuador* (Ethnic Folkways Album FE 4386, 1972) prepared by Michael J. Harner. Additional sources on Jivaroan magical songs include Guallart 1974, Pellizzaro 1977, and Tsamaraint et al. 1977.

Below are two *anen* texts (from which accent marks have been deleted) with their literal and free translations. Both are drawn from previous chapters. The abbreviations "onomat." and "ideophon." are used respectively for onomatopoeic and ideophonetic.

ANEN 20. Singer: Inancia Bashigkásh Entsákua
1. *aishijua   aishijua*
   husband   husband
2. *aishijua   aishijua*
   husband   husband
3. *bukintitkumesha*
   the palm grub [*bukin = datunch*]
4. *chaitu   ijagmasmeke*
   onomat.: sound of grub   you fast
5. *jachachaka   wajakiabai*
   onomat.: stomach growling   let you be
6. *jachachaka   wajakiabai*
   stomach growling   let you be
7. *minig   anentaimsameke*
   to me   you think
8. *jachachaka   wajakiabai*
   onomat.: stomach grumbling   let you be
9. *jititina   wajakiabai*
   onomat.: throbbing   let you be
10. *kurasunchimeka*
   little heart [from Spanish, *corazón*]

11. *kurasunchimeka*
    little heart

12. *nema nema*   *wajakiabai*
    ideophon.: movement of tethered animal   let you be

13. *nema nema*   *wajakiabai*
    movement of tethered animal   let you be

14. *jaucha   wajukawajak*
    oh dear!   how is it with me?

15. *nuwash   pujugtaimpash*
    wife   can you perhaps be alive?

16. *wika   jegataja*
    I myself   I shall arrive

17. *wika   anentaimjai*
    I myself   I think

18. *uchi   waitu   wekagai wekagai*
    child   suffering   walking, walking

19. *juniatsashit*
    here is it not? [transcription uncertain]

20. *tu   anentaimjai*
    where   I think

21. *wamak   jegatajaita*
    quickly   I shall arrive

22. *tu   anentaimsamek*
    where   are you thinking?

23. *jachachaka*   *wajakiabai*
    stomach growling   let him be

24. *kurasunchimeka*
    little heart

25. *nema nema*   *wajakiabai*
    movement of tethered animal   let him be

26. *tututura*   *wajakiabai*
    onomat.: sound of running feet   let him be

27. *tututura*   *wajakiabai*
    sound of running feet   let him be

28. *naynta   tsutsupauchinum*
    the hill   the little pointed

29. *naynta   tsutsupauchinma*
    the hill   the little pointed

30. *tsekentu*   *wekaesamake*
    ideophon.: suddenly appearing   you walk

31. *jania jania*   *wajakabai*
    onomat.: whining of dog   let him be

32. *jau jau jau jau*   *wajakiabai*
    onomat.: barking of dog   let him be

33. *anasuchimeka*
    little thorns

34. *dekapeagchauchi*
    not feeling
35. *tu tu tu tu   wajakiabai*
    running feet   let him be
36. *jika jikania   wajakiabai*
    ideophon.: sadness, longing   let him be
37. *bikun   bikunmatsjai*
    food   I don't eat
38. *tu   anentaimusha*
    where   are you thinking?
39. *mina   anentain   wajakiabai*
    my   to the heart   let him be
40. *kutat   pujukameka*
    onomat.: thudding to ground   you are
41. *jau jau jau jau   wajakiabai*
    barking dogs   let him be
42. *jau jau jau jau   wajakiabai*
    barking dogs   let him be
43. *kurasunchimeka*
    little heart
44. *nema nema   wajakiabai*
    movement of tethered animal   let him be
45. *jania jania   wajakiabai*
    whining dogs   let him be
46. *mina   anentain   egketjuakia*
    my   heart   fill
47. *mina   anentain   anentaimsamek*
    my   heart   are you thinking?
48. *jania jania   wajakiabai*
    whining dogs   let him be
49. *suni suni   wajakiabai*
    ideophon.: sighing, shaking   let him be

ANEN 20. Free translation
 1. Husband, husband
 2. Husband, husband
 3. Like the palm grub *datúnch*
 4. You will fast [i.e., be unable to eat from sadness]
 5. Let your stomach rumble "jachachaka"
 6. Let your stomach rumble "jachachaka"
 7. Thinking of me
 8. Let your stomach rumble "jachachaka"
 9. Let it throb
10. Little heart

11. Little heart
12. Let it move like a tethered animal
13. Let it move like a tethered animal
14. "Oh dear! What am I doing?
15. Is my wife still alive?
16. I shall return
17. Thus I think
18. Are my children suffering
19. While I travel like this?
20. Thus I think
21. Rapidly I shall arrive"
22. Do you think this?
23. Let your stomach rumble "jachachaka"
24. Little heart
25. Let it move like a tethered animal
26. Let your feet run "tu tu tu ra"
27. Let your feet run "tu tu tu ra"
28. On the little pointed hill
29. On the little pointed hill
30. You walk, appearing suddenly
31. Let the dogs whine
32. Let the dogs bark [i.e., announcing his arrival]
33. Passing over little thorns
34. Feeling nothing
35. Let your feet run "tu tu tu ra"
36. You will be lonely
37. "I do not eat"
38. Are you thinking this?
39. Let you be in my heart
40. Sitting with a thud on the ground [like dog with master]
41. Let the dogs bark
42. Let the dogs whine
43. Little heart
44. Let it move like a tethered animal
45. Let it whine
46. Fill my heart
47. Are you thinking as my heart thinks?
48. Let it [i.e., your heart] whine
49. Let it shake with emotion

ANEN 4. Singer: Samuel Wajajái Kasép
 1. *jukmagkuita   wiisham* (four times)
    gatherer   wiisham-bird [species info. unavailable]

2. *pawina*   *anea*   *wiisham*
   curassow [*Mitu mitu*]   loving   wiisham-bird

3. *pawina*   *anea*   *wiisham*
   curassow   loving   wiisham-bird

4. *jukag*   *jukag*   *wiisham*
   gathering   gathering   wiisham-bird

5. *jukag*   *jukag*   *wiisham*
   gathering   gathering   wiisham-bird

6. *kuntinun*   *aneawai*   *wiisham*
   game   he loves   wiisham-bird

7. *kuntinun*   *aneawai*   *wiisham*
   game   he loves   wiisham-bird

8. *japana*   *aneawa*   *wiisham*
   deer   he loves   wiisham-bird

9. *wagana*   *aneawa*   *wiisham*
   tinamou [*Tinamus major*]   he loves   wiisham-bird

10. *jukmagkuita*   *wiisham* (four times)

11. *kuntinun*   *aneawa*   *wiisham*
   game   he loves   wiisham-bird

12. *pawina*   *aneawa*   *wiisham*
   curassow   he loves   wiisham-bird

13. *pawujun*   *aneawa*   *wiisham*
   guan [*Pipile cumanensis*]   he loves   wiisham-bird

14. *chikiwi pinchu,*   *chikiwi pinchu*
   hawk [species info. unavailable]   hawk

15. *uwetjachu*   *aneawa*   *wiisham* (three times)
   not missing   he loves   wiisham-bird

16. *kuntinun*   *aneawa*   *wiisham*
   game   he loves   wiisham-bird

17. *jukmagkuita*   *wiisham*
   gatherer   wiisham-bird

18. *chikiwi pinchu,*   *chikiwi pinchu*
   hawk   hawk

19. *pawi*   *ujuitugkata*
   curassow   attract

20. *pawi*   *ujuitugkata*
   curassow   attract

21. *pawi*   *usupagtatjai*
   curassow   I shall have miscarriage

22. *Nugkui*   *nuwana*
   Nugkui   to the woman

23. *pawi*   *usupikagtatjai* (three times)
   curassow   I shall give miscarriage

24. *japa*   *uwaintugkata*
   deer   make me find, see

---

25. *Nugkui   nuwana*
    Nugkui   to the woman
26. *pawi   usupikagtatjai*
    curassow   I shall give miscarriage
27. *pawi   usupikagtatjai*
    curassow   I shall give miscarriage
28. *Tsewa,*   *Tsewa* (three times)
    Tsewa [mythical spider monkey]   Tsewa
29. *chupa   iwaintugkata* (three times)
    spider monkey   make me find
30. *chupa   usupagtatjai*
    spider monkey   I shall have miscarriage
31. *chupa   usupagtatjai*
    spider monkey   I shall have miscarriage
32. *bacha   usupagtatjai*
    monkey fat   I shall have miscarriage
33. *bacha   usupagtatjai*
    monkey fat   I shall have miscarriage
34. *Nugkui   nuwana*
    Nugkui   to the woman
35. *bacha   usupikagtatjai* (three times)
    monkey fat   I shall give miscarriage
36. *Tsewa,   Tsewa*
    Tsewa   Tsewa
37. *chupa   iwaintugkakia* (four times)
    spider monkey   make me find
38. *chikiwi pinchu,   chikiwi pinchu*
    hawk   hawk
39. *chupa   ujuitugkata* (four times)
    spider monkey   attract
40. *pawi   iwaintugkata*
    curassow   make me find
41. *pawa   iwaintugkata*
    guan   make me find
42. *kuntin   ujuitugkata*
    game   attract

ANEN 4. Free translation.
  1. Gatherer *wiisham* [four times]
  2. *Wiisham* that loves curassow
  3. *Wiisham* that loves curassow
  4. Gathering, gathering *wiisham*
  5. Gathering, gathering *wiisham*
  6. *Wiisham* that loves game
  7. *Wiisham* that loves game
  8. *Wiisham* that loves the deer

9. *Wiisham* that loves the tinamou
10. Gatherer *wiisham* [four times]
11. *Wiisham* that loves game
12. *Wiisham* that loves curassow
13. *Wiisham* that loves the guan
14. Hawk, hawk
15. Unerring *wiisham*
16. *Wiisham* that loves game
17. Gatherer *wiisham*
18. Hawk, hawk
19. Attract the curassow
20. Attract the curassow
21. I will have a miscarriage for curassow
22. To the Nugkui woman [i.e., the singer's wife]
23. I will give a miscarriage for curassow [three times]
24. Make me find deer
25. To the Nugkui woman
26. I will give a miscarriage for curassow
27. I will give a miscarriage for curassow
28. Tsewa, Tsewa [mythical spider monkey]
29. Make me find spider monkey [three times]
30. I will have a miscarriage for spider monkey
31. I will have a miscarriage for spider monkey
32. I will have a miscarriage for monkey fat
33. I will have a miscarriage for monkey fat
34. To the Nugkui woman
35. I will give a miscarriage for monkey fat [three times]
36. Tsewa, Tsewa
37. Make me find spider monkey [four times]
38. Hawk, hawk
39. Attract the spider monkey [four times]
40. Make me find the curassow
41. Make me find the guan
42. Attract game

Notes

1. For a more detailed review of the literature on magic and the debate between those who see magic as a cognitive process ("intellectualists") and those who analyze it as symbolic action ("symbolists"), see Peel 1969, Skorupski 1976, Brown 1984a, and the essays gathered in volumes edited by Wilson (1970), Horton and Finnegan (1973), and Hollis and Lukes (1982). Some recent articles (e.g., Ahern 1979, Weiner 1983) contribute implicit critiques of the symbolist position, even if they do not confront it head on.

2. The complexity involved in applying ethnic labels and determining the distribution of ethnic groups in the Upper Amazon is signaled by the following explanation of the status of the "Mayna" Jívaro, a group whose name appears in the literature about Jivaroan societies. The information below was kindly provided by Luis M. Uriarte, who has spent more than a decade pursuing ethnographic research in eastern Peru:

> The Mayna Shuar . . . are those Achuara who occupy the zone of the Río Corrientes, particularly its tributaries, the rivers Mancusari and Paantamentsa (Platanoyacu). The mestizos call these people Jívaro or Mayna indiscriminately. They identify themselves as Jívaros in some cases and Mayna Shiviara in others. When I visited this zone with some Achuaras of the Río Huasaga (a tributary of the Pastaza), both groups recognized each other as Achuara and lost little time in determining their kinship links. There were only a few linguistic differences between them, and perhaps differences in pottery style. The interpretation given to me by the Achuara of the Pastaza . . . is that these people were *"Maínia aents."* *Maín* means riverbank or the other side of the river. And the ending *-ia* indicates origin. Thus *Maínia aents . . .* means in Achuara: "Achuara people who live across the river"—the great river Pastaza or *Kanus* (Luis M. Uriarte, personal communication).

Elsewhere, Uriarte (1976:44) implies that the Huambisa are essentially Shuar who happen to live on the Peruvian side of the Peru–Ecuador frontier.

3. Whitten (1981:122) takes strong exception to the idea of tribal boundaries on the grounds that they abet "imperialistic imposition of internal colonial 'order.' " Since Jivaroans intermarry so frequently with other ethnic groups, (e.g., Quichua, Záparo), rigidly defined tribal "territories" are meaningless. Whitten's legitimate concerns notwithstanding, I feel that it is only fair to indicate to the reader the approximate location of the societies under discussion.

4. Comprehensive bibliographies on the Aguaruna and Jivaroan peoples in general are to be found in O'Leary 1963 and García-Rendueles 1977. See Mundo Shuar 1984 for the proceedings of a 1982 symposium on Jivaroan research.

5. Ironically, significant interethnic medical exchanges began to develop in late 1978 as I concluded my fieldwork. Colonists new to the Alto Mayo started appearing at the houses of Aguaruna shamans in search of cures for witchcraft-induced ailments.

6. With the exception of bilingual assistants, who were paid in cash on an hourly basis, I did not pay people for interviews, nor did they seek payment. Payment (usually in the form of trade goods) was made in exchange for performance of certain magical songs, however, since this is the practice that the Aguaruna follow among themselves. When staying as someone's guest at a village other than Huascayacu or Alto Naranjillo, I often gave the host family gifts of shotgun shells and other goods.

Chapter 1: Alto Mayo

Notes to pages 35–45

1. The arrival date of the Aguaruna to the Alto Mayo was determined by estimating the age of the oldest living people actually born in the Alto Mayo. I tried to cross-check this with mestizos who had first made contact with the Indians, but their recollection of dates was no more precise than that of the Aguaruna. The date given should therefore be considered approximate. The Aguaruna may well have been exploiting the Alto Mayo as a hunting area long before they settled there permanently.

2. The latter figure does not include data from three Aguaruna communities in the Department of Loreto that were issued very large land grants. The land grant and population data on which I based my calculations were obtained from the *Atlas de Comunidades Nativas* (Chirif and Mora 1977).

3. At the time of my return visit to the Alto Mayo in 1981, the Aguaruna themselves were citing a figure of fourteen hundred for the population of the Alto Mayo communities. Although I cannot verify the accuracy of this figure, it is certain that the population is growing rapidly because of a high birth rate and a steady flow of Aguaruna immigrants from land-poor communities in the Alto Marañón.

4. During a major public meeting between Aguaruna leaders and government officials in 1977, one well-meaning functionary suggested to the assembly that a matter of "highest priority" was the rearrangement of Aguaruna houses in straight lines around a central clearing or, as he called it, a *plaza de armas*. Given the urgent issues that the Aguaruna communities were confronting at the time, his listeners found the suggestion baffling.

5. In the late 1970s, there was a witchcraft-related murder in the Alto Mayo. The killing put several Alto Mayo villages on a war footing with communities in the Río Cahuapanas area, the home of the murder victim. As far as I know, the score has still not been settled. Relations between the two areas remain tense.

Tsewa's Gift

1. Aside from the three comprehensive collections of Aguaruna myths currently available (Jordana Laguna 1974, Chumap Lucía and García-Rendueles 1978, Akuts Nugkai et al. 1977, 1979), the interested reader should consult several shorter essays on topics related to specific myths. These include García-Rendueles 1979, Ballón and García-Rendueles 1979, Berlin 1978, and Brown 1978.

2. Some knowledgeable people in the Alto Mayo insist that the first shaman was a man named Pugku. Interestingly enough, *pugku* means "rapids," a hydrographic feature that is associated with Tsugki.

In the Alto Mayo, I found less interest in Tsugki than has been reported for the Aguaruna elsewhere. Perhaps this stems from the prevailing hydrographic conditions; the deep whirlpools with which Tsugki is primarily associated are not found in the Alto Mayo, nor does one see the aquatic animals (anacondas and dolphins) most closely linked to Tsugki in Aguaruna lore. Nevertheless, allusions to Tsugki continue to figure prominently in the healing songs of shamans.

3. Apajuí figures in at least one myth (see Akuts Nugkai et al. 1977, II:222) in which he is paired with an Aguaruna named Kumpanám. The translators gloss Kumpanám as Compañero, "companion," on the plausible assumption that the name is a loan word from Spanish. Curiously, Métraux (1948:626) reports that the Jívaro recognize a high god named Cumbanamba. The precise connection between Kumpanám and Métraux's Cumbanamba needs to be sorted out through additional research.

4. I was never able to determine to my own satisfaction whether the reflection in the eye and the human shadow are indices of their respective souls or whether they are thought to be the souls themselves. Neither could I find mention of the eye soul in other ethnographic sources on Jivaroans. Larson (1966:29), for instance, simply defines *iwaji* as "the child of the eye (the human image that one sometimes sees in a person's eye)."

5. Although this illness category bears a strong formal resemblance to *susto*, a well-known syndrome found throughout Spanish-speaking America, I have no evidence to indicate that it is not traditional to Aguaruna culture.

6. For a detailed analysis of the significance of intracultural variation in soul concepts within a North American Indian society, see Merrill 1981.

7. Other terms used to classify specific kinds of shamans include *uuk tunchi*, "hidden shaman" (i.e., sorcerer), *yapu* (a powerful kind of curing shaman), and *kukam* (a powerful sorcerer, the term being derived from Cocama, a neighboring ethnolinguistic group reputed to be well versed in the black arts).

8. I have used the masculine pronoun in this discussion because Aguaruna shamans are virtually always men. Women are occasionally accused of being sorcerers, but I recorded only one case (regarded as highly unusual by my informants) in which a woman functioned briefly as a publicly recognized curing shaman.

1. For an opposing view, see Beckerman 1979.

2. The fact that the success of each individual hunter is unpredictable does not, however, mean that the Aguaruna suffer from a chronic shortage of protein. Berlin and Berlin (1977) found that the diet of the Río Cenepa Aguaruna meets or exceeds the minimum requirements established by the World Health Organization with respect to protein (see also Berlin and Markell 1977). I saw no signs of protein-deficiency malnutrition in the Alto Mayo.

3. Saliva and the act of spitting are important in many magical acts performed by the Aguaruna, and they also figure prominently in the mythical conjurations of Etsa, the sun. A special kind of saliva, called *kaag*, is the medium in which shamans reveal their spirit darts.

4. One person said that the *wiisham* bird has the habit of following spider monkeys as they move through the forest canopy, but I could not verify this.

5. The following comment by Karsten (1935:172–73) echoes this view:
> Just as the married Jíbaro woman is believed to have a mysterious influence upon the field which she cultivates, so she is supposed to exert a similar influence upon the hunting dogs confided to her care. The competence of the dogs and the plentifulness of game in the house thus correspond to the ability of its mistress.

Harner (1972:75) confirms Karsten's observation, while stressing the importance of the woman's link to Nugkui:
> It is believed that the presence of the woman, through her connection to Nunkui, will help the man have better luck, and she constantly (and usually silently) sings to Nunkui for success in getting game.

6. The herb *kunakip* (*Bonafousia* sp.) is sometimes mixed with "dog" *tsumáik* to further increase the dog's ability to follow a scent.

7. In free conversation, the Aguaruna sometimes use the terms *tsumáik* and *pijipíg* as generic labels for any kind of hunting or love charm of botanical origin. It is possible, therefore, that the plant mentioned in this narrative might be something other than a species of *Cyperus* or *Carex*.

8. Beliefs about human exuviae can take the form of positive prescriptions as well as avoidances. People dispose of their hair in the dense, aboveground buttress roots of the peach palm "so that our hair will grow fast like peach palm roots." Children's milk teeth are thrown onto the roof of a house while the parents say, "Vampire bat, take this tooth and replace it with one of palm wood." This diminutive rite makes the child's adult teeth as hard as palm wood and as unbreakable as a bat's tooth.

9. In one myth, Etsa converts bones into each animal's present-day form and decrees its characteristic behavior. See Akuts Nugkai et al. 1977, II: 51.

10. Young men at the beginning of their hunting careers are especially vulnerable to *shimpankámu*. According to some informants, if a young man gives away meat from his first kill he can share meat from subsequent kills without fear. But if his first kill isn't shared in this way, he should avoid making gifts until he is "used to hunting," after killing perhaps two dozen animals. One man remarked:

> My young son has *shimpankámu*. He went hunting to bring back meat for a feast. He lost his ability to find game because the meat was given away to others. When he approaches, birds fly away, animals avoid him.

Chapter 4: The Garden's Children
Notes to pages 97–132

1. The rapid development of cash-crop agriculture in the Alto Mayo since the mid–1970s has changed this picture radically. Some communities have experimented with enormous (i.e., five hectares or greater) clear-cut fields, and there have been a few awkward attempts at mechanized forest clearance. As far as I know, however, traditional techniques are still used in the preparation of fields intended for the production of root crops.

2. Boster (1980:47), who conducted an exhaustive study of Jivaroan manioc classification, notes that it is exceedingly difficult to cite an exact figure for the number of manioc varieties cultivated by the Aguaruna because informants often disagree about the validity of a given varietal distinction. Any such figure, Boster argues, would have to be "qualified by the proportion of informants who agree on the existence of the cultivars."

3. Owing to the influence of evangelical Christianity, consumption of manioc beer has declined dramatically in at least two of the communities of the Alto Mayo. Aguaruna Christians oppose the use of all intoxicating substances, preferring instead to drink an unfermented beverage made from ripe plantains.

4. Brent Berlin (1978) has published a fascinating analysis of the transformation of domesticates to morphologically similar weeds in the Nugkui myth. The myth mentions that *tsanímtsanim* was created from manioc (*tsaním*) after Nugkui's daughter was mistreated by the children of her adoptive mother.

5. Swain (1981:107) reports that duckweed is one of the most productive and nutritious species in the plant kingdom. The Aguaruna belief that feeding duckweed to poultry can improve egg production is thus quite accurate.

6. Some women mentioned the existence of a special kind of *nantag* used to make manioc beer sweet and intoxicating. This stone is reportedly kept in the large urns in which the manioc mash ferments. I never succeeded in verifying personally whether these stones exist, but I have no reason to doubt that they do.

7. This procedure bears a striking similarity to the Shuar planting ritual described by Karsten (1935:126–33). The rite in Karsten's account, which involved the participation of several women, was performed when planting a garden intended to provide manioc for a feast.

---

8. Harner (1972:75) reports that Shuar women instruct their manioc plants to drink the blood of would-be attackers who approach through surrounding gardens. In this case, the propensity of the manioc to eat souls or drink blood is directed to ends that are socially useful, at least from the point of view of the household defending itself from attack.

9. A few women mentioned other plants that "bring water" to the manioc. These include *pina* (*Calathea* sp., a plant that produces edible tubers), the air potato (*Dioscorea bulbifera*, which has aerial tubers that are occasionally eaten), and taro (*Colocasia esculenta*, also edible). However, cocoyam, arrowroot, and achira were by far the most frequently mentioned species attributed this property.

10. Harner (1962:269) says that Stirling's inclusion of "Piribri" (actually *pirípiri* in Shuar, which becomes *pijipíg* in Aguaruna) among Jívaro deities is erroneous. He adds:

> *Pirípiri* is the correct term and refers to a plant which the Jívaro use magically to cause rain to swell rivers so that their enemies cannot cross them successfully (ibid.).

I did not record this use of *pijipíg* among the Aguaruna, but various people mentioned that when it is used for magical ends, *pijipíg* sometimes causes rain as an unwanted side effect. As Harner states, the plant is never thought to be a deity, nor is it consistently attributed souls or "people."

11. To do justice to ethnographic reality, I should point out that this male bias is tempered by countervailing customs and institutions: a bilateral system of kinship reckoning, a pattern of bride-service, the absence of extreme fears of feminine pollution, and lack of an overt preference for male offspring. While far from egalitarian in gender roles, Aguaruna society has not developed male chauvinism to the extent that one finds among some other warlike tribal horticulturalists.

12. Boster (1980:40) reports a slightly different version of the same process:

> A second source of new cultivars is from volunteer manioc seedlings. According to my informants, sometimes manioc fruits in abandoned gardens fall into the ground and lie dormant through the period of secondary forest succession. When the site is cleared once again for a garden, the seeds sprout and grow. . . .
>
> Some women on finding a volunteer note its location and wait until the plant is mature. . . . These cultivars are called x *yagkuji*, "x's flower," or x *tsapainu*, "x's sprout," indicating its origin.

Chapter 5: A Technology of Sentiment
Notes to pages 133–61

1. Anne Christine Taylor (1984:101) has found a similar rate of "incorrect" marriages among the Ecuadorian Achuar. She argues that these improper unions are not deviations from the norm but rather the inevitable result of structural forces favoring endogamous marriage alliances in certain circumstances.

2. Data on adult mortality collected in the Alto Mayo in 1976–78 suggest that the Aguaruna suicide rate may be ten times higher than rates reported for Western European countries. The majority of suicide victims are women. See Brown (1984b) for details, and Siverts (in press) for comparative data from Aguaruna communities in the Alto Río Marañón.

3. The themes of Shuar and Achuar love songs found in Pellizzaro 1977 and Tsamaraint et al. 1977 tend to bear out this observation. That is, most of the magical songs identified as being women's deal with the affection of their husbands, whereas men's songs are concerned with arousing affection in their sweethearts rather than in their wives.

4. "The wife sings her songs all the times that something is not going well in the home so that the matrimonial difficulties will be favorably resolved. With these songs, she sends souls, spirits, or animals to her husband so that they will strengthen in him the bonds of love or concern for his family" (Pellizzaro 1977:4, my translation). Pellizzaro's comments refer specifically to the Shuar.

5. I strongly suspect, but was never able to prove, that there exist bewitching or cursing songs using even stronger language.

6. *Puságki* is a phonological variant of the noun *puság*. I use *puságki* in preference to *puság* because of its obvious similarity to *pusanga*, a term widely used in the Peruvian Amazon to denote love charms. *Pusanga* may be derived from the Quechua word *pusamuy*, "to attract," or it may be a loan word from Amazonian Brazil (Chevalier 1982:384, n.2). The Aguaruna also refer to *puságki* as "woman grabbers" (*nuwa achitai*).

7. The tale of the blood-taking power of cetaceans is structurally similar to the myth of UwanchÁu cited in chapter 4. The propensity to drink human blood seems to be a quality of many powerful beings and objects in the Aguaruna world. I have heard people say, for example, that children should not touch jaguar teeth because the teeth can "drink their blood" or "eat their soul." As noted earlier, the same is said of *nantag* stones.

8. Similar bird substances used as love charms by the Campa are listed in Chevalier 1982:385–86.

9. Examples of sexual commerce between snakes and human beings in mythical times are to be found in Akuts Nugkai et al. 1977, I:281–83, and Chumap Lucía and García-Rendueles 1979:104–15. More prominent are stories of intercourse between women and worms; see Akuts Nugkai et al. 1977, II:135, 143. Snakes do figure in at least one commonly used sexual metaphor: the verb *shagkuímat*, which is probably derived from the noun *shagkuím*, terrestrial boa, is used in joking contexts to mean "to have intercourse."

10. "[A]n important role is played by a small plant which among the Ecuadorian Indians is best known under its Quichua name *simayuca*, of which the Jíbaro name *simaika* is but a corruption. . . . The plant is used in different ways as a love charm; any part of it is believed to have a wonderful power of exciting the sexual passions of the opposite sex when it is brought into some contact with his or her body" (Karsten 1935:214).

11. Most versions of this formula for obtaining *tsumáik* or *pijipíg* stress the need to cover the rotting vulture lest its powerful substance be taken away by other animals. One man told me, "The most dangerous kind of *pijipíg* is that of the vulture *chuág*, because all sorts of snakes come to take away the plant. And if it isn't snakes, it's jaguars, pumas, or foxes." To prevent this, the vulture is covered with a gridwork of sticks, then leaves, and finally with a structure of palm wood slats (*tanísh*) securely tied at the top.

12. I recorded another variant of this method of obtaining *tsumáik* in which an otter is killed and burned instead of a vulture.

13. The danger that *puságki* pose to the health of domestic animals is independently confirmed by a Shuar informant's description of the preparation of a love charm (called *musap*) cited in Pellizzaro 1978a: "The elders saw to it that no one had this charm, because the owner who was accustomed to touch it with frequency caused domestic animals—above all, chickens and pigs—to die when they came near him" (295). The account goes on to describe the cruel fate that awaited those who abused the power of love charms: "Furthermore, its owner was filled with evil desires, always corrupting him further; for bothering the wives of others he was murdered or killed by witchcraft in the form of leishmaniasis or madness" (296, translations mine).

Chapter 6: Working Metaphors

Notes to pages 162–77

1. Avoidances do exist as a discrete, marked category in Aguaruna health maintenance strategies, where they are referred to as *wakemtái*. These consist of foods that should be avoided to recover from specific illnesses.

2. Whitten uses slightly different spellings of Nugkui and Tsugki, but I have followed Aguaruna usage for the sake of consistency.

3. People in the Alto May disagree about the fate of the other souls belonging to men or women who produce *ajútap* souls at death. The prevailing opinion is that the eye soul of such a person, that is, the soul that normally ascends into heaven, would not be admitted to heaven "because God does not want killers." The underlying assumption is that people who have had *ajútap* visions have used their power to kill many enemies.

4. The only example of a Jivaroan dream revelation text that I have been able to find is in Larson 1978:398–99.

5. Rosaldo (1975:178) observes an identical process in Ilongot spells:
> By combining rich and vivid imagery with a limited and formulaic use of language . . . [the magician] subordinates the natural world's diversity to a simple and compelling conception of the world that he, through magic, can control.

6. Still to be reckoned with is the contribution of music to the power of magical songs. Although music is an important part of several manipulative or therapeutic utterance forms—shamanistic healing performances being the most conspicuous example after *anen*—I had little success in eliciting comments that might clarify its ontological significance. The key to understanding why *anen* are sung rather than simply spoken may lie in two attri-

Tsewa's Gift

butes of music identified by Merriam (1964:85, 233). First, music induces synesthesia, or connections between the senses. Second, it has the ability to call forth specific emotions. If a function of *anen* is to alter the world through the intentional ordering of the performer's thoughts and utterances, then it follows that the creation of specific emotions and the restructuring of sensory experience through song would contribute to the ordering process.

7. To correct this flaw in the theory of ritual performatives, Ahern proposes a distinction between "weak illocutionary acts," in which the performer intends no practical results, and "strong illocutionary acts," in which the performer "regards considerations related to the effect of his act as relevant, intends his act to have certain consequences, and wants what he requests" (1979:9). The Aguaruna practices I describe here fall within the "strong" end of the illocutionary spectrum. Note that Ahern's modifications in no way counter the objections of Gardner (1983) to the application of the concept of performativity to ritual.

Bibliography

Ahern, Emily Martin
   1979 The Problem of Efficacy: Strong and Weak Illocutionary Acts.
      Man, n.s., 14:1–17.
Akuts Nugkai, T., A. Kuji Javián, and J. Grover
   1977 *Historia Aguaruna: Primera Etapa*. Comunidades y Culturas
      Peruanas, No. 15. 2 Vols. Summer Institute of Linguistics.
      Yarinacocha, Peru.
Akuts Nugkai, T., A. Paati Dusiya, A. Shawit Piitug, and J. Grover
   1979 *Historia Aguaruna: Primera Etapa, Segunda Parte*. Comunidades
      y Culturas Peruanas, No. 16. Summer Institute of Linguistics.
      Yarinacocha, Peru.
Austin, John L.
   1962 *How To Do Things With Words*. Oxford: Clarendon Press.
Ballón, Enrique, and M. García-Rendueles
   1978 Analisis del Mito de Nunkui. *Amazonía Peruana* 3: 99–158.
Beattie, J. H. M.
   1970 On Understanding Ritual. In *Rationality*, ed. B. R. Wilson, 240–
      68. New York: Harper and Row Publishers/Torchbooks.
Beckerman, Stephen
   1979 The Abundance of Protein in Amazonia: A Reply to Gross.
      American Anthropologist 81:533–60.
Belzner, William
   1981 Music, Modernization, and Westernization among the Macuma
      Shuar. In *Cultural Transformations and Ethnicity in Modern
      Ecuador*, ed. Norman E. Whitten, Jr., 731–48. Urbana: University
      of Illinois Press.
Berlin, Brent
   1976 Some Evidence from Aguaruna Folk Botany for the Concept of
      Rank in Ethnobiological Classification. *American Ethnologist*
      3:381–99.

1978 Bases Empíricas de la Cosmología Botanica Aguaruna Jíbaro, Amazonas, Peru. *Amazonía Peruana* 3:187–98.

Berlin, Brent, and Elois Ann Berlin
1975 Aguaruna Color Categories. *American Ethnologist* 2:61–87.
1977 *Ethnobiology, Subsistence, and Nutrition in a Tropical Forest Society: The Aguaruna Jívaro.* Studies in Aguaruna Jívaro Ethnobiology, Report No. 1. Language Behavior Research Laboratory, University of California, Berkeley.

Berlin, Elois Ann
1977 *Aspects of Aguaruna Fertility Regulation.* Studies in Aguaruna Jívaro Ethnobiology, Report No. 2. Language Behavior Research Laboratory, University of California, Berkeley.

Berlin, Elois Ann, and Edward K. Markell
1977 An Assessment of the Nutritional and Health Status of an Aguaruna Jívaro Community, Amazonas, Peru. *Ecology of Food and Nutrition* 6:69–81.

Bloch, Maurice
1974 Symbols, Song, Dance, and Features of Articulation: Is Religion an Extreme Form of Traditional Authority? *European Journal of Sociology* 15:55–81.

Borges, José Luis
1970 The Garden of Forking Paths. In *Labyrinths*, ed. D.A. Yates and J. E. Irby, 44–54. Harmondsworth: Penguin Books.

Boster, James S.
1980 *How the Exceptions Prove the Rule: An Analysis of Informant Disagreement in Aguaruna Manioc Classification.* Ph.D. Diss., University of California, Berkeley.
1983 A Comparison of the Diversity of Jivaroan Gardens with That of the Tropical Forest. *Human Ecology* 11:47–68.

Brown, Michael F.
1978 From the Hero's Bones: Three Aguaruna Hallucinogens and Their Uses. In *The Nature and Status of Ethnobotany*, ed. Richard I. Ford, 119–36. Anthropological Papers No. 67. Museum of Anthropology, University of Michigan, Ann Arbor.
1982 Art of Darkness. *The Progressive* 46(8):20–21.
1984a The Role of Words in Aguaruna Hunting Magic. *American Ethnologist* 11:545–58.
1984b La Cara Oscura del Progreso: El Suicidio Entre Los Aguarunas del Alto Mayo, Peru. In *Relaciones Interétnicas y la Adaptación Cultural.* Sucua, Ecuador: Ediciones Mundo Shuar. pp. 76–88.
1984c *Una Paz Incierta: Historia y Cultura de las Comunidades Aguarunas Frente al Impacto de la Carretera Marginal.* Lima, Peru: Centro Amazónico de Antropología y Aplicación Práctica.

1985 Individual Experience, Dreams, and the Identification of Magical Stones in an Amazonian Society. In *Directions in Cognitive Anthropology*, ed. Janet W. D. Dougherty, 373–87. Urbana: University of Illinois Press.

Brown, Michael F., and Margaret L. Van Bolt
1980 Aguaruna Jívaro Gardening Magic in the Alto Río Mayo, Peru. *Ethnology* 19:169–90.

Carneiro, Robert L.
1970 Hunting and Hunting Magic Among the Amahuaca of the Peruvian Montaña. *Ethnology* 9:331–41.

Chevalier, Jacques M.
1982 *Civilization and the Stolen Gift: Capital, Kin, and Cult in Eastern Peru*. Toronto: University of Toronto Press.

Chirif, Alberto
1980 El Discreto Encanto de un Director. *Marka*. February 21, 1980, 24–25.

Chirif, Alberto, and Carlos Mora
1977 *Atlas de Comunidades Nativas*. Sistema Nacional de Apoyo a la Movilización Social, Dirección General de Organizaciones Rurales. Lima, Peru.

Chumap Lucía, A., and Manuel García-Rendueles
1979 *Duik Muun: Universo Mítico de los Aguaruna*. Lima: Centro Amazónico de Antropología y Aplicación Práctica.

Dougherty, Janet W. D., and James W. Fernandez
1982 Afterword. *American Ethnologist* 9:820–32.

Evans-Pritchard, E. E.
1937 *Witchcraft, Oracles, and Magic Among the Azande*. London: Oxford University Press.

Fabian, Johannes
1983 *Time and the Other*. New York: Columbia University Press.

Favret-Saada, Jeanne
1980 *Deadly Words: Witchcraft in the Bocage*. Cambridge: Cambridge University Press.

Feeley-Harnik, Gillian
1984 The Political Economy of Death: Communication and Change in Malagasy Colonial History. *American Ethnologist* 11:1–19.

Flornoy, Bertrand
1957 *Jívaro: Among the Headhunters of the Amazon*. London: Elek.

Frazer, Sir James G.
1958 *The Golden Bough*. Abridged edition. New York:
[1890] MacMillan Publishing Co.

García-Rendueles, Manuel
1977 Bibliografía de la Familia Lingüística Jibaroana. *Amazonía Peruana* 2:171–78.

1978 Versión Primera y Segunda del Mito de Nunkui en Aguaruna y Españól. *Amazonía Peruana* 3:10–52.

Garcilaso de la Vega (El Inca)

1966 *Royal Commentaries of the Incas*, Part I, [1609] trans. Harold V. Livermore. Austin: University of Texas Press.

Gardner, D. S.

1983 Performativity in Ritual: The Mianmin Case. *Man*, n.s., 18:346–60.

Geertz, Clifford

1973 *The Interpretation of Cultures.* New York: Basic Books.

Goodwin, Michael

1982 Herzog, the God of Wrath. *American Film* 7:36. June 1982.

Grohs, Waltraud

1974 *Los Indios del Alto Amazonas del Siglo XVI a XVIII.* Estudios Americanistas de Bonn, No. 2. Bonn.

Gross, Daniel R.

1975 Protein Capture and Cultural Development in the Amazon Basin. *American Anthropologist* 77:526–49.

Guallart, J. M.

1962 Nomenclatura Jíbaro-Aguaruna de Mamíferos en el Alto Marañón. *Biota* 4(32):155–64.

1964 Nomenclatura Jíbaro-Aguaruna de Especies de Aves en el Alto Marañón. *Biota* 5(41):210–22.

1968a Nomenclatura Jíbaro-Aguaruna de la Fauna del Alto Marañón (Reptiles, Peces, y Anfíbios). *Biota* 7(56):177–209.

1968b Nomenclatura Jíbaro-Aguaruna de Palmeras en el Distrito de Cenepa. *Biota* 7(57):230–51.

1974 *Poesía Lírica Aguaruna.* Serie Ensayos, No. 3. Lima: Centro Amazónico de Antropología y Aplicación Práctica.

1975 Contribución al Estudio de la Etnobotánica Aguaruna. *Biota* 10(83):336–51.

Hallpike, C. R.

1979 *The Foundations of Primitive Thought.* New York: Oxford University Press.

Harner, Michael J.

1962 Jívaro Souls. *American Anthropologist* 64:258–72.

1972 *The Jívaro: People of the Sacred Waterfalls.* Garden City, N.Y.: Doubleday and Co./Anchor Books.

Hollis, Martin, and Steven Lukes (eds.)

1982 *Rationality and Relativism.* Cambridge, Mass.: MIT Press.

Horton, Robin

1967 African Traditional Thought and Western Science. *Africa* 37 (Nos. 1 and 2):50–71 and 155–87.

Horton, Robin, and Ruth Finnegan (eds.)
1973 *Modes of Thought*. London: Faber and Faber.

IWGIA
1979 How Not to Make Movies in Peru. *Newsletter*, International Work Group for Indigenous Affairs, 8–10. November 1979.

Jordana Laguna, José Luis
1974 *Mitos e Historias Aguarunas*. Lima: Retablo de Papel Ediciones.

Karsten, Rafael
1935 *The Head-Hunters of Western Amazonas*. Societas Scientiarum Fennica. Commentationes Humanarum Litterarum, Vol. 7, No. 1. Helsingfors.

Kelekna, Pita
1982 The Achuará Shaman: Mediation and Transition. Paper presented at 44th International Congress of Americanists. Manchester, England.

Kensinger, Kenneth M.
1975 Studying the Cashinahua. In *The Cashinahua of Eastern Peru*, ed. Jane P. Dwyer. Haffenreffer Museum of Anthropology, Brown University. Studies in Anthropology and Material Culture, Vol. 1., 9–86.

1983 On Meat and Hunting. *Current Anthropology* 24:128–29.

Kirchheimer, Anne
1979 Indians in Peru Want Film Maker to Get Out. *Boston Globe*, Aug. 31, 1979, 1.

Larson, Mildred L.
1966 *Vocabulario Aguaruna de Amazonas*. Serie Lingüística Peruana, No. 3. Summer Institute of Linguistics. Yarinacocha, Peru.

1978 *The Functions of Reported Speech in Discourse*. Summer Institute of Linguistics Publications in Linguistics and Related Fields, No. 59. Arlington, Texas.

Leach, Edmund
1968 Ritual. In *International Encyclopaedia of the Social Sciences*, Vol. 13, ed. David L. Sills. New York: MacMillan Publishing Co.

1976 *Culture and Communication*. Cambridge: Cambridge University Press.

Lévi-Strauss, Claude
1973 *From Honey to Ashes*. New York: Harper and Row Publishers/ Torchbooks.

Lieberson, Jonathan
1984 Interpreting the Interpreter. *New York Review of Books* 31(4):39–46.

Malinowski, Bronislaw
1935 *Coral Gardens and Their Magic*. 2 Vols. New York: American Book Co.

Marwick, M. G.
  1965 *Sorcery in Its Social Setting*. Manchester: Manchester University Press.
Mauss, Marcel, and Henri Hubert
  1972 *A General Theory of Magic*. New York: W. W. Norton and Co.
Meggers, Betty J.
  1973 *Amazonia: Man and Culture in a Counterfeit Paradise*. Chicago: Aldine Publishing Co.
Merriam, Alan P.
  1964 *The Anthropology of Music*. Evanston: Northwestern University Press.
Merrill, William L.
  1981 *The Concept of Soul Among the Rarámuri of Chihuahua, Mexico: A Study in World View*. Ph.D. diss., University of Michigan, Ann Arbor.
Métraux, Alfred
  1948 Tribes of the Peruvian and Ecuadorian Montaña. In *Handbook of South American Indians*, Vol. 3, ed. Julian Steward, 535–656. Bureau of American Ethnology, Bulletin 143. Smithsonian Institution, Washington, D.C.
Mundo Shuar
  1984 *Relaciones Interétnicas y la Adaptación Cultural*. Sucua, Ecuador: Ediciones Mundo Shuar.
Needham, Rodney
  1983 *Against the Tranquility of Axioms*. Berkeley: University of California Press.
O'Keefe, Daniel L.
  1982 *Stolen Lightning: The Social Theory of Magic*. New York: Random House/Vintage.
O'Leary, Timothy J.
  1963 *Ethnographic Bibliography of South America*. New Haven: Human Relations Area Files.
Peel, J. D. Y.
  1969 Understanding Alien Belief-Systems. *British Journal of Sociology* 20:69–84.
Pellizzaro, S.
  1977 *Cantos de Amor de la Esposa Shuar*. Mundo Shuar, Series G, No. 2. Sucua, Ecuador.
  1978a *El Uwishin*. Mundo Shuar, Series F, No. 3. Sucua, Ecuador.
  1978b *Shakaim*. Mundo Shuar, Series F, No. 10. Sucua, Ecuador.
Pike, Kenneth L., and Mildred Larson
  1964 Hyperphonemes and Non-Systematic Features of Aguaruna Phonetics. In *Studies of Language and Linguistics in Honor of Charles C. Fries*, ed. Albert H. Marckwardt, 55–67. English Language Institute. University of Michigan, Ann Arbor.

Tsewa's Gift

Rogers, David, and S. G. Appan
1973 *Manihot and Manihotoides (Euphorbiaceae)*. Flora Neotropica,
No. 13. New York Botanical Gardens. Bronx, New York.

Rosaldo, Michelle Z.
1975 It's All Uphill: The Creative Metaphors of Ilongot Magical Spells.
In *Sociocultural Dimensions of Language Use*, ed. Mary Sanches
and Ben Blount, 177–203. New York: Academic Press.

Rosaldo, Michelle Z., and J. M. Atkinson
1975 Man the Hunter and Woman: Metaphors for the Sexes in Ilongot
Magical Spells. In *The Interpretation of Symbolism*, ed. Roy
Willis, 43–75. New York: John Wiley and Sons.

Rosengren, Karl E.
1976 Malinowski's Magic: The Riddle of the Empty Cell. *Current
Anthropology* 17: 667–85.

Ross, Eric B.
1976 *The Achuarä Jívaro: Cultural Adaptation in the Upper Amazon*.
Ph.D. Diss., Columbia University.

1978 Food Taboos, Diet, and Hunting Strategy: The Adaptation to
Animals in Amazon Cultural Ecology. *Current Anthropology*
19:1–36.

Sahlins, Marshall
1976 *Culture and Practical Reason*. Chicago: University of Chicago
Press.

Sauer, Carl O.
1969 *Seeds, Spades, Hearths, and Herds*. Cambridge, Mass.: MIT Press.

Siskind, Janet
1973 *To Hunt in the Morning*. New York: Oxford University Press.

Siverts, Henning
1972 *Tribal Survival in the Alto Marañón: The Aguaruna Case*.
International Work Group for Indigenous Affairs, Document No.
10. Copenhagen.

n.d. Broken Hearts and Pots: Suicide and Patterns of Signification
Among the Aguaruna Jívaro of the Alto Rio Marañón, Peru. In *Sign
and Scarcity: Some Further Steps Toward a Generative Analysis of
Reciprocity*, ed. Reider Grønhaug. Bergen: Universitetsforlaget.
Forthcoming.

Skorupski, John
1976 *Symbol and Theory*. Cambridge: Cambridge University Press.

Sperber, Dan
1975 *Rethinking Symbolism*. Cambridge: Cambridge University Press.

1980 Is Symbolic Thought Prerational? In *Symbol as Sense*, ed. M.
LeCron Foster and S. H. Brandes, 25–44. London: Academic Press.

1982 Apparently Irrational Beliefs. In *Rationality and Relativism*, ed.
Martin Hollis and Steven Lukes, 149–80. Cambridge, Mass.: MIT
Press.

Stirling, Matthew W.
1938 *Historical and Ethnographic Material on the Jívaro Indians.*
Bureau of American Ethnology, Bulletin No. 117. Smithsonian
Institution, Washington, D.C.

Swain, Roger
1981 *Earthly Pleasures: Tales From a Biologist's Garden.* New York:
Charles Scribner's Sons.

Tambiah, S. J.
1968 The Magical Power of Words. *Man*, n.s., 3:175–208.

1973 Form and Meaning of Magical Acts: A Point of View. In *Modes of
Thought*, ed. Robin Horton and Ruth Finnegan, 199–229. London:
Faber and Faber.

Taussig, Michael T.
1980 *The Devil and Commodity Fetishism in South America.* Chapel
Hill: University of North Carolina Press.

Taylor, Anne Christine
1984 La Alianza Matrimonial y Sus Variaciones Estructurales En Las
Sociedades Jívaro. In *Relaciones Interétnicas y Adaptación
Cultural*, 89–108. Sucua, Ecuador: Ediciones Mundo Shuar.

Tsamaraint, A., B. Mashumar, and S. Pellizzaro
1977 *Cantos de Amor.* Mundo Shuar, Series G, No. 1. Sucua, Ecuador.

Turner, Victor
1967 *The Forest of Symbols.* Ithaca, N.Y.: Cornell University Press.

Uriarte, Luis M.
1976 Poblaciones Nativas de la Amazonía Peruana. *Amazonía Peruana*
1:9–58.

Van Baal, J.
1971 *Symbols for Communication.* Assen: Van Gorcum and Co.

Weiner, Annette B.
1983 From Words to Objects to Magic: Hard Words and the Boundaries
of Social Interaction. *Man*, n.s., 18: 690–709.

Whitten, Norman E., Jr.
1976 *Sacha Runa: Ethnicity and Adaptation of Ecuadorian Jungle
Quichua.* Urbana: University of Illinois Press.

1978a *Amazonian Ecuador: An Ethnic Interface in Ecological, Social,
and Ideological Perspectives.* International Work Group in
Indigenous Affairs, Document No. 34. Copenhagen.

1978b Ecological Imagery and Cultural Adaptability: The Canelos
Quichua of Eastern Ecuador. *American Anthropologist* 80:836–
59.

1981 Amazonia Today at the Base of the Andes: An Ethnic Interface in
Ecological, Social, and Ideological Perspectives. In *Cultural
Transformations and Ethnicity in Modern Ecuador*, ed. Norman E.
Whitten, Jr., 121–61. Urbana: University of Illinois Press.

Wilson, Bryan (ed.)

1970 *Rationality.* New York: Harper and Row Publishers/Torchbooks.

Wistrand, Lila

1969 Music and Song Texts of Amazonian Indians. *Journal of the Society of Ethnomusicology* 13:469–88.

Works, Martha A.

1982 Economic Development and Cultural Change: The Situation of the Alto Mayo Aguaruna. Unpublished report.

1984a *Agricultural Change among the Alto Mayo Aguaruna, Eastern Peru: The Effects on Culture and Environment.* Ph.D. diss., Louisiana State University.

1984b El Proceso de Desarrollo y la Experiencia de Cambio: Situación de los Aguaruna del Valle del Alto Mayo. *Amazonía Peruana* 10:119–28.

Index

References to notes are indicated by "n." followed by the number that corresponds to the note.

Evans-Pritchard, E. E., 22

Family structure, 42–43
Fertility, blood as symbol of, 129
Fitzcarraldo, 182–83
Food. *See* Diet
Frazer, Sir James, 21–22, 171
"Fright," 56, 199 n. 5

Game grabbers, 83–90
Gardening
    cultivation and planting, 98–
        101, 201 n. 1
    magic, generally, 125–30
    planting ritual, 118–21, 201 n. 7
    powerful beings, 103, 105–8,
        114–15
    songs, 107–15, 126
    stones, magical, 115–22, 126
    taboos, 124–25, 126
    types of crops grown, 98, 101–2
Geertz, Clifford, 24–25, 162
Gender roles, 103, 126–28,
    202 n. 11
Gods. *See* Powerful beings

Hallpike, C. R., 169
Hallucinogens, 49, 57–62, 184
    See also Plants, psychoactive
Healing sessions, 61–64
Herzog, Werner, 182–83
Horton, Robin, 22
Housing, 44, 198 n. 4 (chap. 1)

Hunting, 67–70
    charms, 83–90, 160–61, 200 n.
        7
    dogs, 79–82, 89, 92–93, 200 nn.
        5, 6
    dreams about, 81–82, 95
    reasons for failure in, 91–96,
        201 n. 10
    sexual symbolism and, 76–77,
        95–96
    songs, 70–83
        dogs in, 79–82
        dreams in, 81–82, 94–95
        myths about, 75
        purpose of, 75–76
        sexual imagery in, 76–77
        synonyms for animals in, 73–
            74
        women in, 76–82
    taboos, 91–93, 200 n. 9
    technology of, 68–70

Illness, 56, 61–64, 174–76, 198 n.
    5 (intro.), 204 n. 1
Insects, as hunting charms, 87–88
Iwanch, 51, 55, 85

Jivaroans, 26–28, 32, 198 n. 4 (in-
    tro.)
Juép, Adolfo, 38

Katíp, Israel, 38
Kinship, 42–43, 136
Knowledge, Aguaruna view of,
    48–49

Leach, Edmund, 23–24
Lévi-Strauss, Claude, 22–23, 90,
    155, 156
Love charms, 153–61, 170, 173,
    200 n. 7, 203 nn. 8, 10, 204 n.
    13
Love songs. *See* Romantic songs